Nepal

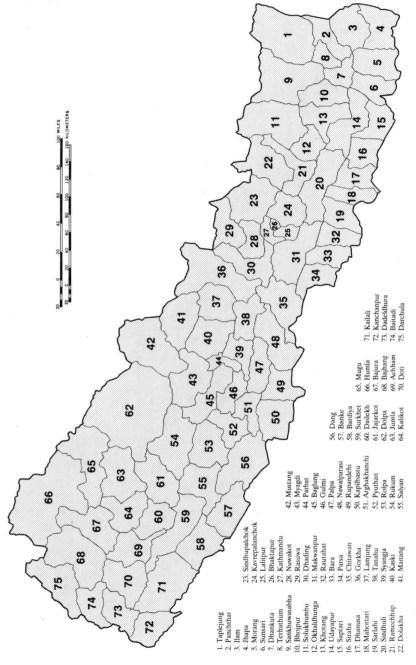

Administrative districts

1. Taplejung
2. Panchthar
3. Ilam
4. Jhapa
5. Morang
6. Sunsari
7. Dhankuta
8. Terhathum
9. Sankhuwasabha
10. Bhojpur
11. Solukhumbu
12. Okhaldhunga
13. Khotang
14. Udayapur
15. Saptari
16. Siraha
17. Dhanusa
18. Mahottari
19. Sarlahi
20. Sindhuli
21. Ramechhap
22. Dolakha

23. Sindhupalchok
24. Kavrepalanchok
25. Lalitpur
26. Bhaktapur
27. Kathmandu
28. Nuwakot
29. Rasuwa
30. Dhading
31. Makwanpur
32. Rautahat
33. Bara
34. Parsa
35. Chitawan
36. Gorkha
37. Lamjung
38. Tanahu
39. Syanga
40. Kaski
41. Manang

42. Mustang
43. Myagdi
44. Parbat
45. Baglung
46. Gulmi
47. Palpa
48. Nawalparasi
49. Rupandehi
50. Kapilbastu
51. Arghakhanchi
52. Pyuthan
53. Rolpa
54. Rukum
55. Salyan

56. Dang
57. Banke
58. Bardiya
59. Surkhet
60. Dailekh
61. Jajarkot
62. Dolpa
63. Jumla
64. Kalikot

65. Mugu
66. Humla
67. Bajura
68. Bajhang
69. Achham
70. Doti

71. Kailali
72. Kanchanpur
73. Dadeldhura
74. Baitadi
75. Darchula

Nepal:
A Himalayan kingdom in transition

Pradyumna P. Karan, University of Kentucky
Hiroshi Ishii, ILCAA, Tokyo University of
Foreign Studies

with the collaboration of:
Yuki Ito, Saitama University
Masao Kobayashi, Tokyo University
Mohan Shrestha, Bowling Green State University
Chakramehr Vajracharya, Nepal Rural Reconstruction
Association
David Zurick, Eastern Kentucky University

Cartography: Gyula Pauer, University of Kentucky

**United Nations
University Press**

TOKYO · NEW YORK · PARIS

United Nations University Press
The United Nations University, 53-70, Jingumae 5-chome,
Shibuya-ku, Tokyo 150, Japan
Tel: (03) 3499-2811   Fax: (03) 3406-7345
Telex: J25442   Cable: UNATUNIV TOKYO

UNU Office in North America
2 United Nations Plaza, Room DC2-1462-70, New York, NY 10017
Tel: (212) 963-6387   Fax: (212) 371-9454   Telex: 422311 UN UI

United Nations University Press is the publishing division of the United Nations University.

Typeset by Asco Trade Typesetting Limited, Hong Kong
Printed by Edwards Brothers, Ann Arbor, Michigan, USA
Cover design by Joyce C. Weston

UNUP-924
ISBN 92-808-0924-5
02500 P

Contents

Illustrations

Figures

Photographs

Preface

Since 1951 Nepal has achieved much in its quest for economic and social development, but much is left undone. Significant achievements in developing transport infrastructure since 1951 have not been accompanied by faster economic growth, reduction in the rate of population growth, increase in food production, and employment generation needed to alleviate poverty. This book is a brief and highly selective introduction to growth and change in Nepal since the 1950s. Various aspects of the development, environment, and human resources are discussed in the context of the mountainous terrain and landlocked character of the country.

Nepal's development experience and the challenges it faces are of practical as well as academic relevance to readers who have an interest in the development of small, resource poor, mountainous, and landlocked nations. The views expressed here are based on observations made during numerous visits to all parts of the Kingdom since the opening of the country in the 1950s.

Professor Masao Kobayashi prepared materials on urbanization and migration; Chakramehr Vajracharya contributed materials on settlements; and Professor Mohan Shrestha helped us with new data and prepared the sections on population, urbanization, and settlements. Yuki Ito did research on communication patterns and prepared the section on communications in Nepal. Professor David Zurick prepared the chapter on tourism. The members of the Nepal Study Group, which meets regularly at the Institute for the Study of Languages and Cultures of Asia and Africa, Tokyo, helped us refine and interpret many ideas concerning changes taking place in Nepal.

Preface

We gratefully acknowledge the assistance of several individuals: Shobhana Chitrakar and Anirudha Man Shrestha in Kathmandu; Kenichi Tachibana, a member of the Nepal Study Group at the Institute for the Study of Languages and Cultures of Asia and Africa in Tokyo; Professor Zenjiro Tamura, the late Machiko Tamura, and Kyoko Inoue who provided us with some of the photographs used in this book. We are indebted to Professor Mohan Shrestha for updating many of the tables and providing us with much needed statistical information on Nepal. Dr. Gyula Pauer, Director of the University of Kentucky Cartography and Geographic Information Systems Laboratory prepared all the maps and charts for the book.

Nepal is now experiencing a period of major change in economy, society, and environment. The general aim of this book is to provide an outline of some of the crucial issues facing the country. We hope this book can contribute to their understanding and management.

Pradyumna P. Karan and Hiroshi Ishii
Lexington, Kentucky and Tokyo

1

Introduction to a landlocked kingdom

Locked within rugged mountain ranges, Nepal was cut off from the mainstream of societal development for centuries. Divided into small princedoms, it was not until the latter half of the eighteenth century that a unified kingdom was forged by Prithvi Narayan Shah of the House of Gorkha, the first political organization in the area to resemble the modern conception of a nation state. Nepal's chaotic political development in the first half of the nineteenth century precluded any real attention to the economic needs of its people. When autocratic stability was imposed by the prime ministers of the Rana regime after 1846, the administrative structure was reinforced to provide economic aggrandizement for the extensive Rana family, to the extent that Nepal's revenues, land ownership, and economic opportunities were almost totally the prerogatives of the ruling family (Regmi, 1950; Joshi and Rose, 1966; Regmi, 1963).

Nepal began to break away from its complete dependence on agriculture and the traditional but limited trans-Himalayan trade routes for its economic livelihood in the twentieth century. During the Rana period, little attention was paid to the systematic development of the country's resources, although a Development Board was established in 1936 and industrial surveys in selected districts promoted economic activities. With little organization and few capital resources, these efforts were not much more than random attempts to promote very limited development (Shrestha, 1967).

At the start of World War II, Nepal was still isolated physically as well as psychologically. Its internal economic transactions were handicapped by many factors: only the most primitive of local bank-

1

ing facilities existed in the Kathmandu Valley, and the sovereignty of Nepalese currency had not been established nor was it widely respected internally; foreign exchange was derived almost exclusively from the exportation of manpower to the British armies; communications with even the areas adjacent to the capital were maintained by runners and porters; and electric power was restricted to the luxury use of the Rana family in Kathmandu at a high cost to the treasury. However, with the forces of change emerging elsewhere in Asia, especially in India, the Ranas were compelled to lift a few of the restrictions that had previously stifled local initiative and non-Rana activity.

The palace revolution of 1950–1951 and the subsequent overthrow of the Rana regime marked the beginning of Nepal's emergence into the modern world, but its economy was still rooted in the medieval past. One of the early objectives of the Nepali Congress government was the rapid adjustment of economic inequalities. Commissions to study Nepal's land reform and taxation policies were conceived and created during the early years of the post revolution period as vehicles for immediate change. Development assistance from various foreign sources began to flow into the country although the fledgling government had virtually no idea of its own resources. It was not until late in 1955 that Nepal took its first concrete steps to formulate a development plan.

Although the new activities promised rapid improvement in the lot of the common man in a land where the government had previously exploited the populace for the sake of an already wealthy oligarchy, attempts to modernize the economy were frustrated, and perhaps even doomed, by the lack of social and economic data concerning the country. No accurate census had been taken, no regulations or registration of Nepal's embryonic industrial establishments existed, and no one could reliably estimate the national income. Knowledge of Nepal's arable land potential was still fragmentary (Karan, 1960), based primarily on venerable but ossified and misleading land office records. The population distribution was unknown and no profile of the labour force existed. The lack of fundamental data was accompanied by archaic administrative practices, which compounded the problem of analysis and the formulation of a development policy.

Non-economic factors also affected Nepal's low level of economic advancement. The emergence of a middle class, independent of connections with either foreign nationalities or the Rana regime, had not occurred. Much of Nepal's ability to utilize its manpower re-

2

sources fully depended on the development of an educational system to train the population for needed skills, yet Nepal's literacy rate was among the lowest in the world and schools were unknown to the vast majority of its people. A 1947 survey indicated that there were only seven Nepalese who had college or graduate degrees and only 48 undergraduate students in the country (Reed, 1968: 48). Traditional social patterns – caste and ethnic associations, attitudes towards mobility, and an understandable suspicion of the government – were deeply ingrained and very slow to change. There was also the factor of Nepal's strategic location between India and China, which prompted 10 countries as well as international aid organizations to extend development assistance. Thus Nepal's economic problems were taken out of the realm of its local policies and decison-making processes. These seemingly unrelated problems are unquantifiable, yet their roles as inhibitors of well-thought-out growth and change are obvious.

A least developed country

The United Nations Committee for Development Planning includes Nepal among the "least developed countries," or poorest of the world's poor countries (United Nations, 1985). These countries are characterized by a number of economic and social features. In Nepal, as well as in the other least developed countries, an extremely low economic growth rate combined with the rate of population growth has brought about a stagnation in the already low level of per capita income. Most of the population is dependent on agriculture, primarily subsistence agriculture; access to modern money-economy activities is limited. Inadequate means of transportation and communication intensify the isolation of most of the population, who live in rural areas. As a general rule these poor countries have not been able to create an export sector – more or less commensurate with their import needs – to help finance a sustained development effort. In most cases, their export trade involves a small number of primary products with very little or no processing. Not much is known about the natural resource endowment of these countries due to inadequate exploration and evaluation.

Nepal has considerable hydroelectric potential, which should enable the country to meet the needs of its fledgling industries and even to provide export earnings. It must be stressed, however, that both the exploitation of resources and the installation of hydroelectric power stations require technologies and capital investments that are generally not available in Nepal. In most of the least developed countries the skilled personnel and administrative staff needed to organize and manage development is extremely limited due to the very low literacy rates. The percentage of the population that has received primary, secondary, and higher-level education is very small. The per capita consumption of energy is not only extremely low, it also involves resources, such as wood, which are not easily renewable. Nepal and several other countries are facing disastrous consequences due to the over-exploitation of timber as their main source of energy.

As to the social needs, these countries face malnutrition, a shortage of safe drinking water, and poor health services and educational systems. Their birth and death rates are among the highest in the world. Most of the countries are heavily dependent on foreign aid to pay for their imports and to finance investments, but the total amount of available foreign-currency resources to purchase from abroad the goods essential to their development remains excessively low in both absolute and per capita terms, and the gap continues to grow between these least developed countries and other developing countries, not to mention the industrialized nations.

Most of these countries also face a serious transfer-of-technology problem. The exploitation of certain resources sometimes involves the use of expensive technologies beyond the scope of their people. Also, personnel trained at great expense in such technologies tend to go abroad to find work commensurate with their qualifications, leading to a reverse transfer of technology. Finally, many of these least developed countries, including Nepal, are geographically handicapped by their landlocked location, the mountainous terrain (fig. 1) with little arable land, and other physical disadvantages.

The landlocked situation and least developed status

There is a close link between the landlocked situation and the least developed status of Nepal with its low levels of income and labour productivity, very scarce skilled manpower, and heavy dependence on a very narrow range of primary commodities in its export structure. Nepal is one of the 38 landlocked states (10 in Asia, 2 in Latin America, 12 in Europe, and 14 in Africa) that has no seacoast. Most of the landlocked states have small or medium-sized territories; with the exception of those in Europe, all are developing countries. Land-

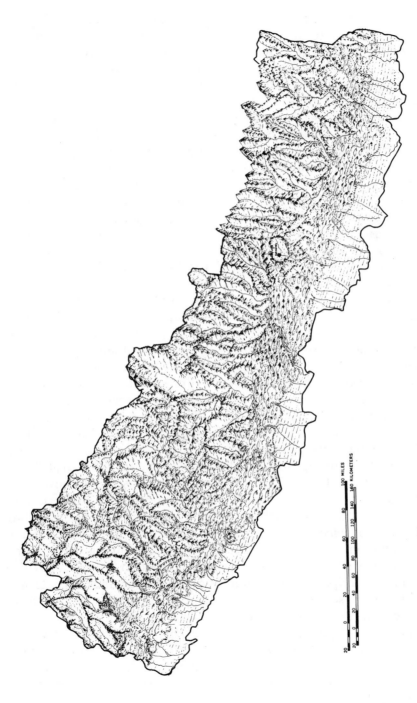

Fig. 1 **Landforms**

100 MILES
160 KILOMETERS

5

locked states are handicapped by not having direct access to the sea. They must enter into agreements with coastal states in order to use their port facilities. They are also disadvantaged with respect to the exploitation of the sea's natural resources. In the case of Nepal these disadvantages are accentuated by the lack of an infrastructure for an adequate system of transportation.

The right of landlocked countries to free access to the sea has been noted in various documents, such as the Barcelona Declaration of 1921, the Geneva Convention on the High Seas of 1958, and the New York Convention on Transit Trade of Landlocked States of 1965 (United Nations, 1987). At the same time the right of free access is exercised in the sovereign territory of neighbouring coastal states, thus the exercise of that right should not be detrimental to the equally legitimate and reasonable interests of the transit states. Therefore, bilateral or regional negotiations and agreements between coastal and landlocked states are essential for the implementation of the right of access to and from the sea.

Because of legal and practical considerations, the claims of land-locked Nepal could not be asserted independently of appropriate agreements with India. The use of Indian ports by Nepal must be limited to principal ports of transit only and to mutually agreed upon prescribed routes. The New York Convention on Transit Trade of Landlocked States contains provisions that stipulate that the access and transit rights should be subject to common agreements between the states concerned and be based on the principle of reciprocity.

As a direct result of its disadvantageous geographical situation, Nepal has experienced difficulties and restrictions in its trade and development. Its foreign trade is largely dependent on transit facilities provided by India. The ever-increasing costs of transit and transportation have led to higher-priced imports and exports. The consequences of the landlocked situation is difficult to quantify, but Nepal's lack of access to the sea is compounded by its remoteness and its isolation from world markets, which are among the reasons for its relative poverty. Overall growth, export expansion, and the utilization of foreign capital resources generate demands for international transport services. Greater difficulties and the cost of these services constitute an extra hurdle for Nepal's development.

Reducing the high transport costs not only requires action within Nepal's own frontiers but also depends heavily on improvements in the transport policies and facilities of neighbouring India. A key element in Nepal's development strategy must be the harmonious

Bheri Kola in west Nepal (courtesy Z. Tamura)

Middle Mountain valley seen from a Chepang village in central Nepal

planning of the transport section with that of its neighbour within a climate of friendly relations. However, the effective cooperation between landlocked Nepal and transit countries such as India raises many complex economic issues and requires a clearer understanding of the real costs and benefits involved for the development of the economy. An integrated approach, tailored to the actual transport and transit circumstances facing Nepal's development, is needed to promote the economic development of the country.

Nepal, wedged between China and India, the world's two most populous nations, has only one reliable outlet to the sea – overland through the Indian port of Calcutta, more than 1,150 km away. In 1989, after failing to negotiate lapsed trade and transit treaties, 19 of the 21 border crossings between Nepal and India were closed, severing links not only to the port of Calcutta but also to northern Indian cities. At the end of March 1989 two more agreements – covering Nepal's imports of petroleum products and coal through

Hillside village near Okhaldhunga in east Nepal (courtesy M. Tamura)

India – expired. Almost immediately, there was a sharp drop in the supplies of kerosene for cooking and gasoline for the buses and trucks that carried food, medicine, and other necessities to remote areas. Petroleum products were rationed. The prices of other commodities such as sugar, salt, and processed foods – many imported from India – rose. Even protected trees were cut to meet fuel shortages.

Nepal, which has benefited from nearly 45 years of Indian aid, special trade concessions, and an open-door policy for millions of Nepalese job seekers, wants to end its economic dependence on India. In spite of a 1950 friendship treaty, which has been the foundation of Indo-Nepal relations ever since, Nepal had made efforts to introduce work permits for Indian nationals in Nepal although the Nepalese in India are not required to have them. Also, Nepal has been levying tariffs on Indian goods not covered by the trade and transit treaties. Nepal's landlocked situation with vital trade links to the outside world through India makes it very difficult for the country to follow an independent economic policy. The communist leaders

9

Winding road from Birganj to Kathmandu (courtesy K. Inoue)

were elected in 1994 on the basis of anti-India rhetoric. But since coming to power the communist government has become more pragmatic, toning down its anti-India stance. No major change is expected in Nepal's relation with India.

10

Political economy and history prior to 1950

The economic policies of the Kingdom of Nepal, established in 1769 by Prithvi Narayan Shah, were tailored to the requirements of well-organized interest groups with a great deal at stake. In general, economic policies were designed to channel resources to specific groups and classes in the country. In the seclusion of a land protected by treacherous mountain peaks to the north and malarial jungles to the south, Nepal developed in its own way, preserving the feudal economy.

At the end of the Anglo-Nepali War of 1814–1816, the Treaty of Sugauli, signed on 4 March 1816, reduced Nepal to approximately its present boundaries (Aitchison, 1929: 54–56). The rulers, having experienced at first hand the impact of western militarism, organized the government along strict military lines; even minor officials were given military titles.

In negotiating the Treaty of Sugauli, Nepal's Prime Minister Bhimsen Thapa made an effort to end the war, which would guarantee Nepal's independence. He consolidated his power at the expense of the King and pushed through taxation to benefit the wealthy landowners. Tactful as he was, Thapa could not escape the intrigue and strife in the royal court, government, and royal family which had plagued Nepal even before the Shah period. He left the scene by committing suicide.

The strife for power in the court continued and became more intense, culminating in an 1846 *kot* massacre, in which Jang Bahadur killed most of his opponents and assumed the prime ministership. Jang Bahadur, who held power until his death in 1877 except for a short time in 1856–1857, was pro-British; after 1848 he made frequent offers of Gorkha troops to serve the British. His offer of 12,000 troops to the British in the Indian Mutiny of 1857–1858 was a typical example. A tract of territory along the Audh frontier, which was ceded to the British under the Treaty of Sugauli, was restored to Nepal in return for this service.

In 1854 the Nepalese clashed with the Tibetans over the treatment of Nepalese nationals in Lhasa. After a fierce struggle, notable for the hardships under which it was fought on the high Tibetan plateau, the Tibetans admitted defeat. In a peace treaty signed in March 1856, they submitted to an annual tribute of Rs 10,000 and agreed to abolish customs duties on Nepalese goods. In addition, a representative of the Nepalese government was stationed in Lhasa to assure Nepalese

11

traders of fair treatment. By this time, China had become too weak to help Tibet because of the Opium War and internal revolts.

The Ranas, as Jang Bahadur and his successors called themselves, had monopolized power by making the king a nominal figure. They distributed land, gave important offices to their kin, and made the office of the prime minister hereditary. This institution, which persisted until 1951, did not eliminate the office as the focus of intrigue and revolution; it made it more so because in the beginning it was stipulated that the prime minister's office was to be handed down to the younger brother who was next in seniority to the one in office.

The Rana were not on the whole progressive. They occupied a dominant position in the political economy of Nepal. Their economic and political interests within the context of institutions existing in the country determined government policies and created a new environment within which their socio-economic objectives continued to thrive. The Rana controlled great wealth, and the continuance of their position seemed to rest on an economically depressed Nepal. The last two prime ministers of the Rana line did attempt reforms. Juddha Shamsher announced a 20-year plan for progress prior to World War II, and in October 1949 his successor, Mohan Shamsher, set up a National Planning Committee to develop a 15-year economic plan. Despite these efforts, and acknowledging the limited resources of the country, one finds little to praise in the role of the Ranas; under their rule nobility flourished but the masses were left to their own devices.

In February 1951, following the 1950 palace revolt in which King Tribhuvan Bir Vikram Shah sought refuge in the Indian Embassy at Kathmandu and asked for India's assistance in restoring Nepal's constitutional monarchy, the hereditary rule of the Ranas was abolished. Under this enlightened monarch, Nepal ended its policy of isolation and seclusion and entered the world community of nations.

Development policy during the past 44 years, 1951–1995

In 1951, after the Rana autocracy ended, Nepal embarked on the task of economic and social development. Serious efforts to plan development took place after a Planning Board was established in 1955. The First Five-Year Plan, prepared by the Board, covered the period 1956–1961. Because of limited knowledge concerning the actual resources, development potential, and population of the country, there were serious shortcomings in the plan itself. Despite this, some significant results were achieved, although expenditures were only Rs 210 million, or Rs 42 million annually. There was some progress in the fields of education and health, yet little progress was made in road construction, power, and industrial development. The plan did stimulate public interest in planning, but made little headway in creating the necessary base for development. Many problems arose in the government itself. Late in 1960, midway during the last year of the First Plan, the parliament was disbanded and the multiparty system of government was dissolved. A new partyless panchayat system of government was formed in 1961. The upheaval associated with this political change did not permit the formulation of a second plan before the end of the First Plan period.

When the Second Plan 1962–1965 was prepared, knowledge of Nepal's economic and social geography was still extremely limited. In the absence of surveys and studies of natural resources, agricultural output, national income and other variables, the existing economic and social conditions could not be accurately ascertained to set overall targets and goals. The absence of data also prevented the formulation of a long-range perspective within which the second plan was to operate.

Due to these shortcomings, the Second Plan tried to give priority to activities that could establish the foundation for more comprehensive future plans. Emphasis was placed on the collection of data on economic conditions and on the development of an economic infrastructure. Emphasis was also placed on the development of transportation, communications, and power, and on agricultural extension and irrigation. For social services, efforts were directed more toward improvement than toward the expansion of schools and health centres. The Second Plan was limited to three years (1962–1965), which was considered adequate for collecting data in preparation for more comprehensive plans in the future. During this period there were surveys of irrigation and power potential, mineral exploration, transport surveys, a population census, a sample agricultural survey, a national income estimate, and other resource inventories, which provided greater knowledge of the economy's spatial structure.

In formulating the Third Plan 1965–1970, an important step was taken: the long-term goal of doubling the gross domestic product (GDP) within 15 years. This was the first attempt by Nepal to fit a five-year plan into a long-term perspective. However, this third plan,

13

as well as subsequent plans, failed to formulate explicitly policies and programmes to double the GDP. The Third Plan was followed by four consecutive five-year plans: the Fourth Plan 1970–1975, the Fifth Plan 1975–1980, the Sixth Plan 1980–1985, and the Seventh Plan 1985–1990. Nepal is currently implementing the Eighth Plan 1992–1997, which was formulated in 1991 after political changes and the general elections.

Nepal's trade and transit impasse with India in 1989 contributed to a period of high inflation and slow economic growth. The effects of this impasse, which lasted for over a year, were severe. Per capita income declined, since the economic growth was less than the rate of population increase. Nepal's high fertility rate combined with its lower mortality rate contributed to a rapid population growth of 2.1 per cent (2.6 per cent in the 1970s) annually, which aggravated the poverty problem and eroded many of its economic gains. The temporary resolution of the trade and transit problem with India in June 1990 eased the economic situation and provided opportunities for greater growth and employment, but prospects for the medium term are difficult to assess because of the various uncertainties facing the country.

A review of Nepal's 42 years of development planning reveals that the five-year plans failed to fulfil their purpose. The lives of most of the Nepalese people remained unchanged; in many ways they were worse off than they were four decades ago. Major breakthroughs were made in road construction, communications, literacy rates, and health services. But the per capita income of the people remained low. There was only marginal growth in real per capita income between 1964 and 1965 (Rs 1,303) and 1989 and 1990 (Rs 1,598) – a meagre increase of Rs 295 over a period of 25 years at 1974–1975 prices. The wealthier classes and some politicians have benefited from public investments and development projects financed through foreign aid, and they have used these new resources to protect and defend their domestic political and economic positions. Consequently, there have been growing disparities in income and in development during recent decades.

Nearly half of Nepal's total population – about 9 million people – is estimated to be below the poverty line, deprived of even the basic minimum needs for living (National Planning Commission, 1991: 2). The process of development has brought little improvement in the rural areas; development benefits are largely concentrated in the cities. As a result, poverty in the rural areas – where the basic amen-

Hydro-electric plant in Kulekhani

ities such as drinking water, health services, and transport facilities are lacking – has worsened. At the same time, urban centres such as Kathmandu, Biratnagar, and Pokhara are showing signs of poorly planned growth with increased demands on their limited public utilities.

Four decades of planning have also increased the development disparities between the mountains and the tarai regions of the country as a result of unequal investments in various geographic areas. The urban-centred development approach has not only widened the spatial disparities between various areas, but it has also led to the emergence of a non-sustainable and fragile economic base. Environmental degradation has accelerated, and the sustainability of subsistence agriculture has diminished. The depletion of natural resources has occurred to such an extent in some areas that the very sustainability

15

of the villages is threatened. The agriculture sector, which contributes more than 60 per cent of GDP, performed unsatisfactorily; productivity either declined or remained unchanged.

Despite the huge investments made in Nepal's economy through foreign aid from the United States, Japan, China, India, and the European countries during the past 40 years, Nepal remains one of the poorest or least developed countries in the world. Economic growth in 1992 was 3.1 per cent, not much more than the population growth; inflation was 30 per cent. Balanced and sustained development remains an elusive goal. The economy is characterized by its heavy dependence on foreign aid, a low export base, its vulnerability in agricultural production, increasingly unbalanced regional development, high population growth, excessive control and regulation, and inefficient public enterprises and administration.

Nepal's failure in development planning can be attributed to several factors. A weak and poorly developed organizational structure to formulate and implement the plans contributed to disappointing results. In addition, the top-down, donor-driven planning process, which characterized development planning until 1990, was devoid of concern for the common people of Nepal. Development projects were selected on an ad hoc basis, depending on the availability of external aid without regard to their overall integration, socio-economic justification, or long-range sustainability. The planning process was unable to generate genuine citizen participation and the development decisions were made by largely autocratic and feudal bureaucrats under the influence of foreign aid donors.

During the 1990s Nepal faces major challenges in its development effort. Foremost among these are the alleviation of poverty and the reduction of high rates of population growth through a variety of innovative programmes. The large disparities in income distribution – a heavy concentration of wealth among a small section of the population (1 per cent of the families share 14 per cent of the annual income) – poses another challenge. The remedial measures to remove this inequality will require reforms in Nepal's economic structure. Though progress has been made in recent years in restructuring the economy, there is an urgent need for further measures to remedy structural weaknesses.

Further tax reforms to rationalize the tax system are also needed, especially the reduction of exemptions and the broadening of the base, so that additional resources for the public sector can be mobilized. The privatization process needs to be hastened, and industrial

16

and trade policies need further reforms. Improving the low productivity of agriculture – the largest sector of the economy – must be
given high priority. All development programmes should be integrated into the environmental conservation policy. This last problem
is most pervasive in Nepal, where poverty and population pressures
compel the people to deplete natural resources to meet their immediate needs for survival.

The government elected in 1991 under the new constitution of 1990
gave cause for some optimism: in the Eighth Plan the government
had focused attention on development issues, examining the environmental effects of various economic policies, and taking the necessary steps to preserve the environment. However, political uncertainties have dogged Nepal since it took the path of multiparty
democracy. In 1994 the parliament was dissolved and new elections
were called that produced no clear majority. The Communist Party of
Nepal – Unified Marxist-Leninist (CPN-UML) – was returned as the
largest single party (with 88 members in a house of 205). A minority
Marxist-Leninist (UML) government came into office in 1994 with
issue-based support from the main opposition parties, the Nepali
Congress (NC) with 83 members and Rashtriya Prajatantra Party
(RPP) with 20 members. But after six months in power, the Marxist-
Leninist (UML) government opted for dissolution of the parliament
in June 1995 to secure a clear mandate in a new election scheduled
for November 1995. The Supreme Court of Nepal declared in August
1995 that the prime minister's recommendation to dissolve the parliament was unconstitutional and ordered its restoration. In a sense,
the UML government became a victim of its own inability to deliver
results. In its election campaign, the UML had promised to reduce
the prices of essential commodities and provide jobs for at least one
member of each family. None of these promises were nearer fulfil-
ment. The poor are unhappy with rising prices, and the intelligentsia
are concerned with the communist government's lack of accountability. For the average Nepali, double-digit inflation and large-scale
unemployment leave little ground for cheer. With the recent ruling
by the Supreme Court it is doubtful whether Nepal will go to the polls
for the third time since 1991. Political uncertainty will have a negative
impact on the pace and quality of development.

Like many other less developed countries, Nepal is at a crossroads
in the mid-1990s in its quest for economic and social development. It
has achieved much since the end of the Rana autocracy and its self-
imposed isolation in 1951, but much is left undone. Economic activity

remains weak, and investment growth is feeble. The absolute number of poor in Nepal has grown steadily in recent decades. Nepal's progress in poverty reduction has been among the slowest in Asia. Rapid population growth is one of the factors undermining the environmental resource base upon which sustainable development depends. Although the nature and strength of the reciprocal impacts between economic, environmental, and population phenomena vary in different regions of Nepal, strong links exist between population, environment, and development in the Kingdom.

The government's choice of the road ahead in meeting the challenges of growth and change will determine the pace and quality of development over the next decade and beyond. It is hoped that Nepal's economic development and environmental protection do not stand as unalterably opposed choices; they must walk hand in hand. Systematic evaluations and assessments of both environmental and economic costs and benefits often prove that sensible policies and actions that protect the environment can contribute to economic progress at the same time.

2

Environment and natural resource base

No other single factor dominates and influences the social and economic patterns of Nepal as does the natural environment and mountainous land. Not only do more than 90 per cent of the people depend on the land for their livelihood, but the nature of the land itself inhibits the process of development, both through natural diffusion processes and by planned efforts for development. Only a few countries in the world have such diverse extremes in topography, climate, soil conditions, vegetation cover, and land use encompassed in such a small geographical area. These factors naturally affect the population distribution and the effective relationship between man and the land in terms of the utilization of labour inputs, mobility, transportation, and social and economic interaction. Thus, the environmental conditions and interrelationships assume unusual importance in Nepal's development process.

Environmental factors in the development context

Within an area of 147,181 sq. km there are extremes of alluvial plain and the highest concentration of 8,000 metre peaks in the world. There are rich lake-deposit soils in the Kathmandu Valley and unfertile, rocky-soil terraces in the higher hill regions. There are gorges, torrential rivers, and semi-arid valleys. Estimates of the various classifications of land patterns are conflicting and unreliable, but in general terms, forests cover about one-third of the entire area while cropland occupies approximately one-sixth of the total land area. The remainder is made up of pasture, barren land, and areas of perpetual snow and ice.

Geoecological zones

Nepal can be divided into four geoecological zones: the Tarai, the Outer Himalaya, the Middle Mountains, and the Great Himalaya (fig. 2).

The highest geoecological zone is the Great Himalaya, which consists of a series of high peaks such as Mount Everest (8,848 m), Makalu (8,470 m), Dhaulagiri (8,172 m) and Annapurna (8,091 m). To the north of the Great Himalaya, a chain of arid mountains marks the southern boundary of the Tibetan plateau within the territory of Nepal. Although they are not the highest peaks in the system, these mountains form the watershed between the Ganges and the Tsangpo rivers and also separate the Himalaya from the Tibetan plateau.

Across the Great Himalaya and the Tibetan marginal mountains are a series of passes which are open to caravans during the summer months. A new highway, which was completed in the 1970s, links Nepal and Tibet as it crosses the Great Himalayan Range at the Kodari Pass. The Great Himalaya is sparsely populated; settlements are restricted to clearings in the high mountain valleys. An increased demand for firewood and overgrazing by livestock associated with high-altitude trekking and tourism have depleted the forests and alpine pastures in many areas. Tourism has created demands for services and materials that are slowly changing the ecology, environment, and the economy of the Great Himalayan zone.

The Middle Mountain zone consists principally of branches which run obliquely from the Great Range and other disconnected units. The chief oblique branches are the ranges of the Mahabharat that stretch on an east-west axis across Nepal. The Middle Mountain zone has a remarkable uniformity of elevation – between 3,000 and 5,000 m. This zone is dissected by a series of rivers: the Seti, Karnali, Bheri, Kali Gandaki, Trisuli, Sun Kosi, Arun, and Tamur. In the Middle Mountain zone most rivers converge and form four main systems – the Karnali, Narayani, Gandaki, and Kosi – which traverse the Mahabharat via deep gorges. Thus, east-west transportation has been very difficult if not impossible. In some places, in order to travel from one place to another only a few miles apart in air distance, it is still necessary to descend to the tarai, travel laterally (often in Indian territory), and then return to Nepalese territory and ascend the hills and mountains.

In the 1960s about 60 per cent of Nepal's population was living in the valleys and on the slopes of this geoecological zone. By the

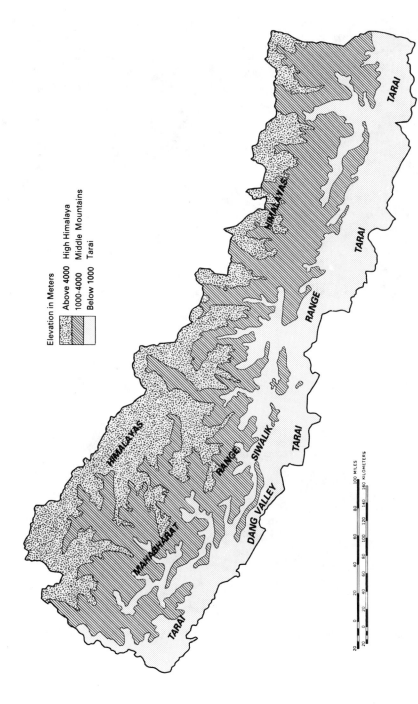

Elevation in Meters

Above 4000   High Himalaya
1000-4000   Middle Mountains
Below 1000   Tarai

Fig. 2 Geoecological regions

21

Glacier in the Dhaulagiri Range

Juniper trees to the east of Jumla in north-west Nepal (courtesy Z. Tamura)

Denuded slopes and deciduous trees, north of Okhaldhunga, east Nepal (courtesy M. Tamura)

1980s the population had decreased to about 45 per cent as a result of out-migration from the mountains. Sizeable populations exist in some large valleys like the Kathmandu and Pokhara. The population density in the Kathmandu Valley is more than 960 persons per sq. km and more than 385 in the Pokhara Valley. There are fewer people in the small valleys and basins, but even in the steepest and most rugged areas every patch of arable land has been settled, so that the most thinly populated regions still have densities of approximately 20 persons per sq. km.

Most cultivators in the Middle Mountains – each sustained by less than a quarter of a hectare of land – supplement their incomes by raising livestock. The forests in this zone have deteriorated, the result of clearing the land for cultivation, uncontrolled grazing, and the gathering of wood for fuel. The clearing of forests along road construction routes also contributes to the loss of top soil, landslides, and excessive water run-off. The people who live in the Middle Mountains are precariously dependent on the natural environment; any negative change in the physical environment adversely affects their survival. Environmental stress has generated a rural-to-rural migration flow within this geoecological zone and from it to the piedmont plain and on to Indian cities, where thousands of Nepalese find work in a variety of jobs ranging from security guard to domestic worker.

A 1993 field survey of several Parbasi Nepali Sanghs – organizations of Nepalese which provide assistance to new immigrants in north Indian cities – revealed that nearly 1.5 million Nepalese have left the Middle Himalaya area for jobs in India.

To the south of the Middle Himalaya lies the Siwalik Range of the Outer Himalaya, with an average elevation of between 1,000 and 2,000 m. This zone has a number of longitudinal flat-bottomed valleys, called *dun*s, which are usually spindle-shaped and filled with gravelly alluvium. The largest of the duns are the Rapti, Chitwan, and Dang, which are significant for agriculture. In many places the Siwaliks merge with the Mahabharat Range.

One malarial dun, the Rapti Valley, was transformed by an 80 km road built with United States aid in the late 1950s. The new road and a DDT-spraying programme opened the valley, which previously had been a hunting preserve for the Rana rulers, for the settlement of more than 30,000 homeless, landless farmers from the Middle Mountains. The success of the malaria-eradication programme led to other resettlements and land distribution efforts in southern Nepal. The resettlement programmes in the Outer Himalaya resulted in the widespread clearing of the forests to make land available for newcomers. Forests of this zone in most of Nepal are now restricted to small, scattered patches.

The Tarai forms the fourth geoecological zone of Nepal. Geographically, much of the Tarai is related to the Ganges plain of India and shares a common physiography. Nevertheless, the area is greatly influenced by the mountains, particularly by the complex of rivers that rise in the Himalayan region and flow southward through the Tarai. In recent geological times rivers such as the Sarda (Mahakali), Gogra, Greater Rapti, Narayani (Great Gandak), Bagmati, Sapta Kosi, Kanki, and Mechi have brought alluvium – either loamy and permeated with limestone or clayey and permeated with sand – down from the mountains. Those portions of the Tarai which have clayey/loamy alluvium and water are generally the most productive agriculturally.

Three regions can be distinguished in the Tarai: the eastern Tarai, the mid-western Tarai, and the far-western Tarai. The eastern and mid-western areas are much alike; both contain thousands of hectares of fertile land and have a year-round growing season in a fully tropical climate. The soil is fine-grained and very fertile. The far-western Tarai is a drier area with less rainfall; irrigation is often necessary for intensive agriculture.

Tarai village in east Nepal (courtesy M. Tamura)

The Tarai region is susceptible to flooding, which occurs regularly
with the monsoon run-off from the mountains. Most rivers have
changed their courses within historic times, thus altering established
patterns of cultivation. The large amount of silt and sediment carried
by the rivers from the higher elevations are deposited in their channels, until the channels can no longer accommodate the huge volume
of water during the monsoon. Consequently, water floods over the
countryside. The flooding of the land leads to the deposition of sediment, which each year replenishes the fertility of the land. However,
the sediment load is a major problem in the design of hydropower
and irrigation works.

Some observers have attributed the large volume of sediment carried by the rivers to man-made factors such as deforestation and
the resultant soil erosion in the catchment of the river basins. Others
attribute the heavy sediment to the natural dynamics of the Himalaya. The Himalayan chain is rising from its parent continental crust
far more swiftly than was previously thought. Some parts of the range
are moving skyward at about 1 cm a year, or about 30,000 feet every
million years. Since uplift is faster, down-cutting is faster, and the
rivers carry more sediment. No one has made a precise determination
of the sediment load attributable to deforestation and land use practices or to the sediment load attributable to the natural dynamics of
the mountains.

Multi-purpose dam in eastern Tarai (courtesy K. Inoue)

Nepal's landforms impose impressive constraints on the potential of its economic system. Agriculture can be practised on a scale exceeding subsistence levels only in portions of the Tarai, in a limited number of Siwalik duns where water can be made available, and in a few valleys in the Middle Mountains. Elsewhere subsistence cultivation is practised, but at great cost to man. The difficulty of land communications hinders the flow of marketable goods and creates a psychological sense of isolation, which inhibits efforts toward national integration. By its very diversity, the landform makes it difficult to formulate an economic development programme that can deal successfully with the particular problems of various geoecological regions.

Climatic configurations

Nepal's climate is characterized by marked changes in elevation and is subject to classification into different vertical zones. The variations of exposure to sunlight and to rain-bearing winds produce very intricate patterns of local climate, but there are also broad climatic areas based chiefly on lower temperatures with increasing elevation.

The Tarai area of south Nepal, like adjoining India, has a tropical monsoon climate. The monsoonal rhythm, characterized by seasonal rainfalls associated with the south-west winds of the summer monsoon and almost dry winters, extends into the mountain valleys. The Great Himalaya protects the southern part of Nepal from the bitterly cold winter winds – air masses generated in the Central Asian source regions. The winter high pressure is much weaker and produces much lighter winds (winter monsoon) than that of Tibet. On the other hand, the extremely intense heat of the Tarai in the summer (along with northern India) produces steep, low-pressure gradients, and the south-west wind (summer monsoon) is much stronger in Nepal.

Most of Nepal's rainfall (fig. 3) is associated with the south-west monsoon, which "breaks" in about mid-June and spreads throughout the country in July. The south-west monsoon usually lasts from June to September. There is a fairly steady east-to-west decrease in the amount of rainfall. For instance, in the tarai the rainfall decreases from 2,800 mm to 3,000 mm near Biratnagar in the east, to 1,200 mm to 1,400 mm near Mahendranagar in the far-western Tarai. The rainfall also increases from the south to the north with proximity to the Siwaliks. The areas near the Indian border receive less annual rainfall than the areas near the foot of the Siwaliks. The Himalayan slopes also show a comparable decrease in the amount of rainfall from the east to the west. The rainfall is strongly orographical on the Himalayan slopes, with higher totals than in the tarai.

In the Middle Mountain valleys the amount of precipitation varies with the extent of exposure to the rain-bearing monsoon winds. Several high valleys located in the well-marked rain-shadow of the mountains are extremely dry. In the Kathmandu Valley the average annual rainfall is about 2,285 mm, most of which occurs from June to September. In the north-west corner of the country in the upper reaches of the Karnali River Basin, in the upper regions of the Gandaki catchment in central Nepal, and in the tarai in west Nepal, the north-west winds bring 200 mm to 400 mm of precipitation during the winter months of December and January (fig. 4).

Evapotranspiration, when compared with effective rainfall, is an important indicator of the water needed for agricultural activities. The rainfall, estimated evapotranspiration, and the deficit in millimetres for a representative tarai location are noted in table 2.

The high moisture deficit during March and April in the tarai has considerable importance in relation to paddy cultivation. Temperatures in the tarai in the months of December, January, and February are considered to be too cold for paddy cultivation. Since paddy cultivation requires at least four months, the paddy must be planted in March or April. In addition to satisfying the large moisture deficit during these months, irrigation water must also be used to saturate and flood the paddy fields. The river flow is also at its lowest during

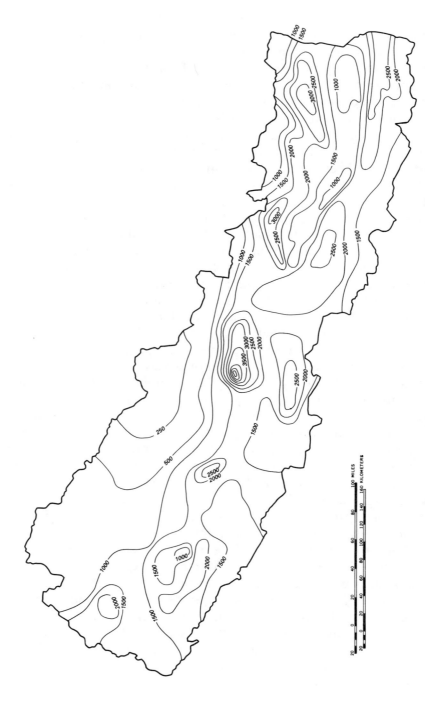

Fig. 3 Mean annual precipitation (After Nayava: Geographical Society of Nepal)

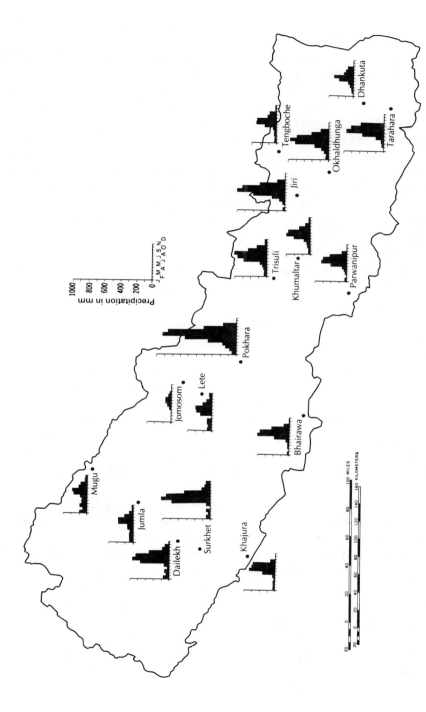

Fig. 4 Mean monthly rainfall at selected places (After Nayava: Geographical Society of Nepal)

29

this time. These rainfall and evapotranspiration factors have a bearing on the potential of the tarai for double or triple-cropping paddy.

Applying Thornthwaite's thermal efficiency index to temperature and precipitation data for Nepal, four climatic zones have been identified in the country (fig. 5). The lowlands – about 100 to 500 m above sea level – experience a sub-tropical climate with summer temperatures of 30°C and winter temperatures of about 18°C. The rainfall varies from 1,200 to 3,000 mm. Between 500 and 2,700 m a mesothermal climate (warm temperate) prevails. Summer temperatures are above 25°C and winters are cold. Rainfall varies from 250 to 6,500 mm on the leeward and windward sides respectively. A microthermal climate (cool temperate) prevails between 2,700 and 3,600 m. Maximum temperatures in the summer are 15–18°C; minimum temperatures in the winter are below 0°C. The average precipitation is 1,000 to 3,000 mm.

The taiga zone is dominant between 3,500 to 4,100 m. Summers are cool and winters are severe. Finally, the zone from 4,100 m has a tundra-type (alpine-arctic) climate.

Water resources

The climatic configuration influences the availability of water resources and is an important factor in the evaluation of land resources. Nepal's potential for water resources has frequently been compared to Switzerland's. However, the capacity of the rivers, especially the great transverse rivers, has yet to be completely assessed (fig. 6). Hydropower in relation to industrial development is discussed later in chapter 8. Here it may be appropriate to discuss the water resources for irrigation in the tarai.

The availability and use of water resources for agricultural purposes is a long-standing problem. It is one of the ironies of nature that the total volume of water which passes beyond Nepal's borders is so vast (estimated at about 150 billion cubic metres), yet some inner regions are uncultivated for want of water. Nepal is only beginning to tap the potential water resources of its river systems for irrigation. Only about 33,000 acres of land were irrigated in the tarai before 1952, mostly by the Chandra Canal (Saptari district) which was built in 1926, and by the Juddha Canal on the Manusmara River. Since 1955 a number of projects have been undertaken with foreign aid; the two largest are the barrages on the Kosi and Gandaki Rivers, which were built with Indian assistance.

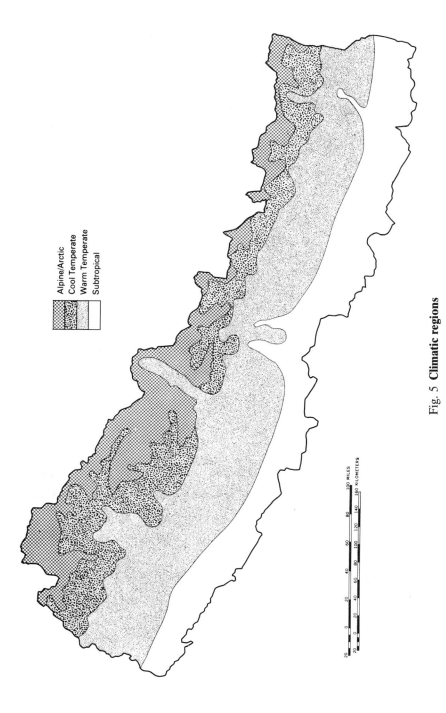

Alpine/Arctic
Cool Temperate
Warm Temperate
Subtropical

100 MILES
160 KILOMETERS

Fig. 5 **Climatic regions**

31

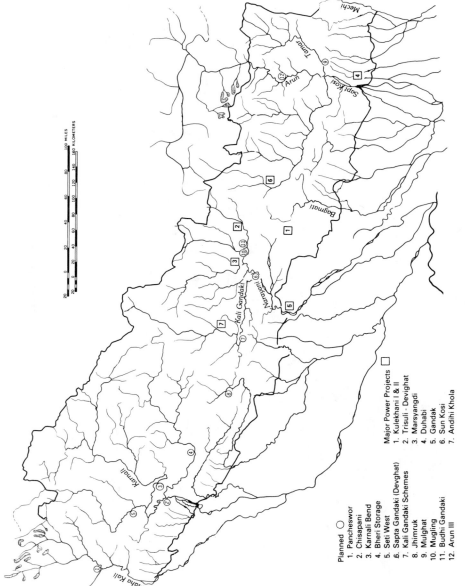

Planned ○
1. Pancheswor
2. Chisapani
3. Karnali Bend
4. Bheri Storage
5. Seti West
6. Sapta Gandaki (Devghat)
7. Kali Gandaki Schemes
8. Jhimruk
9. Mugling
10. Mughat
11. Budhi Gandaki
12. Arun III

Major Power Projects ☐
1. Kulekhani I & II
2. Trisuli - Devighat
3. Marsyangdi
4. Duhabi
5. Gandak
6. Sun Kosi
7. Andihi Khola

Fig. 6 **Drainage, water resources, and power projects**

32

Only a preliminary assessment of groundwater resources has been carried out in the tarai. No systematic investigation of groundwater resources in the mountainous area north of the tarai has been conducted so far, except in the Kathmandu Valley. Unconfined groundwater only a few metres deep flows throughout most of the tarai. Aquifers suitable for development by wells with the capacity of 50 to 80 litres/sec range in depth from 150 to 250 m. In this case, conventional deep-well turbine pumps, powered by electric or diesel motors, must be installed. Even where the artesian head of the aquifer in this depth range is a few metres or so above the land surface following the monsoon rains, the decline of the head during the dry season – with the resultant decrease in yield – usually requires the installation of pumping equipment.

Groundwater exploitation in the tarai is more promising than in the mountainous portions of the country. The areas offering the greatest potential for groundwater exploitation are those with flowing artesian conditions. These areas are found immediately south of the Siwaliks and in the central, interfluvial portions of the tarai. Such areas constitute nearly one-quarter of the total area of the tarai. Groundwater can be exploited through the construction of deep wells and the installation of pumping equipment.

The assessment of groundwater irrigation potential ranges from 0.4 million hectares (Upadhyay, 1993) to about 1 million hectares (Deo, 1993). The large difference in estimates of groundwater irrigation potential highlights how little accurate information is available on groundwater development. About 100,000 hectares are estimated to be irrigated with groundwater.

In addition, groundwater can also be exploited from shallow hand-dug wells, pumped by hand or animals, or by diesel or electric power. Such wells are found in areas of shallow water. These wells have a very low capital cost and command a very small area. Generally, each well is owned by one farmer, leading to high water-use efficiency and low capital and operating costs in relation to gains in agricultural productivity.

Public water-supply systems, which make use of abundant water resources, have not been developed. Consequently, there are intermittent or chronic scarcities of potable water in both the urban and rural areas. Even in places where wells, springs, and rivers provide an adequate supply of water, it is generally contaminated and dangerous to drink unless boiled.

Groundwater is not widely used. In 1987 the share of groundwater in total water use from all sources equalling 1,620 million cubic metres was 25 per cent, or 410 million cubic metres (United Nations, 1989). Groundwater is used mainly for irrigation (380 million cubic metres per year) and rural water supplies (25 million cubic metres per year), accounting for 24 per cent and 74 per cent respectively of the available water supply in those sectors. In several urban settlements in the tarai groundwater is used in limited amounts for domestic and industrial supplies.

The quality of groundwater is generally good for drinking water or for irrigation. The concentration of dissolved solids in groundwater is usually low to moderate, although it is higher in the shallow ground-water in the tarai. In some places, such as the Kathmandu Valley, the iron content slightly exceeds the permissible level for drinking water; therefore the groundwater is treated before it is used.

In 1987–1988 the average cost of developing groundwater was estimated by the United Nations Economic and Social Commission for Asia and the Pacific (ESCAP) at eight US cents per cubic metre for shallow, diesel-powered tube wells and two US cents per cubic metre for deep, electrically operated tube wells. In both cases, the cost of the tubes, pumps, and other equipment accounted for more than 50 per cent of the total development costs.

Farmers pay a water charge of two-tenths of one US cent per cubic metre in deep-tube well-irrigation projects, while for shallow-tube well-irrigation projects the consumers bear 90 per cent of the initial investment and 100 per cent of the operation and maintenance costs. For municipal water supplies consumers are charged at the rate of about 35 US cents per cubic metre.

No groundwater legislation is in force in Nepal. The responsibility for groundwater exploration and irrigation development in the country is vested in the groundwater section of the Department of Irrigation, Hydrology and Meteorology. Decisions on groundwater investigation programmes are made by an inter-ministerial body – the Groundwater Resources Board.

The groundwater resources of the tarai offer great potential for developing and expanding areas under perennial irrigation and for providing safe drinking water. There is a complex interaction between land ownership, tenure, and leasing systems, and the development of groundwater irrigation. Improving the access of poor farmers to groundwater resources can have an impact on alleviating poverty in Nepal. Some policy changes are necessary to make groundwater more accessible to small farmers. Increased and more effective farmer participation is needed in the development operations and maintenance of tube well-irrigation systems. A policy to encourage group ownership and operation will bring tube wells within the reach of the small farmers.

Mineral resources

The nature and extent of Nepal's mineral resources are very limited. While it is assumed that there may be undiscovered deposits of commercially valuable minerals, to date they have not been found in economically significant deposits. The fact that the Himalaya is geologically young contributes to the general paucity of significant resources.

Low-grade iron ore deposits are found at Phulchoki, near Kathmandu. The lack of coal and coking coal makes any development unfeasible without importing fuel. There are copper deposits scattered in many sections of Nepal, especially in Palpa and Okhaldunga, but the deposits are so small that any kind of mining industry based on them is highly impractical. Small home smelters are found in many parts of the country, but the resultant product is inferior and used only locally.

Throughout the length of the Kali Gandaki River to Mustangbhot and on the Marsyandi River to Dhaulagiri, gold is panned by the local people during periods of low water, usually in January. This gold is sold within Nepal. The primitive mining techniques and short period of time in which panning can be done make this at best a secondary occupation for a very small percentage of the population.

Small deposits of mica have been found in the hills north-east of the Kathmandu Valley, but the problem of extraction and transportation to the nearest market in Calcutta precludes their development. Limestone deposits have been located at Godavari and Nagarjung near Kathmandu. The Godavari deposit is of a decorative quality. Other deposits, notably along the Rajpath near Bhainse, have been cited as the resource for the establishment of a mini cement factory. Much of Nepal's limestone deposit has either a high silica or magnesium content, which makes it unsuitable for cement.

Deposits of talc have been found to the east of the Kathmandu Valley, close to the road to Kodari. However, the market for talc – used by the cosmetic industry – is in India, which would make transportation costly. There is the possibility of some petroleum reserves in the Siwaliks, where the geographic configuration might be favourable. In 1963 Shell International conducted an exploration for oil in Nepal's southern border areas, but did not find any deposits.

Several common problems confront the exploitation of Nepal's mineral resources. The lack of adequate fuel supplies for the extraction process not only increases the cost but also contributes to the rapid depletion of the forest resources in the surrounding area. The lack of adequate transportation to processing centres makes any exploitation costly. Finally, the markets for most of the minerals or products are not in Nepal but in India, thus adding to the high cost before the final product reaches the markets. An American aid programme financed the establishment of the Bureau of Mines for surveying the mineral resources. However, exploration has been phased out with the argument that known deposits must wait for improved transportation facilities or an increase in local demand (Malla, 1987).

Forest and scenic resources

The forest resources of Nepal and the environmental problems associated with their exploitation are discussed in chapter 3. Scenic resources, tourism, and the trekking industry are very important in Nepal and are discussed in chapter 10.

Natural resource management issues in Nepal

The major question concerning Nepal's natural resource management is how to manage the land, forest, and water resources in order to maintain both their productive capacities and ecological functions. Nepal is not the only country where improving natural resource management is a development issue. However, during the past two decades the significant loss and damage to the forests, soils, and riverine systems in many areas of Nepal have led to widespread environmental damage and declining agricultural productivity, underscoring the urgency of developing practical measures to re-establish a sustainable agricultural production system.

The situation in Nepal is complicated by three factors. First, like many low-income developing countries, the degradation of Nepal's natural resources is closely tied to the unrelenting pressure exerted on limited arable land by a large and rapidly growing population, almost 90 per cent of whom depend solely on agriculture for their livelihood. Over the past three decades, Nepal's high population growth rate has consistently outpaced the growth of the agricultural sector. Population growth has also resulted in the expansion of agricultural activities into marginally arable lands, causing a rapid depletion in resources and related environmental degradation. Therefore, any long-term effort to improve the management of Nepal's natural resources must be based on programmes that increase agricultural productivity through intensified cultivation rather than through expansion and a curb in population growth.

Secondly, until the late 1970s, Nepal's development policies did not emphasize natural resource management issues. From the 1950s through the early 1970s, government policies concentrated instead on developing power, transportation, and communication facilities, and on agricultural production in the Kathmandu Valley and in the lowland tarai. The government's strategy was to increase food-crop production in the tarai by adopting higher-yielding crops and by investing in irrigation facilities. In addition, the government claimed ownership over forest resources and established a government-owned forest-products industry.

During the late 1970s, the government of Nepal became increasingly committed to promoting economic development in other parts of the country. The government also became aware of the environmental degradation caused by clearing extensive tracts of forest for agricultural activity and by over-cutting and overgrazing forest and shrubland adjacent to farming areas. In many localities, the forest cover needed to maintain an ecological balance had either been destroyed or degraded to the point where natural regeneration was not occurring. Moreover, it had become clear that enforcing forest protection laws through legislation alone was virtually impossible.

Therefore, the government of Nepal began to take steps to reverse environmental degradation by supporting foreign donor-funded reafforestation and resource conservation projects and by addressing related policy issues. In short, natural resource management issues have only recently been incorporated into government and donor-sponsored development activities. In fact, serious attempts to deal with these issues began only in the 1980s. As a result natural resource management strategies and activities in Nepal are still experimental.

Thirdly, the country's mountainous terrain, landlocked situation, geographic diversity, and dispersed settlement pattern present formidable challenges for implementing development projects with infrastructure and service delivery components. The construction, operation, and maintenance costs of transportation and service networks in Nepal are very high, especially in isolated regions of the country.

Similarly, natural resource management approaches that rely on substantial investments in engineering works such as river training structures, fences, and other physical barriers that protect forest land or
prevent landslides can be very costly to implement and maintain.
Therefore, the cost-effectiveness of natural resource management
approaches in Nepal must be considered carefully.

Nepal's four decades of natural resource management experience
offer several insights. The most important lesson concerns the generating of government support for policy changes and related institution-building activities to facilitate the nationwide implementation
of natural resource management activities. In Nepal, the main issue
has been to draw the government's attention to the inadequacies of its
natural resource development policy and to invest in a long-term programme to integrate resource conservation activities into the government's development programme. Efforts towards this goal have
been generally ineffective in the past.

The emphasis on technology development and wide geographic
coverage have proved inappropriate, given the lack of institutional
support for the implementation of field activities associated with natural resource development projects and the lack of local management
and private enterprise in the effort. A major concern emerging from
Nepal's resource management experience is the question of how to
develop a strategy to address complex natural resource management
issues such as watershed management, and the development of scenic
resources, whose ramifications are not apparent during the initial
project design stage.

The implementation problems encountered in Nepal by resource
development programmes caution against the temptation to start a
natural resource management programme with "big fixes." The
implementation of large-scale projects involving technologies and
approaches that far exceed the country's capabilities can quickly turn
into a management nightmare. Technically sophisticated solutions
are not always required. On the contrary, Nepal's experience shows
that community-level resource management and conservation activities can be undertaken with minimum technical assistance and subsequently managed on a self-sustaining basis.

A small-scale programme to promote natural resource management need not start with policy reform or institution-building projects. Instead, initial support can focus on resource conservation
activities that can be integrated into existing agricultural or rural
development programmes. Such activities can concentrate on devel-

oping low-cost simple measures, such as curbing soil erosion on hill slopes and catchment areas, that can be undertaken by individual people or on a communal basis to improve the local resource base. Apart from teaching farmers to conserve soil and water resources, the objective would be to increase the production of livestock and tree products without compromising the production of food crops.

Finally, problems with the implementation of resource management clearly indicate that the process of planning natural resource management activities should not stop at the local government level. Groups in the local population – especially women – affected by the programme should be actively involved in planning conservation activities and maintaining the resource base. Nepal is taking an important step in this direction by introducing legislation and economic incentives to encourage the formation of groups that will be responsible for restoring and maintaining the natural resources, such as forests. The effectiveness of these measures in drawing genuine community support for resource management will not be known for some time.

3

Land use, forest cover, and environmental problems

During the past few decades, governments have paid considerable attention to spatial organizations at the national and regional levels of land use patterns to protect and maintain the integrity of the environment. The concept of rational land use – a sensible distribution of land between agriculture, forestry, and grazing – has been evolving rapidly in the direction of integrated land resource management towards a condition in which the goods and services of the different subsectors combine to achieve the best possible result to sustain the environment and the ecology. At a more restricted local or regional level, this management of space finds application in integrated watershed management, in specific natural resources management (forest, grazing land, and farm management) and in community development, according to the priority given to physical, economic, social, and environmental criteria.

Unfortunately, there are few land use theories that relate to the mountain ecosystems such as those of Nepal. Very often land management concepts and methods originally developed in industrialized countries have been transferred to countries like Nepal. Often theoretical models do not take into account the difficult mountainous terrain, although in practice it has been proposed to set aside areas in need of protection, using as criteria the steepness of the slopes, erodibility, or poor productivity of the land.

The development of a sound land use pattern is the key to protecting the environment and the ecology. The final decision on land use is always a political one, even if this decision is taken with regard to the existing ecological, economic, and social factors. Despite the importance of a land use pattern in environmental management, accurate data on Nepal's land use is not available. During the last four decades planning and development activities have been based on only rough estimates of land use made at various times. No effort has been made to attempt a complete inventory of land resources or to produce a comprehensive land use map of the country to formulate and implement plans and projects pertaining to the growth of agriculture, forest management, resettlement programmes, and urban and rural development.

Land use pattern

A brief inventory of the general pattern of distribution of the land for important use – cultivation and forestry, for example – seems appropriate at this time. Estimates of land use under various categories, which have been made by scholars and government agencies from time to time since 1954, are summarized in table 3.

The land use estimates are beset with a number of limitations in terms of spatial coverage and procedures employed to collect data. They give only a generalized view of major land use in Nepal between 1954 and 1990. Nearly one-third (33 per cent) of the land area of Nepal is economically unfit for agriculture or forestry; it is covered with permanent snow or consists of steep, rocky, barren slopes. The remaining two-thirds of the land area are suitable for agriculture, forestry, and grazing, as well as for a variety of other uses, depending on the physical attributes of the land.

According to various estimates, forests have occupied (fig. 7) about one-third of the land area, which indicates that the area under forest has remained relatively stable; some recent figures even show a substantial increase in forest cover. Robbe's estimated cultivated area appears exaggerated, but it is evident that the area under cultivation has increased from about 10 per cent in the 1960s to about 20 per cent in the 1980s. The cultivated area shrank to 18 per cent in 1990.

Forest cover

Precise estimates of forest cover in Nepal are not available. Differences in the definition of "forest land" in various estimates make comparisons of the area under forest cover difficult. For example, the Land Resource Mapping Project by Kenting Earth Sciences Ltd. of Canada revealed the area with forest cover to be 42.69 per cent of the

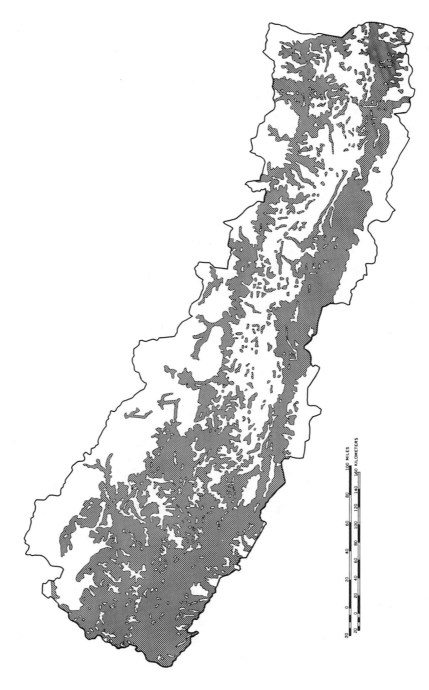

Fig. 7 **Forest cover**

100 MILES
160 KILOMETERS

42

total area of the country. In this study three classes of forest cover – namely 10–40 per cent, 40–70 per cent, and 70–100 per cent – and shrubland were combined. The Land Resource Mapping Project used 1:50,000 stereo photographs along with detailed field work. The Land Resource Mapping Project data provide a much more intensive and complete forest cover inventory than earlier surveys (Kenting Earth Sciences Ltd., 1986).

The first scientific measurement of forest resources was undertaken in 1963 by the Forest Resources Survey Office of Nepal's Department of Forests, assisted by the US Agency for International Development. This survey was based on aerial photographs taken over a 15-year period – 1953–1967 – and adjusted by strip photographs covering 10 per cent of the surveyed area.

The high Himalayan area – a mostly barren tract of roughly 3 million hectares – was not covered at all, and there were gaps in the coverage of the Middle Mountain region of over 1 million hectares. The area under forest cover in this survey was estimated at 6.5 million hectares with 5.7 million hectares in the Middle Mountains and 0.8 million hectares in the tarai (Water and Energy Commission, 1987: 27). This figure is not comparable with land use data for 1964 as reported in the Agricultural Statistics of Nepal and reproduced in table 3.

In 1977 the FAO/UNDP Integrated Watershed Management Project in the Department of Soil Conservation and Watershed Management made the next inventory of forest cover. This was based on 1975 satellite imagery and supplemented by air and ground field work. The main purpose of this survey was to identify the major ecological and land units and their watershed conditions. The total area under forest in 1975 was estimated at 6.1 million hectares with 3.7 million hectares in the Middle Mountains and 0.4 million hectares in the tarai (Nelson et al., 1980). The 1964 and 1977 surveys used different definitions of forest land and were not directly comparable. The 1964 survey considered land with more than 10 per cent of crown cover as forest land, while the FAO/UNDP survey included only land with more than 50 per cent of crown cover.

A comparison of the Land Resource Mapping Project data and the FAO/UNDP data for equivalent land types indicates that they agree within 1 per cent. Thus, forest areas (more than 50 per cent of crown cover) comprised 29.1 per cent of the area of Nepal in the FAO/UNDP inventory and 28.1 per cent (more than 40 per cent of crown cover) in the Land Resource Mapping Project. The area under forest

43

cover declined. The Middle Mountain area lost less than 4 per cent of its forest area, while the tarai lost nearly 25 per cent (Nield, 1985; Water and Energy Commission, 1987: 27).

Data from Karan's land use mapping in 1960, field reconnaissance in Nepal during 1991–1992, and an analysis of figures of forest cover given in various reports indicate that with the exception of the tarai, the area under forest has not changed very much during the last 30 years. This is corroborated in recent works by Mahat (1985) and Gilmour (1987). However, the forest area has been considerably degraded. Valleys which were covered with forests in 1960 have been cleared in many areas where access to inputs or outside employment made conversion profitable. A depletion in forests means less fuel-wood, fodder, and timber. It means the loss of soil fertility, increased soil erosion, and the degradation of fragile lands. It means changes in the water supply for agriculture and energy, as well as increased flooding caused by the rapid run-off.

Hillsides damaged by landslides, north of Okhaldhunga, east Nepal (courtesy M. Tamura)

Forest typologies

Although there is an enormous variation in forest types, for analytical purposes three types can be distinguished: tropical moist deciduous, sub-tropical moist hill-pine, and temperate conifer (fig. 8). There is considerable variation within all three types. The output of a particular forest depends greatly on management and silvicultural intensity, and on the level and type of human interference.

Tropical moist deciduous forest

This forest occupies the moist area of higher temperatures in the tarai and in the Churia Hills along the southern part of Nepal. The dominant tree in the Churia Hills is the *sal (shorea robusta)* whereas in the tarai *khair, sisso, semal,* and *karma* predominate.

The forests of the lowland tarai may be divided into: (1) new riverain species found abundantly in the main river beds and on the islands, and (2) old riverain species found further away from river beds where the soil is no longer subject to flooding. The new riverain forests contain mainly the *khair (acacia catechu)* and *sisso (dalbergia sisso)* species, often in association with tall grasses. *Sisso* is used in furniture making. From *khair* catechu is extracted and used in the making of *pan* (a mixture of betel nuts, betel leaves, and catechu), which is chewed by the local people. The new riverain forests hold together the gravel, boulders, and sand brought down by the rivers from the Churia Hills and the Mahabharat Range. In the early 1950s there were at least 210,000 hectares of this forest in the tarai; most of it has been cleared during the last 40 years.

Away from the river banks *semal (bombax malabaricum), karma (adina cordifolia), siris (albizzia sp.), bot dongero (lagerstroemia), latikarma (hymenodycton),* and many other species of the old riverain forests appear. These forests occur throughout Nepal between the new riverain and the *sal* forests of the foothills. *Semal* is one of the most valuable species of this type of forest. In the early 1950s it was intensively exploited in the western districts of Banke, Bardiya, Kailali, and Kanchanpur, and in the central tarai districts, except for Chitwan. This wood can be used for plywood, matches, and paper. *Karma* also has a high commercial value in furniture and veneer manufacturing.

Sal appears where the land starts to rise beyond the old riverain forests. The *sal* forest once extended over an estimated area of

46

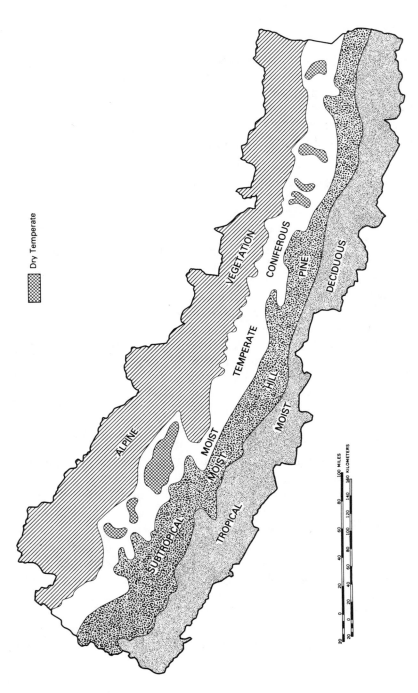

Dry Temperate

ALPINE

MOIST TEMPERATE VEGETATION

SUBTROPICAL

MOIST

CONIFEROUS

PINE

MOIST HILL

TROPICAL

DECIDUOUS

20   0   20   40   60   80   100 MILES

20   0   20   40   60   80   100 120 140 160 KILOMETERS

Fig. 8 **Natural vegetation**

907,000 hectares in the 1950s, based on the author's reconnaissance survey. Economically, *sal*, which is used for building and to make railroad ties, is the most valuable forest in Nepal; it has a vast market in India. All of the readily accessible areas of the *sal* forests have been depleted during the last four decades. Once the Chitwan and Morang districts had very extensive and healthy stands of *sal* forest; these lands have now been converted to an alternative use, such as agricultural land or urban development.

In the Churia Hills *sal* – associated with pine – is found between 300 and 1,200 m. This *sal* is of an inferior quality. Because of the distance from road and rail terminals, the stands have not been exploited as intensively as in the tarai plain. *Chir* (*pinus longifolia*) grows in the drier parts of the Churia Hills. There are other species of lesser commercial value, but the ground cover of *babai* grass is an important resource for the manufacture of paper and pulp.

Tropical moist forests, which contain a large biomass, represent one of the densest terrestrial ecosystems of Nepal. Only a small segment of these – where human activity has had little impact on the ecosystem – remains intact. In most of the tropical moist deciduous forests, human interference, including logging and agriculture, has resulted in damage that ranges from slight to severe.

Subtropical moist hill pine

The subtropical moist hill pine occupies a long belt along the Himalayan slopes (mostly at 900 to 2,100 m). Pine with some oaks predominate in this area. *Sal* may be found in suitable sites on the lower margins. Cultivation of the land has been so intensive in this zone that very little of the forest remains.

On the Mahabharat Range – a broad sweep of country (1,500 to 2,750 m) stretching along the whole length of Nepal – the forests consist of a great mixture of species such as pine, oak, rhododendron, poplar, walnut, alder, magnolia, and conifer. In the east, the main species are oak, magnolia, larch, and pine. Except for the remote and inaccessible areas, most of this forest land has been cleared; some inferior clusters on the steep slopes and rocky terrain remain intact.

In the western part of the Mahabharat Range, the main species are *khair, chir*, walnut, and cedar. In some areas fairly extensive forests still exist. In the upper basins of the Mahakali and Karnali Rivers the large stands of *khair* and cedar (*cedar deodara*) mixed with walnut have been depleted. In the lower basins of the Mahakali and Karnali Rivers the *chir* and deodar have gone through large-scale logging.

The subtropical moist forest zone is mostly open woodland, containing a far less biomass per unit area than tropical moist forests. Overexploitation has caused severe degradation, including soil erosion, weed infestation, and an increased susceptibility to fire and insects. These areas of degraded forests are utilized extensively by thousands of small-scale farmers and local communities, which are highly dependent on the patches of woodland, forest-fallow vegetation, natural shrubs, and planted-on-farm trees for their fuelwood, fodder, building materials, and other basic needs. Depending on the inherent quality of the site, market conditions, and technology, degraded forest land may be suitable for restoration as forest plantations or for conversion to other uses.

Temperate conifers

The temperate coniferous forest of Nepal can be subdivided into two zones, according to the elevation. The upper part (approximately 3,350 to 3,650 m) of the temperate conifers consists of *talispatra* (*abies spectabilis*) mixed with *bhojpatra* (*betula utilis*). Rhododendrons are abundant in this subalpine zone. In the lower part (approximately 2,150 to 3,350 m) various species of oak are dominant, but there are also larch, bamboo, and some hardy deciduous trees. There is a significant difference in vegetation between the northern and southern slopes of the mountain range. On the southern (warm) side conifers are not well developed; here oak forests predominate.

In certain sections of the Middle Mountain ranges, such as the northern flanks of the Dhaulagiri Range, the moist temperate forest is replaced by a rather open xerophytic forest. This dry temperate forest consists mainly of junipers with scattered oak and ash. On the more arid hillsides and terraces junipers are replaced by thorny bushes.

The Middle Mountain ranges bear some of the finest and most valuable forests left in Nepal. At 2,750 m there is *khair*; up to 3,050 m there are magnificent forests of this species mixed with *picea morinda* and *thigo* (*abies pindrow*); above that *khair* gradually gives way to *dhupi* (*cupressus torulosa*) and junipers. Of the hardwoods, oak and maple occur up to 2,900 m, and from there on up to the timberline (4,250 m) there is birch.

Deforestation and degradation

Except for the tarai, the forest area of Nepal is approximately the same as it was 30 years ago. In the tarai the large-scale resettlement programme has led to a dramatic reduction in forest land since 1954. Precise estimates of actual deforested areas vary, but field reconnaissance reveals that areas under forest are very small indeed. The tropical forests of the tarai once formed a nearly continuous dense, green belt. Most of this land has been cleared since the mid-1950s. The tarai has absorbed an ever-increasing stream of migrants from the Middle Himalaya during the last 30 years; according to the 1991 census it contained nearly half of Nepal's population.

According to the 1964 Forest Resources Survey of the Department of Forests with US AID assistance (Water and Energy Commission, 1986: 27) and the FAO/UNDP survey (Nelson et al., 1980), the forest area in the tarai declined from 0.8 million to 0.4 million hectares during the 1964–1975 period. A comparison of the Land Resource Mapping Project data (Kenting Earth Sciences Ltd., 1986) and the FAO/UNDP data shows that the tarai lost one quarter of its forest area between 1964–1965 and 1978–1979 (Mahat, 1985: 4).

In the Middle Mountains and High Himalayan region less than 4 per cent of the forest area was lost during 1964–1965 and 1978–1979. Thus, the forest area (more than 10 per cent of crown cover), excluding the Great Himalaya, declined from 5.6 to 5.4 million hectares. The total forest area declined from 6.4 to 6.0 million hectares (excluding 221 thousand hectares in the High Himalaya), based on the Land Resource Mapping Project and FAO/UNDP data (table 4).

There are several different reasons for the deforestation of Nepal's mountains and tarai. Large-scale deforestation in the tarai was accompanied by resettlement projects and the increasing pressure of migrants from the Middle Himalaya on the already limited tarai forests. Deforestation in the tarai has allowed an alternative use of forested land for agriculture, urbanization, and infrastructural development such as roads. In the mountains the forest area – although damaged and degraded – has stabilized, and the forests have become an important source of leaf fodder, commonly collected from the community forest. The forest is a more important source of fuelwood in the mountains than in the tarai, where villagers have greater access to other energy sources, such as kerosene.

Hillside trees on fire in east Nepal (courtesy M. Tamura)

Principal factors leading to deforestation

Policies and programmes for forest management must be based on an understanding of the principal factors leading to deforestation. Population growth and an increasing demand on forests for fodder, fuelwood, and land-clearing, as well as institutional factors, have contributed to deforestation.

Population growth

Nepal's population increased from 9.4 million in 1961 to 11.6 million in 1971, to 15.0 million in 1981, and to 18.5 million in 1991. Growth in the tarai (4.2 per cent per year during the years 1971 to 1981) is much higher than in the mountains (1.6 per cent). The population, close to 20 million now, is increasing at an annual rate of 2.1 per cent, which would cause it to double in only 33 years. An increasing population over the last 30 years has led to growing demands for farmland to grow food; fodder to feed the livestock that provide manure, milk, and draft power; and fuelwood for cooking, heating, and lighting.

50

Land survey officer at work in a Middle Mountain village in central Nepal

Land clearing

Growing population pressure and a scarcity of agricultural land has increased the pressure to convert forest land into agricultural settlements. The malaria eradication in the tarai, beginning in 1958 with assistance from US AID and WHO, has resulted in an ever-increasing stream of migrants from the Middle Mountains to the tarai during the past 30 years. In the Middle Mountains, forests were earlier converted to grazing land and then to farmland, while in the tarai government resettlement schemes, as well as migrants from the Middle Mountains, converted land directly from forest to farmland. Most cultivable land in the Middle Mountains had already been converted to farmland by 1960 (Karan, 1961). Further increases in farmland during the past three decades have taken place on marginal Middle Mountain land. Additional increases in farmland are likely to come from the conversion of the remaining tarai forest to agriculture. It is likely that all of the tarai forest will be converted to farmland to feed the growing population.

51

Despite land reform efforts beginning in 1964, which placed limits on land ownership, little land has been distributed to poor farmers, and land ownership remains significantly skewed. The poorest half of the population, who own an average of barely 0.1 hectares per household, owns less than 7 per cent of the cultivated land. Even if the population were not increasing, small-scale farmers would need more land in order to grow enough food for their families.

Since crop yields have been stagnant in Nepal, an increase in food production has been achieved by increasing the area of farmland and the number of crops per year. Crop production has not kept pace with the population growth, and per capita crop production has declined. From 1961 to 1981 the production of major food crops increased less than 25 per cent from 3.5 to 4.3 million metric tons (Department of Food and Agricultural Marketing Services, 1983), while the population increased by nearly 60 per cent. Yield increases on irrigated land with improved seed have been offset by declining yields resulting from extensive cultivation on the steep slopes. While potential increases in crop yields with improved seeds are possible, and the number of crops grown each year can be increased if water is available, some increases in crop production will probably come from the further conversion of forest to farmland, particularly in the tarai.

Fodder collection

In Nepal, dependency on forests for fodder is high (Wyatt-Smith, 1982). Almost every household in Nepal maintains some animals. The average number of bovine animals per family was estimated at 4.4 and 6.2 in the Middle Mountains and in the tarai respectively (World Bank, 1974). The bovine population in 1962 was 7.7 million (5.7 million cattle and 2.0 million buffalo); by 1981 it was 8.9 million (6.5 million cattle and 2.4 million buffalo), an increase of less than 1 per cent per year. The goat population increased from less than 2.8 million to over 3.6 million between 1962 and 1981, an increase of less than 1.5 per cent per year. By 1984/85, there were 6.4 million cattle, 2.8 million buffalo, and 4.9 million goats. The goat population is now increasing in response to the increased costs of maintaining animals as the forest resources decline. There is an increasing preference for buffalo over cattle and for goats and sheep over bovines because buffalo, goats, and sheep are more efficient in converting low-grade fodder into milk, meat, and energy. Buffalo produce more and richer milk, and some ethnic groups eat buffalo meat.

The limited amount of grazing land in the Middle Mountains provides enough feed for the animals only during the monsoon season
(between June and September). Private fodder trees and crop residue
provide some feed during other months but it is not enough because
the land holdings are so small. Families rely on the forests to make up
the difference, estimated to be about 23 per cent of the total consumption (Rajbhandary and Shah, 1981). It has been estimated that
the average family requires 3.5 hectares of forest to support its livestock (Wyatt-Smith, 1982). It is difficult to estimate the forest area
currently available to each family for fodder collection. However, the
forest land divided by the number of households gives an area of only
about 1.7 hectares per family (R. L. J. Shrestha, 1982). This is only
half the land needed to support the livestock.

Overgrazing by livestock results in the continuing degradation of
forests and grasslands. Apart from the direct consumption of fodder,
grazing animals degrade the forest and pasture resources by eating
seeds and small tree seedlings, uprooting young grass-shoots, and
trampling both the seedlings and the new grass. While fodder consumption does not directly reduce the forest area, the destruction
of the shrubs and grass layer may be the main cause of forest degradation, which leads to increased erosion as a result of the depleted
ground cover and compacted soil. Goats and sheep, which clip the
grasses close to the ground, are responsible for more overgrazing
than the cattle and buffalo. Often people harvest the fodder from the
trees over a long period of time to prevent regeneration.

Fuelwood

Dependency on forests for essential fuelwood for domestic use is
one of the main factors leading to deforestation. Fuelwood is the
main energy source and is likely to remain so in the near future.
Domestic use accounts for 95 per cent of the energy consumed in
Nepal, and about 87 per cent of the country's total energy needs is
derived from wood (World Bank, 1978). As the population of Nepal
has increased, the consumption of fuelwood has also increased, but at
a slower rate. As fuelwood becomes harder to obtain due to declining
forest resources, people are turning to other forms of energy such as
crop residue in the Middle Mountains and dung-cakes in the tarai.

The estimates of annual per capita fuelwood use has ranged from
0.10 to 6.67 cubic metres; a government report indicates that the
national per capita consumption is about 0.9 cubic metres or 650 kg

53

(Water and Energy Commission, 1988). There is considerable regional variation in fuelwood consumption. In the Middle Mountains, consumption varies from about 0.7 cubic metres in central Nepal to about 1.2 cubic metres in eastern Nepal. Consumption in the tarai varies from 0.6 cubic metres in the central tarai to over 1.4 cubic metres in the western tarai. The Middle Mountain people consume more than the inhabitants of the tarai. Mountain populations have greater heating requirements and have greater access to the forests for fuelwood. But in the tarai, access to forests is relatively difficult. Urban residents of Nepal generally consume the least amount of fuelwood – less than 0.4 cubic metres – because commercial fuels are available and some urban households can afford to buy them.

Shrestha (1986), in a detailed study of two Middle Mountain panchayats (in Syangja and Kaski districts) and one in the eastern tarai (Morang district), reported that the farmers' dependency on different sources of fuelwood is changing. Dependency on the forests for fuelwood supplies declined in the mountains as well as in the tarai during the years 1976–1985. Shrestha notes that people have begun to supplement their supplies of fuelwood by purchasing it from private lands and forests. In the tarai panchayat more people were purchasing fuelwood. In general, one person per household was engaged in collecting fuelwood. The average time taken to collect a load of fuelwood per person in the Middle Mountain panchayat was three hours and in the tarai it was five to eight hours, according to Shrestha's field survey.

The extra time spent in collecting fuelwood and other forest products takes time away from agriculture, which results in reduced income from farming. This adversely affects food consumption and eventually the nutritional status of the population (Kumar and Hotchkiss, 1988). Nepalese women face an increasing workload as deforestation expands. This tends to reduce their overall labour input in agriculture with deforestation, thereby decreasing further the already low productivity of mountain agriculture.

A satisfactory substitute for fuelwood as a source of energy is not readily available in the rural areas of Nepal. Water-power development, with its high construction and distribution costs, may not be available in the near future. Biogas is used by some tarai villagers, but the initial cost is too high for most Nepalese farmers. For the rural populations of Nepal there are no feasible fuelwood substitutes. If fuelwood is not available, rural people will burn crop residue or animal dung. In each case a valuable resource is used, depriving animals of their main source of fodder, depriving the crops of an important source of fertilizer, and depriving the soil of needed organic matter. In urban areas, people are switching to kerosene, electricity, and gas. Increased fuelwood production and increased efficiency in fuelwood use are practical alternatives for the future. Improved stoves have been distributed and adopted by many households in Nepal, but their use has not spread as rapidly as expected.

Forest management in Nepal

Forest management in Nepal has been influenced by a number of economic, social, and political factors. Management systems differ substantially as one moves from west to east and from north to south, through different ecological and cultural settings. In part, this reflects a change in climate and ecology, with the west possessing lower biomass productivity due to lower rainfall levels and consequently greater levels of scarcity. Indigenous forest management institutions and capacity are better developed in the west, perhaps for this reason.

The political history of Nepal has also influenced the evolution of forest management institutions in different parts of the country. From the time of unification, the government's authority over forest land was gradually extended through the collection of revenue. In areas closer to government centres, communities have been less autonomous and have had to share a greater proportion of their forest resources with the state. Less isolated communities have had greater interaction with the Forest Department and its programmes, while remote villages have been left to manage their forests with little interaction from the state, regardless of the nature of the government's forest policies.

Human ecological studies of resource use patterns in Nepal Himalaya indicate that many of the region's cultural communities use the forest, grassland, and water most efficiently (Davis, 1993). Fodder and fuelwood production is often maximized through the periodic lopping and pruning of such multipurpose species as oaks, alders, and willows. Local users often exploit forest resources on a rotational basis, allowing them to recover. The pruning of willows and the lopping of oaks and other fodder trees is usually carried out with care to maximize the yield and avoid injury to the trees. In many mountain villages, resource use patterns reflect the attempts to transfer energy and resources from one part of the ecosystem to another. In the upper Kali Gandaki river valley, Thakali farmers collect large quantities of pine needles from the forests, which are composted with manure to fertilize the better agricultural land. In this way the forest resources enhance the productivity of prime farmland.

More research is needed to determine the impact on the productivity and sustainability of each subecosystem as nutrients and resources are shifted in space and time. Where farmers are maximizing the productivity of the better irrigated farmland – in part driven by the commercialization of the agricultural economy – they may also be relieving pressure on marginal rain-fed land. Further studies of energy transfer patterns are needed to better assess the optimal use systems.

Systems for the utilization of mountain resources mostly appear to be run by small residential or clan-based groups. Generally, they are based on the premise of an equitable division of protection costs and production benefits. In the Middle Mountains, equity involves getting a fair share, not necessarily an equal share, and this will vary according to the social context and economic need. This view of equity allows villages to take family resources into account and to adjust contributions and benefits according to capacity and need. The equitable distribution of produce and benefits becomes more of a problem when the government or outside development agencies invest in projects to optimize or change resource use patterns, creating new resources or upsetting existing distribution arrangements.

Equity has also become an issue in areas where many men seasonally or temporarily migrate, leaving the women to manage the farms and forests. As this male migration has grown in importance in Nepal in supplementing family incomes, the women are playing an increasingly strategic role in decision making and are the primary source of labour. Yet, among some groups women lack the authority to take action in managing the resources. In many Middle Mountain villages the men in the community, who once made resource management decisions and carried on forest protection functions, are increasingly absent. Now the women must take over their roles. Government departments, with their predominantly male staffs, do not have the capacity to work with the women's groups involved in forest management.

In the evolution of forest management systems, Nepal represents a unique case. Nepal was one of the last nations in South Asia to place forest lands legally under central government control through the Forest Nationalization Act of 1956. This occurred approximately a century after state authority was imposed in most south and south-east Asian countries. However, once forest lands were nationalized, the Nepal Forest Department experienced major difficulties in their protection and management. The lack of staff and extreme isolation of much of the forest areas limited the agency's attempts to survey, demarcate, and manage the land under its jurisdiction. Before nationalization, traditional rules existed for forest protection and management by the villagers. However, after the government assumed ownership of all forests, the existing traditional rules faded, and the local people felt they were no longer responsible for the forests.

Traditional forest management

Before 1957 the state exercised little control over the forests. Nepal's forest resources were managed largely as a common property regime, with local villagers controlling forest use and receiving the benefits of conservation.

Before 1957 Nepal's land, including forest land, was held under (1) Raikar (state landlordism and its derivatives): (a) Birta – land granted to individuals as a favour and for specific jobs, (b) Guthi – trust land assigned to religious and philanthropic institutions, and (c) Jagir – land assigned to government employees; and (2) the Kipat (communal ownership) system. Among them Jagir and Birta were abolished in 1951 and 1959 respectively. Kipat, which had a long history in Nepal, was abolished in 1968.

Ethnic groups living in the mountains considered the use and conservation of the forests their local responsibility. With a smaller population and more extensive forest resources, the supply of fodder and fuelwood from the forest was more than adequate to meet the demand in the years before 1957. The absence of property rights, however, led to a lack of investment in forest resources to ensure future supplies. There was no incentive to encourage investments to provide for future consumption.

Nationalization and the government's management of forest resources

The Private Forests Nationalization Act of 1956 gave ownership of Nepal's forest resources to the government. However, the government lacked the technical and administrative resources to manage

Pine forest in Khotan district in east Nepal (courtesy M. Tamura)

the forests. Forest areas were not demarcated; it was not known what areas were under government authority. There were very few trained forest officers to oversee the management of the forests.

The reaction to nationalization varied from one area to another, depending upon the people's awareness of new legislation. In most of the remote areas people were unaware of new legislation due to the lack of forest officials; in these areas the nationalization of the forests had little or no impact. In other areas people reacted negatively to nationalization because their traditional rights to the use of forest resources as well as their responsibility for local management was terminated. In areas where land records did not exist, people cleared the forests and converted them to agriculture to prevent the government from assuming ownership. In this way large sections of the forests were destroyed in Nepal in the years following nationalization, and land was claimed as private property after it was cultivated. In some areas where forest demarcation had begun, irregularities in forest boundaries also provided an incentive to convert land to private ownership.

In many parts of Nepal, nationalization led to the conversion of forests from common property management with restraints on their use and conservation to an open-access resource with overuse and an absence of obligation to conserve. After the forests became an open-access resource in 1957, there was widespread degradation. Several laws were passed from 1957 to 1977 to regulate the use of forest resources, but most of these legislations were not implemented due to the inadequacy of the forestry administration.

Nationalization changed the perceived locus of the decision-making authorities with respect to forest resources. Before nationalization, local individuals and community groups controlled the use of forest resources. After nationalization, in locations where the prospect of government intervention seemed likely, individuals began to convert forests into private property, often by converting them into agricultural land. Where cultivation was not sustainable, erosion increased. Much of this land is now low-grade forest. Where the prospect of government intervention seemed unlikely, traditional management continued.

The 1961 Forest Act was comprehensive forest legislation that prohibited destructive activities. The 1967 Forest Protection Act prohibited damage to, or the removal of, forest products without official permission. The 1970 Forest Products Rules established a system of permits and prices for forest products. Most of these rules and regulations were not enforced. Most forest boundaries are not demarcated, so it is difficult to implement rules concerning damage or the removal of forest products. There have been reports in the Nepali press of local forest guards receiving and transmitting illegal payments to use the forests, and of the sale of permits to cut thousands of hectares of tarai forests at a premium to finance the panchayat referendum of 1980 (*Rising Nepal*, 28 November 1987).

The 20-year period which followed nationalization in 1956 was characterized by the lack of institutional foundations for forest conservation and management, which resulted in the widespread degradation of the forest land.

Community forestry management since 1977

In 1977 the National Forestry Plan – allowing community involvement in managing national forests – was introduced. Under the Panchayat Forestry Acts of 1978 and 1980, Nepal allocated about 40 per cent of all national forest land for participatory management. The

Nepal Forest Department attempted to relay information to the village panchayats about their rights and responsibilities concerning the forests. While some progress has been made in operationalizing the Panchayat Forest and Panchayat Protection Forest programmes, it is clear that the development of the Forest Department's capacity to support community management systems will need a sustained effort for some time to come.

Legislation defined new categories of forests: Panchayat Forests, Panchayat Protected Forests, Religious Forests, and Leasehold Forests. Panchayat Forests are degraded forest areas entrusted to a village panchayat for reafforestation in the interests of the village community. Panchayat Protected Forests are forests entrusted to a local panchayat for protection and proper management. Religious Forests are forests entrusted to religious institutions for protection and management. Leasehold Forests are degraded forests entrusted to individuals or agencies for reafforestation and the production of forest products.

Panchayat Forest Rules limit these forests to about 125 hectares in each panchayat. Government assistance is provided to encourage villages to invest in the forests. The government provides land and seedlings; in return for labour, the village panchayat receives all the income from the sale of forest products. These sales are restricted to ensure that the local villagers benefit from them, and to ensure that the forest is maintained in a productive condition. It is left to the village panchayats to provide incentives for individuals to plant and maintain the Panchayat Forests.

Panchayat Protected Forests are limited to about 500 hectares in each panchayat. Rules for these forests provide an incentive for communities to maintain existing forests through a shareholder arrangement, with the village panchayat receiving three-quarters of all income from the sale of forest products. One major problem is that the income from the Panchayat Forests and Panchayat Protected Forests is not received directly by the villages. Rather, these proceeds are forwarded to the central government, which then grants them back to the villages. A lack of faith in this disbursement process has prevented many villages from moving ahead with this aspect of community forestry.

Leasehold Forest Rules place limits on the size of these forests, varying from 2.5 hectares for individuals in the Kathmandu Valley to 68 hectares for institutions in the tarai. These rules represent a step in the direction of private ownership of forest land. With the exception of a few isolated cases, these rules have not been implemented.

The return of formal control of the forest land to local communities represents a major change in Nepal's forest policy. It was virtually impossible for the government to manage the forests after nationalization. Local management of their forest by village communities seemed to be the best solution. The lack of trained technical and administrative personnel in the Ministry of Forests and Soil Conservation, which is responsible for the implementation of forest policy, hampers the effective functioning of the community forestry programme. Foreign aid projects are primarily responsible for the implementation of the community forestry programme. The programme has been more successful in producing and distributing seedlings than at planting Panchayat Forests or designating Panchayat Protected Forests.

One of the problems facing the local management of forests by the village administrative unit or panchayat is that most often panchayats lack both the experience and operational capacity to manage their resources. In many cases the composition of organization leaders in the panchayat does not necessarily reflect the resource users. In less populated areas, village panchayats have large areas of forest land to oversee.

As the community forestry programme was implemented, it became apparent that many indigenous forest management systems run by individual households, extended families, clan groups, and settlement clusters, were still functioning (Gilmour, 1989; Fisher, 1989). In the early versions of the Panchayat Forestry Act no authority or recognition was given to these "user groups." Later on, however, the Forest Department began modifying procedures to integrate customary management controls and use patterns into the Panchayat Forest programme.

Unlike the uniform organizational structure of village panchayats, user groups varied in size, function, and structure. Nepal's diverse ethnic composition, history, climatic variations, mountain ecology, and isolation have encouraged numerous localized systems of forest management to evolve. While these varied management systems represent a promising human organizational resource for protecting and developing the nation's forest resources, their full management potential will not be realized until local "user groups" are better understood by the Forest Department officials and others, and processes are created to recognize them and formally integrate them into the national management system.

In 1989 the Nepal Forestry Development Plan was formulated and ratified. The plan provides an integrated planning framework to co-ordinate government and foreign assistance investments for the sys-tematization and acceleration of forestry activities. One area identi-fied under the plan is the development of a Forest Department staff capable of working with user groups to formulate community forestry management plans. The creation of such a collaborative process between the Forest Department and forest user groups will allow for a much better integration of local and national needs and interests.

A number of donor agencies are working with the Forest Depart-ment, developing new approaches to community forest manage-ment and formulating new training programmes for the agency's field staff. The ODA-funded Khardep programme places considerable importance on ranger-training and reorientation activities. A Swiss-German funded project in the Tinao watershed has developed an interactive process between farm families and foresters called an approach development. The Nepal-Australia Forestry Project has produced field-worker guides to involve the local people in develop-ing forest management plans and in strengthening user groups. US AID has extended its activities in community forestry by providing further support for the Institute of Forestry (a branch of Tribhuvan University), which is located in Pokhara.

The efforts of the Forest Department and foreign aid agencies during the last decade have generated new ideas and enlarged the pool of experience regarding methods for helping communities mobi-lize their human and material resources for improved forest and watershed management. Yet much of the innovative work has con-centrated on a limited number of project watersheds, while the impact of new panchayat forestry policies on most mountain com-munities is less clear.

The success of Nepal's collaborative forest management will be determined by the extent to which the government agencies and community groups cooperate in meeting both local and national needs. To what extent is this integration of the local and national management systems taking place in the Middle Himalayan region? How effective has the Forest Department's field staff been in assisting community management groups in developing the capacity to admin-ister forest land better so as to meet their fuel and fodder needs? How have the new Panchayat Forest and Panchayat Protected Forest programmes affected the quality of forest management? How have management changes varied from region to region? How do physical characteristics such as topography, elevation, and climate, or such cultural factors as ethnicity or agroeconomics differentially shape local forest management systems? Despite the experiences of the past decade, answers to these questions are not clear.

It is obvious, however, that community forestry projects alone cannot solve Nepal's accelerating rural energy problem. The results of the community forestry programmes cannot keep pace with the incremental fuelwood demands of the growing population. Under the forestry projects there is not enough increased production from newly planted forests or existing forests to provide the fuelwood and fodder needs of the increasing population. Also, community projects will not by themselves solve the problem of deforestation in Nepal.

Increasing population pressure on mountain resources is one of the primary threats to the sustainability of Nepal's forests. Off-farm employment, represented largely by migration, offers an alternative source of income to mountain communities and has played a positive role in reducing pressure on marginal lands. Yet, throughout many of Nepal's Middle Mountains, the pressure on forest resources continues to grow, and it is only through community protection that these resources can be kept from over-exploitation. Some communities have developed forms of access control to guard against resource degradation. Recent legislation in Nepal provides some authority over the actions of local user groups, but many of these groups are still unaware of their rights and responsibilities under the new laws.

The Nepal Forest Department faces a major challenge in implementing the progressive community resource management policies that have been formulated by the government since 1977. While the agency is growing in size and capacity, training the existing and new staff to work with communities in managing the isolated forest resources remains a formidable task. The creation of collaborative agreements between the Department and the forest user groups will require intensive work at the sub-panchayat level. Local administrators, foresters, and village representatives will require substantial guidance and training if decentralized governance and resource policies are to result in more sustainable and productive management. However, an ineffective incentive system in the Forest Department (low pay and an inadequate and uneven recognition of outstanding service) hampers the effective functioning of officials, which results in uneven forest management.

The community management of forests also requires trust in the local authorities; without strong local leaders this may not be possible (Campbell, Shrestha, and Euphrat, 1987). In a few communities, where strong leadership has made a commitment to forest management, the programme has been successful (Gautam and Roche, 1987). In many villages nothing has been done. In areas where the government has exercised little control, the introduction of community forestry is viewed as an unwanted outside intrusion of authority.

Forestry institutions

Forest development requires strong institutions for the prevention and amelioration of environmental damage and the integration of coherent programmes into forest management. The forestry institutions in Nepal have frequently focused on the collection of revenue. They have often been pressured by political demands for concessions to special interest groups and to provide low-cost supplies of fuel and fodder, raw materials to industries, rural employment opportunities to the landless poor, and a multitude of other goods and services.

The first three national plans (1957–1970) gave priority to the development of infrastructures such as boundary demarcation, forest roads and buildings, and the training of technical personnel. The Fourth Five-Year Plan stressed the development of the survey and management aspects of forestry. The Fifth Five-Year Plan emphasized the importance of forests with respect to social, economic, and environmental aspects. In the Sixth Plan, planning was reoriented to include the people's participation in forest management. The Seventh Plan (1985–1990) emphasized the need to tackle the problems associated with the indiscriminate destruction of forest resources.

There was little implementation of the forestry programmes and projects listed in Nepal's national plans. For example, the Sixth Five-Year Plan set a target of planting nearly 43,000 hectares of trees; only about 37,000 hectares were planted. The afforestation target for the Seventh Plan was 175,000 hectares – five times the actual achievement of the Sixth Plan. However, the loss of crown cover from 1964/65 to 1978/79 was more than 68,000 hectares each year, nearly twice the afforestation target (Nield, 1985: 22).

The Eighth Plan (1992–1997) provides for the management of forest land to augment the current supply and to reduce the demand for forest resources. It calls for the rehabilitation of degraded forests and wasteland, further encouragement to small forestry user groups that have been active in the management of forests, and the promotion of private farm forestry on private land. The plan emphasizes the development of alternative energy resources, the use of fuel-efficient stoves, and price reforms or reduced subsidies to reflect the real cost of the forest products sold by the Timber Corporation of Nepal (National Planning Commission, 1991: 24–26).

The Ministry of Forests, now known as the Ministry of Forests and Soil Conservation, was established in 1958. The Ministry has a poor record of managing Nepal's forest resources. Many of the agencies in the Ministry were established by foreign aid projects; foreign aid has financed between 25 and 50 per cent of the development budget in forestry. Four agencies are involved in planting: the Department of Forests, established in 1942 to manage the tarai forests; the Afforestation Division, created in 1966 to carry out afforestation in the Kathmandu Valley; the Department of Soil Conservation and Watershed Management, established in 1974 to protect the watershed areas of Nepal's rivers, to control floods and landslides, and to promote conservation; and the Forest Products Development Board, established in 1976. As compared to the planting efforts that are now needed, the afforestation accomplishments of these agencies have been minimal.

The Timber Corporation of Nepal, the Fuelwood Corporation, and the Forest Products Development Board are responsible for harvesting. The Timber Corporation of Nepal was established in 1955 as a US AID-assisted sawmill project. The Fuelwood Corporation was established in 1962 as a Fuel Committee to ensure a regular supply of fuelwood for Kathmandu; it is supplying half of the firewood used in Kathmandu. Much of the firewood is purchased by brick factories (Kernan, Bender, and Bhatt, 1986: 6).

The Forest Products Development Board was created to make forest products available to consumers and to help build forest processing plants. Timber and fuelwood are sold by the Timber Corporation of Nepal at highly subsidized (low) prices. The market price, which is about three to five times more than the Timber Corporation's price, has encouraged corruption and black marketing. The low price has benefited only a few people at a high social cost. The Timber Corporation has been more concerned with using the tarai forest than in replenishing it. The recent plantation efforts do not match the logging activities (Carter, 1987: 82). In view of the privatization of services policy, the continued existence of the Timber Corporation may be in doubt.

The operations of the Timber Corporation, the Fuelwood Corporation, and the Forest Products Development Board overlap considerably. Their functions are not coordinated. There are other examples of the lack of coordination in the Ministry of Forests and Soil Conservation, which results in waste and the inefficient management of forest land. Generally speaking, the harvesting activities of the agencies within the Ministry are unrelated to afforestation and the planting activities of other agencies in the Ministry. Consequently, the Ministry of Forests has often contributed to deforestation rather than helped to solve the problem. In order to reverse this trend of depleting the forests, a significant coordinated effort by government agencies is needed.

Foreign aid in the form of grants and loans to carry out forest development projects – designed with expatriate assistance – has played a key role in Nepal. The history of expatriate involvement in Nepal's forestry has been documented (Bajracharya, 1986). In the early years, foreign advisers generally encouraged the consumption of forest resources without much concern for replenishing the resources. Later on, foreign advisers were the first to become alarmed at the serious consequences of deforestation in Nepal. Many of the agencies in the Ministry of Forests were established with foreign assistance, and the community forestry programme is funded mostly by external assistance.

Strategies for forest development

The foregoing discussion suggests that the causes of deforestation and the degradation of forest land are numerous and complex. Further, the problems associated with Nepal's forest resources are interrelated with the problems of poverty, population growth, farmland, and livestock. In order to make a significant change, a concerted effort is needed by the government and international agencies as well as the cooperation and involvement of the local population.

Policy shifts in forestry towards the rural poor

Policies to protect the forests or to slow deforestation seem doomed when pitted against the growing tide of poor villagers, who need the land to survive. General economic development, reductions in inequality and poverty, and slower population growth are necessary for a long-term solution to the forest problem in Nepal. For forest conservation, priority must be given to increasing agricultural productivity in poor, densely populated areas, especially those adjacent to forested areas, and to expanding non-farm employment opportunities in these target areas.

A change is needed in forestry policies so that the rural poor can obtain the fullest benefits from the forest and tree resources through direct participation in their management and use, thus helping to combat the pressures leading to their destruction. In 1991 between 7 and 8 million of Nepal's 19 million population lived in absolute poverty, unable to support their minimum daily caloric intake and satisfy their minimum energy needs for cooking and heating (World Bank, 1991). A large section of the population was in a deficit situation, only meeting its needs by depleting the forest reserves. The rural poor, especially women and children, have suffered the most in this declining spiral, since they are the primary users of forest products such as fuelwood, fodder, and handicraft materials. Difficulties in acquiring sufficient wood has led to nutrition and hygiene problems and also to set-backs in food production. Agricultural residue is being increasingly diverted from its traditional fodder or manure use to complement or substitute for scarce fuelwood. The fuelwood problem is thus not only an energy issue, but a symptom of the deteriorating environmental and socioeconomic conditions that lead to greater poverty.

For meeting the rural fuelwood crisis, policies applying participatory approaches to rural development are needed. The principal method of increasing wood supplies for the rural poor has been through the promotion of panchayat-level community forestry. In Nepal, with a significant number of landless persons, policies must be designed to provide access to land for this specific purpose to the landless groups. These programmes are in need of stronger institutional support. The planting of trees has the potential to benefit the small and marginal farmers if it results in economic benefits from the sale of products to the market or from the growth of forest-based industries linked with tree development on small farms.

There are several ways in which forestry policies can be strengthened to meet the employment and income needs of the rural poor. Forestry programmes should be integrated into Nepal's rural employment programme. Small forestry-based enterprises can play an important role in generating non-farm employment and rural industrialization. Through community forestry projects, small-scale processing and marketing enterprises have been pursued in Nepal, but more needs to be done.

67

Increasing the supply of forest products

It is widely recognized that the best way to increase the supply of wood is by mobilizing rural labour and land for the planting of trees and for the better management of non-forest trees. Supplying rural wood through large-scale commercial operations is not viable, nor is the continuation of widespread wood-gathering in the forests and other wooded areas sustainable or even environmentally acceptable.

Community forestry is seen by many as the key to increasing the supply of forest products. Local cooperation is essential for successful community forestry. While villagers do not have to be skilled long-term technical planners, they must be able to see that their long-term interest lies in managing the forests more effectively. They must also know their rights and responsibilities related to community forestry, so that an increased extension effort is required. The Forestry Department needs to be more oriented in the light of this recognition to provide technical advice and input to villagers as they manage the forest.

There is insufficient data to predict the increase in forest yields through community forestry. Based on data in Nepal's Water and Energy Commission's (1987) report on fuelwood, a typical panchayat's population consumes about 4,000 cubic metres of fuelwood per year, while the panchayat's forest produces only 2,500 cubic metres per year. If a new Panchayat Forest can produce 5 cubic metres per hectare annually, and yields on existing Panchayat Protected Forests can be raised from 2 to 5 cubic metres per hectare annually, a community might increase local fuelwood production by 2,125 cubic metres (625 cubic metres per year from Panchayat Forests and 1,500 cubic metres from Panchayat Protected Forests), nearly doubling the current production of 2,500 cubic metres. Combined with trees on private land, this increase could meet the current fuelwood and fodder needs in many areas of Nepal.

However, the typical panchayat must achieve the production mentioned above in less than six years simply to keep pace with the increasing demands of its growing population. With a population growing at over 2.6 per cent annually, demand will increase from 4,000 to over 4,625 cubic metres – the sum of the current (2,500 cubic metres) and new (2,125 cubic metres) production – in less than eight years.

The Eighth Plan target is to allocate 252,000 hectares of forest land to 5,000 local user groups during the period 1992–1997 (National

Planning Commission, 1992). These targets are less than the legal limits of community forestry. The Eighth Plan's afforestation pro- gramme will cover about 80,000 hectares of land during the five-year period. This will not keep pace with forest degradation if the current level of depletion (over 50,000 hectares per year of crown cover) continues on the remaining forests (2.8 million hectares of crown cover).

Regional strategy

The Middle Mountain regions of Nepal have a lot of relatively sparse forest, while the tarai has a little dense forest, mostly in the western part of the country. In the Middle Mountains, community forestry seems to be a good practical solution, while in the tarai private and leased forestry may offer the best solution to the energy problem.

Private management of forest resources includes both managing trees on private land and managing trees on government land through leasehold or other contractual arrangements. In some parts of the tarai it may be possible to establish large commercial planta- tions. However, caring for a few trees near houses and on field bunds (borders) would probably solve Nepal's energy problems more quickly. Secure tenure over forest land is necessary for their efficient man- agement under private ownership. However, there is the possibility that secure individual tenure over forest land in areas where the for- est has been an open-access resource will deprive the poor of their use of the forest. Current regulations limit private forest holdings to small plots of trees and effectively prohibit private forest manage- ment on a commercial basis. The leasehold forest provisions of the community forestry legislation have not yet been implemented except in a few isolated areas. The Eighth Plan states that an unspecified amount of forest land will be leased to economically deprived groups.

Forest officials in Nepal do not support private and leasehold for- estry because this reduces their authority over forest resources. This may be one explanation for the lack of implementation of leasehold forestry.

Implementation of forest development strategies

Implementing the strategies discussed above – with regard to the integration of forestry with rural development, an increasing supply of forest products, a region-based strategy for community forestry,

69

and private and leasehold management – will require stronger and reoriented forestry institutions. Nepal has found it difficult to integrate these multiple functions into coherent programmes. The forestry institution has focused on the extraction of revenue from the forest land.

There are several prerequisites for the effective implementation of forest policy by the Ministry of Forest and Soil Conservation. Adequately-trained forestry personnel with motivation and a willingness to work in remote areas is needed. A change in the attitude of forestry officials is also necessary; they must view the forest as a community resource to be managed for the benefit of the local people. Generally, the forest has been viewed as the government's private property to be exploited for revenue. The forest should be viewed as Nepal's most important resource to meet local forest-based needs.

The forestry staff must also earn the trust of the villagers. Due to corruption and inefficiency at nearly all levels of management, the forestry staff is not trusted. Strong leadership is needed to improve the efficiency of the forest bureaucracy, and dedicated local forestry officials are essential for the successful implementation of the development strategies.

Forty years ago in Nepal, in an era of low demand (small population) and high supply (large forest cover), little formal forest management was needed. Now this situation has changed, and the forestry institutions must also change in order to solve the myriad resource problems facing the country.

4

Agriculture: Patterns and problems

Although agriculture dominates Nepal's economy, accounting for about 60 per cent of GDP, 90 per cent of the employment, and 60 per cent of the country's export income, precise data on agricultural land is not available. The most recent estimate by the Asian Development Bank (1989: 19) states that "only about 18 per cent (2.65 million ha.) of the country's total land area (14.7 million ha.) is cultivated." Ten years earlier, based on 1978–1979 surveys, the Land Resource Mapping Project by Kenting Earth Sciences (1986: 46) reported nearly 2.96 million hectares of cultivated land, or about 20 per cent of the land area. Based on land capability data, Kenting Earth Sciences estimated that a total of 4.96 million hectares, or 33 per cent of Nepal's land area, could be potentially cultivated if irrigation and soil fertility management facilities were available. In 1987 a publication from the International Food Policy Research Institute stated that 16 per cent of the area was cultivated (Yadav, 1987: 14). A report prepared for US AID in 1984 estimated that 20 per cent of the land was cultivated (Fletcher and Sahn, 1984: 1). The Government's Economic Survey (1992) lists 2.96 million hectares under principal food crops in 1991/92.

Nearly 40 years ago Rauch (1954) estimated that 10 per cent of the total land area, or 1.67 million hectares, was under cultivation. In the same year Robbe (1954) placed the area of cultivated land at 2.38 million hectares. As is evident from the above figures, data on agricultural land use in Nepal is very conflicting. However, official data and field observations reveal that the area under agricultural use has increased in Nepal during the last four decades. Deo (1993) estimates

71

2.5 million hectares of agricultural land. About 5 per cent of the agricultural land is in the mountains, 40 per cent is in the Middle Himalaya, and the remainder is in the tarai.

As the population has increased and the demand for food supplies has grown, there has been a trend towards bringing additional areas under cultivation. However, since the possibilities for farming are limited by physical factors such as inadequate precipitation, low temperatures, the mountainous terrain, and thin or infertile soils, large areas in Nepal are either under forest or grazing land, or lie barren and unproductive.

The pattern of agricultural land use (fig. 9) in Nepal has thus been conditioned by two sets of factors: (1) physical factors such as climate, topography, and soils, which set broad limits on the capabilities of the land; and (2) human factors, such as the length of human occupance, density of population, social and economic institutions (especially land tenure), and the technological levels of the Nepalese people, which determine the extent to which the physical capabilities of the land are utilized. The percentages of the areas under cultivation (based on the latest available official data) are shown in fig. 10.

The land use pattern reflects the extraordinary localization of various uses. Agricultural land is concentrated to a marked degree in the tarai and in the central and eastern parts of the country along the major river valleys. Patches of agricultural land have been carved out in the mountainous forested area of western Nepal, but in the mountainous areas in general, agricultural land use has remained fairly constant. In some places there is evidence of abandoned agricultural terraces and a decline in the amount of cultivated land. Generally speaking, cultivation in the mountainous Middle Mountain region is not encroaching on the forest land.

The Middle Mountains, which form the central part of Nepal, constitute about 60.5 per cent of Nepal's total land area but contain less than 35 per cent of the cultivated land. About 47 per cent of Nepal's population lives in the Middle Mountain valleys; about 5 per cent live in Kathmandu. The Great Himalayan region occupies about 16 per cent of the country's land area and contains nearly 8 per cent of the total population. Very little agriculture is practised there.

Both planned and illegal settlements have led to the conversion of large areas of forest land to agricultural use in the tarai. According to Kenting's Land Resource Mapping Project's data, during a 12-year period (1965 to 1979) nearly 15 per cent of the forests in the Siwalik foothills and 24 per cent of the tarai forests were converted to agri-

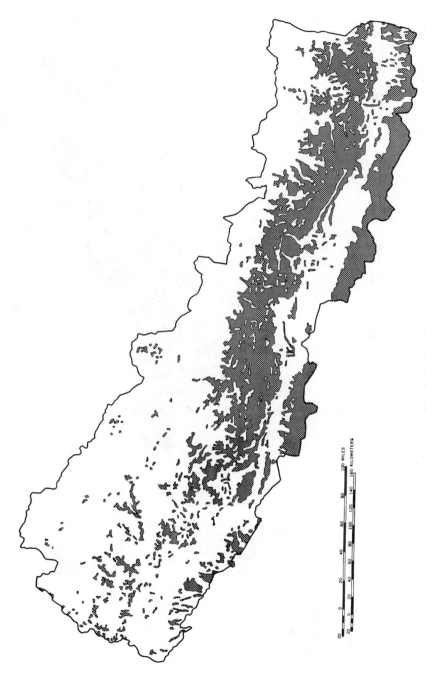

Fig. 9 **Agricultural land use**

73

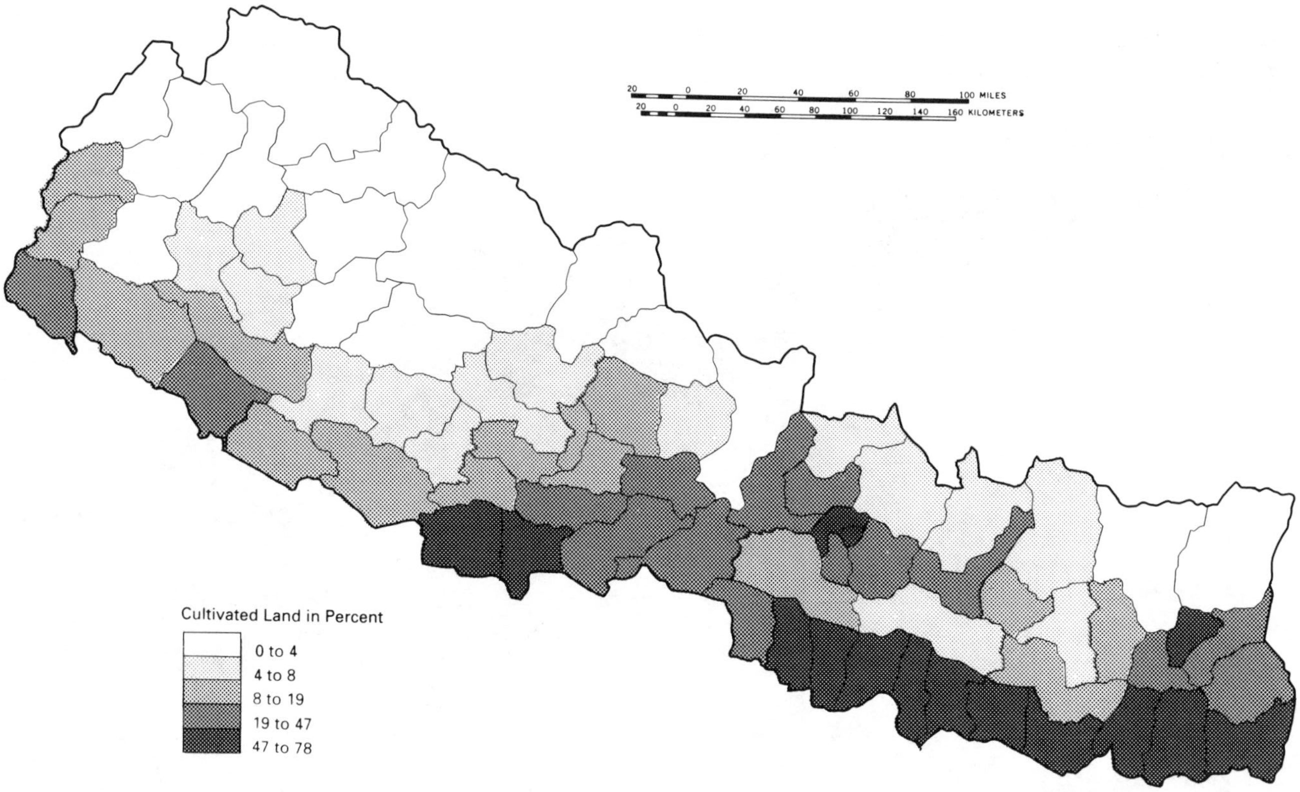

Cultivated Land in Percent

0 to 4
4 to 8
8 to 19
19 to 47
47 to 78

Fig. 10 **Area under cultivation**

74

cultural use. The tarai lowlands (60–330 m above sea level) cover 23.5 per cent of Nepal and account for 65 per cent of all the cultivated land in the country. Malaria hindered settlements and cultivation in the tarai before 1960; the United States's successful malaria eradication programme in the mid-1950s opened up the Rapti Valley in the tarai for settlement. During the last three decades internal migration from the Middle Mountains to the tarai has increased.

Cropping patterns and agricultural productivity

The methods of cultivation in Nepal have changed very little during the last century. Francis (Hamilton) Buchanan, an official of the British Government in India, visited the kingdom early in the nineteenth century and returned with detailed descriptions of the daily lives and practices of its people. His description of farming among the Newars in the Kathmandu Valley could, with slight modifications, be a contemporary report (Buchanan, 1819: 221).

The cropping pattern can best be considered in terms of a vertical alignment of crop zones based on altitude. Kawakita (1955: 87) developed such a schema to account for the pattern and its variations. Spring and summer maize, African millet in the summer and autumn, and irrigated paddy in the summer are cultivated almost exclusively up to altitudes of approximately 1,650 m for the former and 1,800 m for the latter. A transitional zone from 1,500 to 2,500 m is devoted to some paddy at the lowest levels, spring and summer maize, and spring barley. Overlapping this line, from approximately 2,100 to 2,900 m, is the region in which spring barley and summer buckwheat are grown. The zone from 2,900 to 3,200 m is devoted to winter wheat and winter barley, and from 3,200 to approximately 3,700 m – the present upper limit of cultivation in the central region of Nepal – summer wheat is the staple crop. Above that altitude summer barley can be cultivated. Kawakita notes that the crop zones suggest the "rational utilization of growing seasons according to altitude" (Kawakita, 1955: 88).

In north-eastern Nepal, however, the Sherpas cultivate potato in the Khumbu Valley area above 3,800 m. Hagen (1961) noted haymaking in the alpine meadows where yak are pastured up to the permanent snow-line during the summer months. The potato is not native to this area. Estimates of the first appearance of the small white potato range from 65 to 120 years ago. The large red variety was brought into Nepal from Darjeeling for the first time in 1942

(Fürer-Haimendorf, 1964). Since then the potato has become the staple of the Sherpa diet and a product for export to the lower regions of Nepal.

There are two areas which provide exceptions to the generalized scheme: the Kathmandu and Pokhara Valleys. In the Kathmandu Valley wheat is intensively cultivated along with winter vegetables. The Pokhara Valley, which is somewhat lower in elevation than Kathmandu but similarly positioned in the mountains, is not winter-cropped because of the porous gravel stratum, which readily drains the surface water. However, fruits such as oranges grow well and provide an export cash crop.

The tarai constitutes an entirely different agricultural system. In the eastern tarai, the combination of rich alluvial soil and rainfall, which exceeds 2,000 mm per year, makes possible the cultivation of rice, jute, and sugarcane; on the eastern border there are tea plantations. Because of the comparatively heavy rainfall, double and sometimes triple-cropping is possible. Good access to transportation and markets in India enables the export of jute and rice surpluses when they occur. Tropical fruits, tobacco, cotton, mustard, and linseed are also grown.

In the mid-western tarai, where the rainfall averages 1,000 mm and is uncertain, agriculture is less intensive and harvests are often poor. Wheat is the main crop in this region, though rice maintains a position of importance. The soils of the western tarai are fertile, but the rainfall is inadequate to support a substantial agricultural economy without irrigation development.

Ordinarily, variations in the cropping patterns in a geographically diverse country can be explained in terms of elevation, soil, and climate. However, Kawakita (1955) also argues that the patterns are as much a result of ethnographic characteristics as of climate and geographic features. He notes the difference between the cropping patterns in the Hindu and Tibetan culture areas: the Hindu people emphasize the production of summer crops while the people of the Tibetan culture plant winter crops. The transitional zone is inhabited by people with mixed ethnographic affiliations. The Kathmandu Valley – the only area in which intensive winter cropping is practised in the lower elevations – has features attributed to the Tibetan relatedness of the Newars. However, it would seem that in the Tibetan culture area climate may be an important factor because of the prolonged germination period required in the colder climates, while winter is the dry season in the lower altitudes occupied by those people living in the Hindu culture area.

About 85 per cent of Nepal's cropped area is devoted to food grains. Rice, which can be found growing virtually everywhere below 1,800 m where irrigation water is available, is dominant. Fifty-three per cent of Nepal's cultivated land is in rice (Kenting Earth Sciences Ltd., 1986: 46). Some 64 per cent of the rice land is found in the tarai, over 15 per cent is in the alluvial land in the mountains, and the remainder is on the terraced mountain slopes. Maize, the single most important rain-fed crop in Nepal, occupies 1.13 million hectares, or 38 per cent of the total cultivated area. Over 80 per cent of the maize cultivation occurs in terraced land in the mountain regions of Nepal. Other cereal crops are wheat, millet, barley, and buckwheat. Pulses are also an important crop, both as part of the Nepalese diet and as a key component of the cropping system in Nepal. Jute, sugarcane, tobacco, tea, oilseed, and potato are major non foodgrain crops.

Total cereal grain production increased by an annual rate of only 1.10 per cent between 1961/62 and 1980/81 while the productivity or yield declined by 0.58 per cent annually. The cropped area during this period increased by 1.69 per cent annually (Yadav, 1987). In the 1970s total cereal grain production increased by an annual rate of 0.95 per cent compared with 0.75 per cent in the 1960s. Productivity declined at 0.46 per cent annually in the 1970s compared with a decline of 1.0 per cent in the 1960s. Likewise, the cropped area in the 1970s increased at 1.42 per cent compared with 1.77 per cent in the 1960s. Thus, both the decline in productivity and increase in the cropped area were less in the 1970s than in the 1960s.

During the 1980s the area, production, and yield of the principal food crops increased. The area under food crops increased from 124,000 hectares in 1985–1986 to 140,000 hectares in 1989–1990. During the same period production increased from 117,000 metric tons to 150,000 metric tons, and the yield increased from 94.25 to 107 metric tons per hectare (*Economic Survey*, 1992).

The production of all food grains increased in 1990–1991; total food grain production reached 5.8 million metric tons. In 1991–1992, due to adverse weather conditions, total food grain production was estimated to have declined by 6.5 per cent, but the cash crops (except jute and tobacco) increased by 9.1 per cent. During this period the production of sugarcane and potato nearly doubled whereas jute production declined. Thus, in 1991–1992 total food grain production was estimated at 5.4 million metric tons, and the total cash crop production was estimated at 2.1 million metric tons. In 1991–1992 both the area and productivity of food crops were estimated to have declined by 2.3 per cent and 4.3 per cent respectively, compared to 1990–1991. The area and productivity of cash crops, however, were estimated to have increased by 1.7 per cent and 7.3 per cent respectively in 1991–1992 as compared to 1990–1991.

The production of rice paddy, which occupies a dominant position among food crops, was 3.39 million metric tons in 1989–1990 and 3.50 metric tons in 1990–1991. There was a decline of 8 per cent in 1991–1992 in paddy production, which was estimated at 3.22 million metric tons. Likewise, the area under rice paddy declined to 1,412,000 hectares in 1990–1991, a decrease of 3 per cent when compared to the previous year. The paddy yield was estimated to be 2.28 metric tons per hectare.

Maize production was 1.20 million metric tons in 1989–1990. In 1990–1991 maize production increased by 2.5 per cent over the previous year, producing 1.23 million metric tons. In 1991–1992 production declined to 1.20 million metric tons, and the cropped area decreased to 754,000 hectares, a decline of 0.5 per cent from 1990–1991. The yield of maize was estimated at 1.60 metric tons per hectare.

Millet production, which was 225,000 metric tons in 1989–1990, increased to 232,000 metric tons in 1990–1991. During 1991 and 1992 both the area and production of millet declined to 198,000 hectares and 229,000 metric tons respectively. The yield per hectare of millet was estimated at 1.16 metric tons.

Barley production was estimated at 28,000 metric tons in 1990–1991, with about 198,000 hectares under this crop.

The official agricultural statistics for the 1970s reveal that the productivity of maize, paddy, millet, and barley registered a negative growth rate. However, the productivity of wheat showed a positive growth rate of 2.67 per cent in the 1970s. Wheat production was estimated at 855,000 metric tons in 1989–1990, but due to unfavourable weather conditions production declined to 836,000 metric tons in 1990–1991. The cropped area under wheat was 593,000 hectares, and the yield per hectare was 1.41 metric tons in 1990–1991 (Central Bureau of Statistics, 1992c).

The share of cash crops in Nepal's agricultural production is about 25 per cent. The cash crops occupy about 10 per cent of the cropped area, or roughly 0.3 million hectares. The area under cash crops increased at an annual rate of 2.23 per cent from 1961–1962 to 1980–

Rice transplantation in a village in Humla-Karnali area, north-west Nepal (courtesy M. Tamura)

Scattering kodo (millet) seedlings in a Chepang village. They will take root after rain (courtesy K. Tachibana)

1981. Sugarcane had the highest growth rate at 8.86 per cent, while jute production increased only 2.46 per cent. The sugarcane and oilseed yields increased, the tobacco and potato yields declined, and the jute yield remained almost constant. In general the yield of cash crops was better than for cereal crops. The greater use of fertilizer on cash crops may provide an explanation for the higher yields. The national average use of fertilizer per hectare was 29 kg on sugarcane compared with 14 kg on wheat, 3 kg on maize, and 4.5 kg on paddy (Central Bureau of Statistics, 1985b). It is common knowledge that sugarcane is grown where irrigation facilities are available, unlike maize and paddy, which are largely grown under rain-fed conditions.

In 1991–1992 sugarcane production was estimated at 1.29 million metric tons and the cropped area was 37,000 hectares, with an average yield of 34.89 metric tons per hectare. The cropped area under jute was about 15,000 hectares in 1991–1992, with a production of 19,000 metric tons. There were 85,000 hectares under potato in 1991–1992, with a total production of 733,000 metric tons and a yield of 8.62 metric tons per hectare. Oilseed occupied 155,000 hectares, with an estimated production of 88,000 metric tons and a yield of 0.57

metric ton per hectare (*Economic Survey*, 1992). Nepal has a comparative advantage in the production of most of these crops, and the output has increased during the past 10 years. Oilseed, jute, and potato are exported. The changes in the cropping pattern reveals a shift in favour of high-value crops.

The production and yield of crops in the hills and mountains have declined much faster than in the tarai. In the tarai, total cereal grain production increased annually by 1.44 per cent; the yield remained constant from 1970–1971 to 1980–1981 (Yadav, 1987). During the same period production in the Middle Mountains remained constant and the yield declined annually at 1.14 per cent. An increase in the cropped area for the tarai, at the rate of 1.50 per cent annually, kept production rising without any change in the yield, while a decline in the yield for the mountains was offset by a 1.27 per cent increase in the cropped area which left production undiminished.

Food production trends and requirements

Food production in Nepal has not kept up with the population growth. The 1991 census estimated the total population of the country to be 18.49 million. The annual rate of population growth during the 1981–1991 intercensal decade was 2.1 per cent. The distribution of population among the three ecological regions was 7.3, 45.0, and 46.7 per cent in the Great Himalayan valleys, Middle Mountains, and the tarai respectively. The 1991 census data indicates that the population of Nepal continued to migrate from the mountains to the tarai during 1981–1991.

The differential population growth rates have resulted in a significant change in the distribution of population during the last 40 years. These changes have led to a population density in the tarai that exceeds that of the other two regions. From 1952 to 1991 the population density of the country increased from 60 to 125 persons per sq.km. In 1952 the tarai contained 35 per cent of the population, and the Great Himalayan valleys and the Middle Mountain regions had 65 per cent of the country's population. In 1991 the tarai had 47 per cent of the country's population, while the percentage of people living in the Great Himalayan valleys and Middle Mountains had declined to 53 per cent.

Much of the increase in the tarai has been the result of migration from other geoecological regions. Data on cultivated land for 1971 and 1981 – the most recent available – indicates that the cultivated

81

land per capita and per household are larger in the tarai than in the other two regions, but both are declining in all regions (table 5). The Great Himalayan valleys and the Middle Mountain regions contained 53 per cent of the population but supported it on only 38 per cent of the cultivated land. The distribution of cultivated land and the agricultural densities in various districts are given in table 6.

The amount of per capita cultivated land has been declining in all of Nepal's geoecological regions. The yields of major crops are relatively low. Production has increased in some cases because the expanded areas were large enough to offset the decline in yields. Both the yields and production of maize and millet have declined significantly; both are grown mainly in the Middle Mountains. The most disconcerting aspect of agriculture is the stagnant or falling yields of the main food grain commodities. Rice and wheat yields were about as high in the 1960s as they are now. Wheat is the only cereal which shows a positive trend in yield. The expansion of the cultivated areas can no longer be a major factor in expanding food production. Increased yields and cropping intensity are the only remaining sources of the production potential needed to meet the country's future food requirements.

Both the Middle Mountains and the high valleys in the Great Himalayan region have consistent deficits in food production: the largest deficits occur in the more densely populated Middle Mountains. Even in recent good crop years (1991–1992), large deficits existed in the Middle Mountains. All available information points to growing food deficits in the Middle Mountains and increasing malnutrition among the low-income groups in the region.

Overall the tarai shows a strong food surplus but one that is smaller in magnitude than the sum of the deficits in the other two geoecological regions. As a result, for the country as a whole, there has not been enough food to meet the estimated requirements of the population.

Policies for improving food production must include a long-range strategy for the efficient and equitable distribution of food among the needy. Small-scale community-owned and operated irrigation works along with small-scale terracing improvements and small-scale flood control projects – mainly in the Middle Mountain region – should help to increase food production in the region. Pricing and distribution policies are also important. Government intervention in food grain distribution goes back to the Rana period. The main concern of these efforts was to supply adequate food grains to the Kathmandu Valley, where government, army, and police personnel were con-

Terraced fields in Taranagar, central Nepal

centrated. The present system can be traced back to 1962, when the Food Management Committee was created, followed by the Food Management Corporation in 1965.

At the present time, the Nepal Food Corporation, operating under the Ministry of Civil Supplies, is responsible for executing the government's food policies. The main responsibility of the Corporation, which reaches almost all of the deficit districts in the Middle Mountains, is to operate the subsidized food grain distribution programme. The Kathmandu Valley continues to be the main beneficiary of the National Food Corporation programme, receiving 50 per cent or more of the total food grains distributed. Even with its large losses, the Corporation provides only a small fraction of the food grain deficit in the mountain regions.

The National Food Corporation procures its grain by open-market purchases and also by a levy system. Levies on private mills account for a substantial part of the Corporation's supplies. Millers take this factor into account in setting the prices they pay to producers. As such, the levy system, while it reduces the National Food Corporation's outlay for grain procurement, serves as a tax on producers.

83

Little analysis has been done on the benefits of the National Food Corporation's procurement and distribution programme. It is widely believed that the poor people in remote areas have little access to subsidized grains. The main recipients are thought to be civil servants and politically influential people near the distribution points. While anecdotal accounts and field interviews are consistent with this view, there is no empirical data or analysis which clearly substantiates these assertions. Much more needs to be known about the targeting of benefits to evaluate the cost/effectiveness of the programme.

Nepal has used a policy of quantitative restrictions on exports as a means to stabilize the domestic supply of rice. Rice, which is exported, is also taxed. However, quantitative restrictions and taxes on rice exports are patently impossible to enforce along the long open border with India. There is substantial unrecorded trade in many commodities, with rice the most prominent.

The rice market in the tarai is much more closely integrated with North India than with the mountain regions of Nepal. Higher food prices in the neighbouring Indian states of West Bengal, Bihar, and Uttar Pradesh create a movement of food grains from the tarai surplus production area. This means that prices in the tarai are closely related to the market points on the Indian border. Thus, the price is predominantly a derived price, which reflects Indian prices and the cost of transportation and across-the-border movement. Its existence places a constraint on the degree to which Nepal can carry out an independent pricing policy based on domestic production, consumption, and pricing factors.

There is evidence that the overall impact of government intervention in pricing and trade has been unfavourable to agriculture and food production. This intervention occurs extensively in both the product and factor markets. As a result, the barter terms of trade between agriculture and non-agriculture have moved downward in recent years (Svejnar and Thorbecke, 1986). In India, in contrast, the domestic terms of trade for agriculture have risen. Fertilizer and credit, the two subsidized inputs, are scarce and unlikely to reach the small and remote producers. The support price policy has not been effectively implemented for the food grain crops. Taxes, levies, and quantitative controls on rice exports have created uncertainty in the industry and depressed domestic market prices. While definitive evidence of the role of these interventions in the stagnation of Nepal's agriculture is lacking, it is clear that their overall impact has been unfavourable to agricultural growth and has created constraints on the adoption of new technology and the productivity of public investments in irrigation and other infrastructure and services.

Foodgrain production potential and constraints

As noted above, Nepal's food grain production growth has been less than dynamic during the last 30 years. With the exception of wheat, stagnant or declining yields have created a growing gap between the population growth and the foodgrain supply. While an expansion in the area under cultivation concealed this gap somewhat through the 1970s, the gravity of the long-term problem is now beyond dispute.

The scope for expanding the cultivated area is believed to be extremely small. In the Middle Mountains and the Great Himalayan areas substantial portions of marginal land are already in use as a result of increased population density and declining yields. Erosion and the lack of animal manure caused by the growing use of dung for fuel lead to still lower yields, further deforestation, and continued deterioration of the fragile resource base in the mountain environment. While clear evidence of the remaining potential for expanding the cultivated area in the tarai is lacking, that which remains will be more expensive to bring into production and more demanding of technology and management for producing sustained field crops.

This leaves increasing yields per unit of land as the source for production increases in the future. Yield increases result from both higher yields of a given crop and from increased cropping intensity through more double or triple-cropping. Since the yields of foodgrain crops are generally low in Nepal as compared to international standards, the potential for improving yields through improved varieties, new techniques and cropping systems, more fertilizer and other inputs is substantial.

The tarai offers the most readily achievable potential for yield increases of the major foodgrain crops. Extending irrigation is one means, but this requires an investment in both water distribution and organization for efficient water usage. Impressive productivity increases have also been achieved in the tarai under rain-fed production with improved cropping systems and varieties and the increased use of fertilizer. The service and commercial infrastructure that supports yield increases in the tarai is much superior to that of the Middle Mountains. Output growth in the tarai will better supply the domestic economic demand and will provide exportable surpluses, which will benefit the tarai producers, urban consumers, and the

Harvesting kodo (millet) in a Chepang village (courtesy K. Tachibana)

country's balance of payments. It will not solve the food deficit problem in the mountains because of the high transportation costs and the lack of purchasing power by the poor people who live there.

This point provides strong support for programmes that would increase productivity in the mountain region. Experiments conducted under the Integrated Cereals Project provide some grounds for optimism. This project suggests that substantial increases in yields are possible, using the package approach devised by the project. This approach aims at improving the total annual productivity of a farm unit, not just the yields of a single crop. This approach has a special validity where crop and animal production are interdependent, as in the mountains of Nepal. Factors considered in this approach include crop combinations, different varieties, cultivation practices, and, to some extent, fertilizer applications.

Much still needs to be done to create the research base for generating improved technology in the mountains, not to mention the need for an effective extension system to apply the knowledge. The timely provision of inputs, especially fertilizer, is a daunting challenge in areas remote from the nearest road connection point.

Tharus weeding in a vegetable field in Chitwan owned by an Indian (courtesy K. Tachibana)

Farm size, land scarcity, and landlessness

In a predominantly agricultural country like Nepal, rural prosperity depends largely upon the farm size and land holding. The size of the holding is a major determinant of rural income (table 7); there is a close correlation between income and farm size.

Thirty years ago a study by Pant (1962: 8) stated that the holdings of the average farmer were below a normal subsistence level, with vast numbers of cultivators not owning the land they tilled. Since then the situation has worsened. It is estimated that 63.1 per cent of households had holdings of less than one hectare. These landholdings comprised 10.6 per cent of the cultivated land. At the other extreme, 10.4 per cent of the households had holdings in excess of five hectares. Their holdings comprised 60.5 per cent of the cultivated land. In other words, over 60 per cent of the cultivated land is under the control of slightly more than 10 per cent of the households, which indicates a major concentration of land ownership in Nepal (table 8).

A recent World Bank study indicates that 5 per cent of owners control about 40 per cent of the cultivated land, while 60 per cent control about 20 per cent of the cultivated land (World Bank, 1991: 34). In 1986, 45 per cent of the holdings in the tarai had an

Threshing paddy on a foot-pedal thresher in a Newar village in the Kathmandu Valley

average size of 0.09 hectares, comprising 2.8 per cent of the cultivated land. In the Middle Mountains 54 per cent of the holdings, comprising 11 per cent of the cultivated land, had an average size of 0.18 hectares. In the tarai 13.8 per cent of the holdings, with an average size of 6.15 hectares, comprised 57.7 per cent of the cultivated area. In the Middle Mountains 5.1 per cent of the holdings, with an average size of 5.67 hectares, comprised 33.8 per cent of the cultivated land (World Bank, 1991).

The attempt to distribute land in the Rapti Valley and in the tarai among the small cultivators failed. Since then the choice parcels have found their way into the hands of the already landed class. As a result of the general failure of the land distribution efforts and population growth, the incidence of landlessness has increased. The census reports that less than 1 per cent of the households are landless, but other sources report figures of between 10 and 20 per cent. Many households with holdings of 0.09 hectares in the tarai are effectively landless households.

Social and economic conditions of the landless

In Nepal the landless people are made up of agricultural labourers with no ownership of land, and small marginal farmers, owners and/ or tenants with operational land holdings so small or of such poor quality that they do not provide a reasonable livelihood throughout the year. A landless household may possess a homestead or homesite which might be used for kitchen gardening and raising poultry but it does not have enough land for cultivation. In Nepal the problem of the marginal farmer is nearly as acute as that of the landless. A marginal farmer in Nepal is defined as one who owns below 1.02 hectares in the tarai and below 0.20 hectares in the Middle Mountain areas. With such small holdings, the marginal farmers are as vulnerable as the landless people.

As rural poverty has tended to increase in Nepal during the last 30 years, so has the incidence of landlessness (Khan and Lee, 1983). There has been a sharp increase in landlessness along with an increase in landholding (UN-ESCAP, 1985). Deterioration in the economic condition of the rural poor can be traced to their loss of control over the land. There are several factors behind the poverty situation, but land-oriented poverty is a significant component.

The causes of landlessness and near landlessness are many, and it is difficult to rank the various causes with respect to their importance. The scarcity of land, high population growth, low agriculture productivity, unequal agrarian structure, and lack of effective government policies are generally considered to be the major causes of landlessness.

Nepal's National Planning Commission's 1978 survey of 4,037 sample rural households revealed that only 10.4 per cent were landless, that is, they were not operating any land. Small farm households made up 31.2 per cent of the total, followed by marginal farms comprising 25.8 per cent of the total (Katwal, 1986). Tenants and sharecroppers, as well as small farmers operating undersized land holdings, should also be included among the landless. In Nepal, the existing agrarian structure is highly unequal in terms of the ownership of cultivated land. Based on the minimum holding (owned or rented) necessary to secure the basic nutritional and other needs of a farm family in Nepal, Katwal (1986) estimated that 44.88 per cent of the households were landless. In Nepal the scarcity of land, feudal-type institutional arrangements, and concentration of land holdings have resulted in landlessness.

The estimates of potentially cultivable land, the actual area of arable land, and the area under crops together with the total population have been discussed earlier. It is clear that Nepal suffers on both counts. Its per capita arable land (0.17 hectares in 1991–1992) is one of the lowest in the world. Besides, much of the land suitable for agriculture in Nepal is already under cultivation; therefore, the scope for bringing additional land under cultivation is limited. The low productivity of agriculture and the lack of a major manufacturing sector prevent a rapid acceleration of economic development and, as a result, the population pressure on the land continues to increase, especially with the rapid population growth. The problem of landlessness in Nepal is both a cause and effect of underdevelopment.

Assessment of Nepal's efforts to reduce landlessness

The government of Nepal initiated several policies to improve the living conditions and resettlement of the landless people. There have been several resettlement programmes and agrarian reform measures. In addition, the Integrated Rural Development Programme and the Small Farmers Development Programme have tried to reach the rural poor, including the landless. The agrarian structure in Nepal prior to 1950 was essentially feudal. Political changes in 1951 resulted in the following land reform measures: (1) Tenancy Rights Security Act, 1951; (2) Royal Land Reform Commission, 1952; (3) 13-point Programme, 1955; (4) Land and Cultivators Records Compilation Act, 1956; (5) Land Reform Act, 1957; (6) Birta Abolition Act, 1959; (7) Land Reorganization Act, 1962; and (8) Land Reform Act, 1964. The Birta Abolition Act of 1959, which abolished the feudal land tenure system, was the most significant piece of legislation. However, it was not fully implemented. The Land Reform Act of 1964 was introduced to launch a comprehensive reform programme based on equity considerations. The maximum ceiling of ownership of agricultural land was established at 18.4 hectares in the tarai, 2.7 hectares in the Kathmandu Valley, and 4.1 hectares in other Middle Mountain areas. The land above these ceilings was to be purchased from land-lords, then redistributed to tenants or landless farmers.

The amount of land actually redistributed under the Land Reform Act of 1964 was insignificant. It covered only 1.5 per cent of the cultivated land, which was distributed among 10,000 families (World Bank, 1991: 35). In general, it failed to alter the pattern of land-ownership through redistribution. In the tarai there is the possibility of the physical redistribution of the land. If 20 per cent of the tarai land in the largest holdings could be broken into small parcels of 0.5 hectares and redistributed effectively, nearly 40,000 households could be taken out of poverty and landlessness.

In 1956 Nepal announced its land resettlement programme – mainly in the Rapti Valley of the tarai region – to exploit the land resources and settle the marginal and landless farmers. After the implementation of the malaria eradication programme in 1958, the resettlement programme began to take shape. The Nepal Resettle-ment Company, formed in 1965 with the assistance of Israeli experts, began its first project in Nawalparasi district in 1965–1966 (Thapa and Weber, 1986). Since its establishment, the Nepal Resettlement Company has resettled 18,741 families and distributed 25,153 hec-tares of land. In addition, the Resettlement Department, established in 1968 to coordinate resettlement programmes, settled 58,776 families and distributed 44,300 hectares of land. The majority of the benefi-ciaries of the programme were migrants from the mountains, many of whom, although classified as landless, had sizeable land holdings back in the Middle Mountain area. The objective of resettling the landless was not effectively realized.

Policies for reducing the incidence of landlessness

Land is considered to be Nepal's most important economic asset, and the lack of access to it has serious consequences for a vast majority of the population. Therefore, landlessness is considered to be an over-riding development issue, but it still remains as daunting a problem as ever. Since agriculture is an important sector of the economy, access to land is a crucial factor in Nepal. Various interventions by the gov-ernment to combat poverty have failed, mainly because it did not recognize that poverty is grounded in the lack of access to resources, which results from an unequal distribution of assets of all kinds.

Consequently, the majority of rural households are mired in inse-curity, indebtedness, and feelings of powerlessness. There are several broad categories of remedial measures that could reduce the inci-dence of landlessness. They are not necessarily mutually exclusive, since several measures may be applied at the same time to combat the problem of landlessness.

Land reform

Among curative measures, land reform is by far the most important. The implementation of land reform legislation in Nepal has been unsatisfactory. The reforms have not increased the access of the rural poor to land and other productive assets. Without adequate institu-tional and administrative support, legal measures cannot reduce the incidence of rural landlessness. The 1964 reform had set a land ceil-ing, as noted earlier, to further land distribution. It was estimated that 600,000 hectares of land would be available for redistribution, the combined area of all holdings exceeding ceiling levels. Actually less than 3 per cent of the cultivated land was available for redistribution. Less than 1.5 per cent has been legally appropriated or confiscated and only 1 per cent has been distributed (table 9).

The unequal distribution of land has remained intact in Nepal since the land reforms of 1964. One direct result of land concentration is the marginalization of the peasantry and its landless condition. Since land concentration has remained mostly intact, marginal and sub-marginal holdings are increasing rather than decreasing. The ceilings under the land reforms of 1964 were fixed at an arbitrarily high level, nearly 10 to 12 times the average size of a family's cultivated land holding. Also, every son above the age of 16 and every unmarried daughter above the age of 35, even when living with parents as a single family, were counted as separate families. Many landlords transferred their land above the ceiling to other relatives to avoid the confiscation of surplus land, thus effectively defeating the purpose of land reform.

The 1964 reforms were accompanied by a tenant registration drive. An estimated 10–20 per cent of the tenants were certified. Under the law, those with "registered" tenancies can potentially claim title to the land they till. Therefore, landlords prefer to use Indian labourers who do not make claims on the land. A large and growing class of the landless could become tenants if the laws were enforced.

Land settlements

Land development and settlement is one way of providing land to the landless and small-scale peasants. Nepal has attempted to bring additional land under cultivation and to settle the landless and small farmers there. The first resettlement programme was started under the Rapti Valley Development Project in the Chitwan district in 1956 with the objective of relieving population pressure in neighbouring areas, rehabilitating the landless peasants, and partially solving the food problems in the Kathmandu Valley, which resulted from the 1954 flood. However, the programme could resettle families only after the malaria eradication programme became effective in Chitwan in 1958. In fact, the planned resettlement programme began in 1964 with Israeli aid, based on a survey in the tarai which suggested such possible resettlement areas as Nawalpur, Banke, Bardia, Kailali, and Kanchanpur districts. Also, basic land infrastructure and more social amenities, which subsequently became "pull" factors for migrants from the Middle Mountains, were made available in the tarai.

The Nepal Resettlement Company, with His Majesty's Government as shareholder, launched its planned resettlement project at Nawalpur (Nawalparasi district). The main objectives were to bring fallow and uneconomic forest land under cultivation through resettlement, to reduce population pressures on the land in the Middle Mountains, and to remove forest encroachers from protected forests and resettle them in an organized way elsewhere. The company launched other resettlement projects in Nawalpur and Dhanewa (Nawalparasi district), Prithvinagar (Jhapa), Kajura (Banke), Jamuni (Bardia), Parsan (Kanchanpur), Jugeda (Kailali), and Nawalpur (Sarlahi).

Due to high population pressure without matching employment opportunities in the mountains and the easy availability of land and job opportunities in the tarai, migration from the mountains to the plains began. This compelled the government to establish the Resettlement Department to supervise the Resettlement Company, in order to organize land resettlement on a massive scale.

Though the main task of the Department was to look after the coordination and policy matters of the resettlement programmes, it was also involved in programme implementation. Subsequently, the Department started its first resettlement programmes in Sijuwa (Morang district), Murtia (Sarlahi), Sindhureghari (Rautahat), Najgarh (Bara), and Dhanewa (Nawalparasi). Later, as these settlements

93

grew and forest encroachment began, the Department had to establish offices at Jhapa, Morang, Parsa, Rupandehi, Dang, Nepalganj, Dhangadi, and Mahendranagar.

The objectives of resettling the landless and controlling forest encroachment could, however, not be effectively realized. Hence, the government opted for a policy change in 1973, deciding to have two types of resettlement programmes: a resettlement plan and programme, and a disorganized settlement control programme. The objectives of the former were to resettle families displaced by natural calamities and landless families dependent on agriculture, and to increase agricultural production through improved agricultural practices. The objective of the second programme was to control the encroachment on government land and forests by regulated resettlements in specified areas.

Although a large number of migrants from the mountains have been settled in the tarai, the emergence of resettlement as a crash programme without sufficient planning or the basic mechanism to settle landless people and to control forest encroachment has aggravated the problem of landlessness and forest encroachment (Kansakar, 1979: 18–19).

Under the Rapti Development Project in Chitwan district, 29,000 hectares of land were distributed among 5,000 families. The Resettlement Company, under its planned settlement programme, resettled 13,000 families on 23,000 hectares of land. The Department of Resettlement had settled 46,000 families on 39,000 hectares of land.

Of the eight resettlement projects under the Resettlement Company, the largest number of settlers are in Kanchanpur with 3,044 families on 4,261 hectares of land, followed by Nawalparasi with 2,884 families on 3,663 hectares of land, Bardia with 2,838 families on 4,169 hectares, and Banke with 1,520 families on 3,676 hectares. The smallest project is in Sarlahi, where so far 241 families have resettled on 310 hectares of land.

The Resettlement Department – alone and on behalf of other commissions and agencies – has piecemeal resettlement programmes in 29 districts. The Kanchanpur office, under the Resettlement Department, has the largest number of settlers (9,664 on 8,541 hectares of land), followed by Morang (8,691 families on 7,914 hectares), Jhapa (6,343 families on 6,178 hectares), Kailali (5,211 families on 4,195 hectares), Bardia (2,814 families on 1,641 hectares), Nawalparasi (2,630 families on 2,356 hectares), and Banke (1,748 families on 1,462 hectares). Since most of the settlers under Company or Department programmes were given either forest or cultivable wasteland, these programmes have had no direct bearing on land distribution. Some resettlers were genuine victims of natural disasters or were landless, but some took undue and illegal advantage of the resettlement programmes.

Despite growing resettlement programmes (both planned and disorganized), the flow of migrants from the mountain areas continues, and forest encroachments have increased so much that national forest areas have decreased. Since the economy of the mountain areas is still critical and other employment opportunities are lacking, the pressure of the migration flow and the need for resettlement programmes continues. There is limited scope for bringing more forest land under resettlement and cultivation programmes and the government has now terminated resettlement programmes in forest areas. However, the Asian Development Bank (1982: 51) estimates that about 500,000 hectares under forest are suitable for agriculture.

It has been nearly three decades since the resettlement programme began. However, it has neither resolved the problem of the landless nor helped agricultural production. A number of problems have beset the programme, such as the unplanned starting of resettlement programmes, disorganized and ad hoc settlements, the lack of a clear demarcation between the functions of the Company and the Department, the independent functioning of agencies, the absence of an integrated approach in providing necessary services to the resettlement and settlement programmes, and ineffective technical machinery.

Structural transformation

Landlessness can be reduced by providing employment opportunities to the landless people through a structural transformation of the economy, especially by industrialization. Rural growth centres, rural industrial zones, and agro-industries can provide gainful employment to the rural poor, including the landless people. Rural non-farm activities, based on traditional crafts and new technologies, could be developed and integrated with the market system in order to ensure an adequate return to the people engaged at the production level.

The experience of industrialization in Nepal during the previous four decades has not been very encouraging in providing employment to the landless. This raises an important question: how should Nepal plan its industrialization strategy so as to diversify its national economy while at the same time creating additional employment opportunities at a pace capable of absorbing the rapidly growing labour force? This is where rural small-scale industrialization becomes very important for Nepal. However, without adequate infrastructure facilities and training in management, accounting, and finance, any attempt at a rapid expansion of rural industries may not be feasible. The problem of landlessness and unemployment is serious enough, but in view of the scarcity of resources, haphazard expansion would be self-defeating.

Family planning

Family planning is a possible curative measure against landlessness. Since landlessness is at least partly the product of a rapidly growing population, a decreasing birth rate would certainly help. Efforts at population control have had limited success in Nepal, but considerable progress can be attained only when these efforts are combined with the provision of education and employment opportunities, particularly for women, as well as social security for the elderly and infirm.

Support for rural women

The gender dimension of development and policy making is an important element in the alleviation of landlessness. Therefore, landless women should be the direct target of land reforms and other rural development programmes. Programmes for the salaried employment of landless women should have preference over welfare-oriented programmes.

Participatory programmes

The landless and the poor do not get a "fair" share of the resources because of the vested interests of the rich. They need to organize themselves to get their "fair" share. The aims of the participatory measures are to enable the landless and the poor to organize themselves; to identify their needs; and to share in the design, implementation, and evaluation of programmes which meet their needs. Participatory programmes also include action programmes to mobilize the landless workers and the rural poor in associations or unions, which would enable them to act as pressure groups.

Among the measures discussed above, effective land reform would go a long way if Nepal were prepared to take such a radical step. There are no obvious signs of wide acceptability of the idea of a radical redistribution of the land. The real issue is that even if radical redistribution were feasible it would only provide a breathing space in Nepal unless population growth were brought down to manageable proportions and industrial development or other off-farm employment grew fast enough to absorb the additional labour force.

Development theory and agricultural policy

Since the 1950s economic development in Nepal has been to a large extent equated with economic growth rates. The beneficial effects of growth on welfare and living standards have remained implicit. Over time, experience in Nepal and other developing countries changed this perception of economic development into a much more complicated concept.

A major problem with emphasizing economic growth rates was the resultant neglect of distributional and poverty-reduction considerations. In Nepal the neglect led to a marginalization of large segments of the population. Thus, by the 1970s the new concept of "growth with equity" had gained momentum and moved to the centre of the development debate. Agricultural and rural development benefited from this approach, which emphasized the reduction of rural poverty and focused on the small-scale farmer. The human dimensions of development and poverty issues became the forefront of development concerns. Increased emphasis was placed on the democratization of development, whereby the people affected are central to the process. Also, agricultural exports were expected to provide foreign exchange for financing the import of capital goods during the initial phase of industrialization.

The highly stylized development theory noted above had a considerable impact on policy formation in Nepal during the 1970s and 1980s. A number of considerations, in particular the general performance of the rural sector, support the view that agriculture was relatively neglected in Nepal during these decades.

At the present time there is no consensus with regard to the general orientation of policies. Some believe that reliance on market mechanisms produces beneficial economic outcomes for the development of agriculture. They relate agrarian structure and markets, and technological possibilities. In contrast, the structuralist stresses the

97

role of the economic, social, and political structures that makes Nepal unique. Here, emphasis is placed upon inequalities in land ownership, access to credit, and the differential market power of various groups. Rural inequality poses a major barrier to agricultural modernization in Nepal.

To a large extent the debate over relative prices versus social and economic structures reflects an implicit conflict between short and long-term problems of agriculture. Even if a government implements policies of structural change, such as land reform, the results are seen only after several years. In the meantime, there is still a need to improve agricultural performance within existing institutional limits. In the difficult search for an appropriate mix, the theories often provide the reference for a policy formulation.

In the Eighth Plan (1992–1997) Nepal emphasizes agricultural development based on farmers' resource endowments, agro-ecological diversity, and market access. The prices of traded inputs and outputs along the India-Nepal border will be used as a reference point for setting minimum prices of agricultural commodities and agricultural inputs in Nepal. Since agricultural prices are not always an effective policy instrument, non-price variables such as improvement in technology and organization, investments in infrastructure (roads and irrigation), and institutional improvements are planned for increasing agricultural production. It is expected that institutional reforms in the areas of credit, land tenure, and agricultural support services will have a substantial impact on agricultural production and equitable development.

The Eighth Plan is concerned with developing a long-term perspective plan for agricultural development with the goals of poverty alleviation, sustainable growth, and resource conservation. This will involve guiding the structural change in Nepal's economy. Much of the future of economic development in Nepal depends on the success of its agricultural policy. Efforts to date have been either inadequate, misinformed, or at the mercy of variables that could not be changed. Future efforts must look realistically at past records and formulate a paradigm for agricultural policy if a significant level of development is to be achieved.

Because agriculture is the main engine of growth in Nepal, efforts to alleviate poverty and malnutrition largely hinge on increasing agricultural productivity, but this is increasingly hampered by widespread environmental degradation and reduced government investment in rural areas. To meet these challenges, Nepal must adopt strategies to increase investment in the agriculture sector; to enhance access to improved agricultural technologies; to develop productive, sustainable, and environmental friendly technologies; to strengthen efforts to protect the environment; to improve commercialization of agriculture; to increase investment in human resources; to improve trade linkages; and to improve government policies.

5

Human resources

A major factor affecting the development and environment in Nepal is the rapid growth in population, which has almost doubled during the past 20 years. The success of environmental management and economic development will depend in large part on the success of the population policy. The problem of population growth is recognized by the government and international agencies, which have addressed this fundamental issue on both the supply side by providing family planning practices, and on the demand side, primarily through education. Population growth has forced more intensive use of land and water resources, and has thrust people into more marginal, environmentally sensitive areas. Population growth has put pressure on forest resources, and it has also filled cities such as Kathmandu with a relentlessly growing multitude of human beings who have few skills, little resources, and no jobs.

The government of Nepal began to collect population data in 1911 for the purpose of collecting revenue for forced labour and for army recruitment. Population censuses were taken in 1920, 1930, and 1942. Demographic characteristics of the population were ignored in these early population counts until the first regular census was taken in 1952–1954. Because of the political changes that took place in 1951, this census was completed in two parts. The census of the eastern part of the country (except Mohotari) was completed in 1952; the census of the central and western parts of the country, including the Kathmandu Valley and Mohotari, was completed in 1954. There are some earlier population estimates by various authors. Fraser estimated the total population of Nepal in 1820 at 3.6 million, Oldfield thought it was 4 million in the 1950s, and Vansittart estimated it to be between 5.2 to 5.6 million at the beginning of the twentieth century (Kansakar, 1989: 28).

Since 1961 Nepal has had a regular decennial census. However, frequent changes in the census schedules, definitions, enumeration units, and district boundaries make a comparative study of population change at the district level a difficult task. The censuses of 1952–1954 and 1961 used 28,400 villages as the unit of enumeration. The country was divided into 55 administrative districts and four major census regions: Hill, Kathmandu Valley, Inner Tarai, and Tarai. These regions were further subdivided into nine census regions in 1952–1954 and into 10 census regions in 1961. The Western Hill region was subdivided into the Western Hill and Far-western Hill regions in 1961.

With the introduction of the Panchayat system in 1962, the political boundaries as well as the census regions were completely realigned. The country was divided into 14 zones and 75 districts, and 28,400 villages were regrouped into nearly 4,000 village panchayats. In the 1971 census, three major census regions were identified: Mountain, Hill, and Tarai. The Mountain region was created out of the northern part of the Hill region, and the Inner Tarai was either included in the Hill or the tarai regions. These regions were further subdivided into three east-west sectors, excluding the Kathmandu Valley. Thus, there were 10 census regions, but these were totally different from the 10 census regions as defined in 1961.

The 1981 census recognized the three major census regions as before, but they were subdivided according to the five development regions: East, Central, West, Midwest, and Far-west. The Kathmandu Valley was included in the Hill region. Thus, the combination of these two sets of regions yields 15 census regions. The enumeration units (village panchayats) decreased from nearly 4,000 units in 1971 to 2,935 in 1981. The second amendment of the Constitution of Nepal in December 1975 relocated some of these village panchayats to different districts, and thus changed the boundaries and populations of 63 districts.

The Central Bureau of Statistics has not even attempted to adjust the population data of the different censuses to the present district boundaries. The spatial dimension of the censuses has been completely neglected. Boundaries of village panchayats and urban areas were never given, and no attention was paid to the changes in the boundaries while comparing data from the two censuses. How much of the population growth in urban areas, for example, is due to the incorporation of adjacent areas rather than natural population growth? There is no way to discern the effect of various factors in such a situation. This makes any time analysis merely a tentative hypothesis rather than a proven fact.

Even after five censuses and 40 years of experience, the quality of census data is questionable. Some of the problems are due to the social and cultural values of the population while others are due to the lack of proper training and inefficiency of the administrators and bureaucrats. There was a serious undercounting of children under age 5, and an underenumeration of females aged 10 to 24 and of males aged 15 to 24 in the 1952–1954 census. The same kind of undercounting is present in the 1961 census (Krotki and Thakur, 1971). There could be a minimum undercount of about 5 per cent of the total population of the country. If we consider the possibility of missing whole households or whole villages, the undercount could be even greater. Subsequent censuses showed no improvement. Without any significant change in the fertility rate in the country during the past 10 years, the 1991 census indicates the rate of population growth to be 2.1 per cent per year. This is a significant drop in the growth rate from 1981 (table 10). Either there should have been a serious overcount in the 1981 census or a serious undercount in the 1991 census, or both (Dangol, 1992: 2).

Population growth, distribution, and density

In 1911 Nepal's total population was estimated to be 5.6 million. The next two censuses showed successive declines: 5.57 million in 1920 and 5.53 in 1930. The 1941 census showed an increase in the total population by 13.57 per cent over the 1930 population. Several factors, such as deaths due to the influenza epidemic of 1918, the threat of war with Tibet in 1930, and the return of the Nepalese after World War II, have been cited as possible causes of population change during these 40 years (Kansakar, 1989: 32). All of the changes may not be attributed to these factors. These early censuses were not scientifically conducted, and the margins of error are unknown. The undercounting of the population could have been due to a lack of transport facilities, lack of public participation, or lack of adequate methodology. How much these factors contributed to the change in the total population cannot be estimated. Therefore, the earlier population figures in table 10 are not discussed in great detail in the analysis.

According to the first scientific census of 1952–1954, the population of Nepal was found to be 8,256,625. Since this census was conducted during two different time periods two years apart, we need to project the population of eastern Nepal for 1954 on the basis of an assumed growth rate, then add the population of western Nepal, including Mohotari and the Kathmandu Valley, to reach the total. Furthermore, in the censuses of 1952–1954 and 1961 people who were absent from their home for less than six months but were still in Nepal were counted as absentees. Since 1971 the censuses were conducted on a modified de jure basis (Central Bureau of Statistics, 1977: 9–10). Persons living in places other than their permanent residences for less than six months were counted in their original residences. Hence, to make these figures compatible with each other, the persons living away from their permanent residence but within Nepal for less than six months need to be added to the total population (Banister and Thapa, 1981:24). These figures, however, are not used in the later discussion at the regional and district level because of the difficulty in assigning the total number of these people to a particular region or district. Thus, the total population of Nepal in 1954 should be around 8.36 million. This indicates an increase of 33 per cent of the estimated population of 1941 within 13 years (table 10). The error in the count resulting from underestimation was not corrected.

In the latter half of the 1950s the population of Nepal increased at the rate of 1.3 per cent per year. Subsequent censuses indicated a steady population increase at a higher rate. In the 1960s the rate of increase was 2.05 per cent, followed by 2.6 per cent in the seventies and by 2.1 per cent in the eighties. This growth rate fits the exponential growth curve exactly (fig. 11). The population of Nepal in 1991 reached a total of 18,491,097, giving an increase of 23 per cent over the 1981 population. This is considered to be significantly lower than the expected growth rate of 2.57 per cent per year. Without any significant change in the fertility rate, and the lowering of the death rate in the 1970s and 1980s, the population growth rate should have been greater than the rate indicated by the 1991 census. Hence, it is possible that there was a gross overcount in the 1981 census or an undercount in the 1991 census. Another explanation suggested by Shrestha (1992: 12) was an out-migration of Nepalese to India and other countries in search of jobs. The exact cause or an explanation of this lower rate of population growth cannot be given until a detailed census report and the results of a post enumeration survey are published by the Nepalese government.

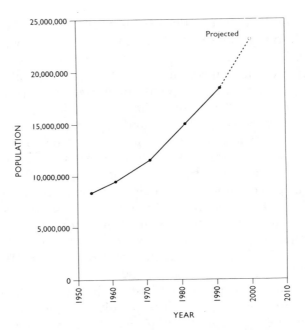

Fig. 11 **Population growth, 1954–1991**

Between 1954 and 1991 the total population of Nepal more than doubled, from 8.4 million to 18.5 million. If this growth rate continues, the population of Nepal will again double in another 33 years. Even with a slight decline in the total fertility rate (TFR = 4.00), the population is expected to reach 23 million by the year 2000. The rapid decline in infant mortality, decline in the death rate, and increase in life expectancy without any decline in the fertility rate explains the current growth. This growth rate will continue for sometime, since the majority of the people are still young and are within the reproductive age group.

The Great Himalaya and the Middle Mountains, which constitute 77 per cent of the total area of Nepal, contained 65 per cent of the total population in 1952–1954. In 1961 the share of the national population in the Great Himalaya and Middle Mountain regions increased a little, but from then on these regions steadily lost their population share (fig. 12). In 1991 these regions accounted for 53 per cent of the total population.

On the other hand, the population of the tarai is rapidly increasing. In 1952–1954 the tarai supported only 35 per cent of the total pop-

104

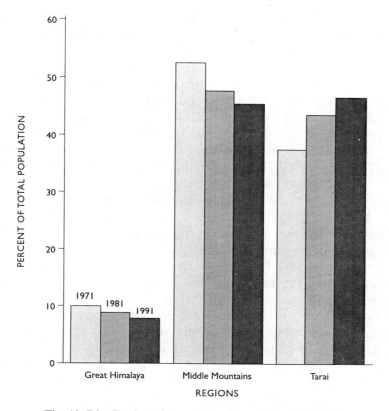

Fig. 12 **Distribution of population by regions, 1971–1991**

ulation. At present, it accounts for almost 47 per cent. The Middle Mountain and Great Himalaya regions have only about 45 and 8 per cent of the population respectively. The rapid population growth in the tarai region is mainly due to the rural-to-rural migration from the mountain areas to the tarai. Now that the tarai is the most populated geoecological region of Nepal, its share of the national population will continue to increase in the future.

There is an east-west variation in the growth pattern of each of these ecological regions (table 11). The largest growth in the mountain region was in the far-west area, followed by the central, midwestern and eastern mountain regions. In absolute terms the central mountain region gained the most population – 54,862. In the Middle Mountain region, the central region gained the most, both in percentage as well as absolute terms. The tarai region gained nearly 32

105

per cent of the total population increase. The far-western tarai had the largest increase whereas the eastern tarai had the least increase. This growth pattern started in the 1970s and continued into the 1980s. It is likely that this trend will also continue into the 1990s.

In 1991, at the district level, Humla had the highest percentage gain followed by Kailali, Kathmandu, and Kanchanpur. In terms of absolute gain, Kathmandu ranked first, followed by Kailali, Rupandehi, and Morang (fig. 13). Because of its small population size, Humla had only a small change in population, but showed a larger percentage change. In the 1970s Humla actually lost its population, partly because three of its panchayats were shifted to the Mugu district.

There are only three districts which actually lost population in the 1980s. The population of Mugu declined by 7,341 (16.80 per cent) persons while Manang and Taplejung lost 1,658 (23.61 per cent) and 727 (0.60 per cent) persons respectively. All of these districts are in the mountain region. Districts in the tarai region gained the most population while the mountain districts gained the least. A gradual increase in the percentage gain is from the eastern districts to the western districts; in the Middle Mountains and the Great Himalayan regions it is somewhat mixed. There is a greater percentage in the west, but a greater increase in absolute numbers is in the eastern districts in the mountain region (fig. 14). These changes in the population were evident even in the 1970s, showing the magnitude and direction of population shifts over time (table 12).

The density of population gives a better picture of the population concentration on land. The average density for the whole country reached 126 persons per sq. km in 1991. Forty-two of the 75 districts had greater densities than the national average. The highest density was recorded in Kathmandu, followed by Bhaktapur, Lalitpur, and Dhanusa districts. Many of the districts with the highest densities were all located in the eastern and central tarai. Districts in the central and western parts of the Middle Mountains and in the western tarai had the second highest densities. Districts in the mountain region had the least densities.

In an agricultural country like Nepal, a more meaningful measure of population pressure on the land is the ratio of people to cultivated land (fig. 15). Since Nepal is a mountainous country, not much land is available for cultivation. According to the 1981 National Sample Census of Agriculture, only about 17 per cent of the total land was under cultivation, which amounts to 610 persons per sq. km of cultivated area. At the district level, the density per cultivated area ranges

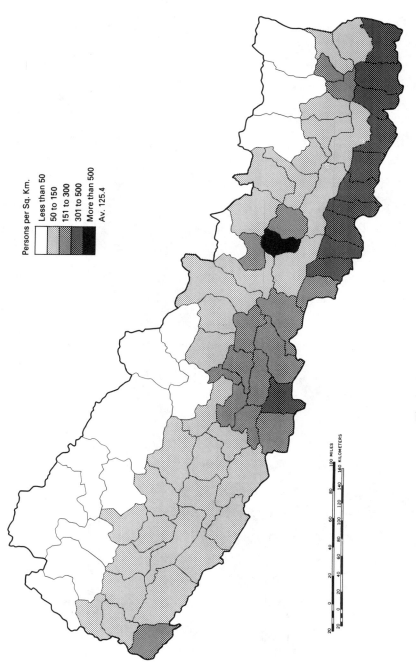

Persons per Sq. Km.

Less than 50
50 to 150
151 to 300
301 to 500
More than 500
Av. 125.4

Fig. 13 **Population density, 1991**

107

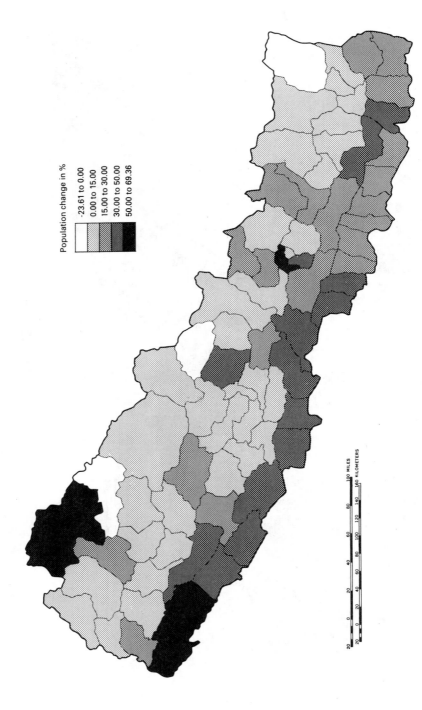

Population change in %

-23.61 to 0.00
0.00 to 15.00
15.00 to 30.00
30.00 to 50.00
50.00 to 69.36

20   0   20   40   60   80   100 MILES
20   0   20   40   60   80   100   120   140   160 KILOMETERS

Fig. 14 **Population change, 1981–1991**

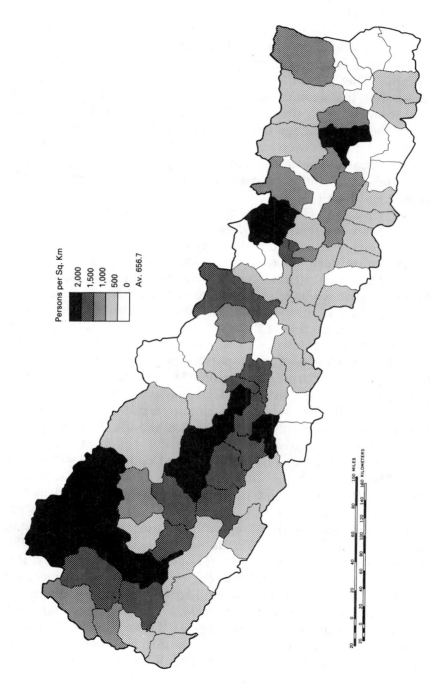

Fig. 15 **Population density per square kilometre of arable land**

Persons per Sq. Km

2,000
1,500
1,000
500
0

Av. 656.7

from almost 3,000 persons per sq. km in Mugu to 191 in Mustang. Much of this variation can be explained by the percentage of land under cultivation, the amount of rainfall, and the type of terrain.

The eastern and central tarai have the highest percentages of cultivated area. The eastern, central, and western areas of the Middle Mountain and the western tarai districts have the second highest concentrations of cultivated areas. The districts in the Great Himalaya have the least acreage under cultivation because of the higher elevation and the snow-covered mountains. Another factor which affects this variation is rainfall; it decreases from east to west. Hence, the potential use of land for agriculture decreases from south to north and from east to west.

A large population concentration with less land available for cultivation increases the density of persons per cultivated area. Hence, many of the districts with the highest densities per cultivated area are found in the western area of the Middle Mountains and Great Himalaya. The tarai districts have a greater percentage of land under cultivation, and hence have a lower density per cultivated area.

It is interesting to note that the density per cultivated area over the 10-year period from 1971 to 1981 actually decreased. In 1971 the average density per cultivated area was 699 persons per sq. km; in 1981 the density decreased to 610 persons per sq. km. This decrease, however, was not uniform in all regions. In the Great Himalaya, the density decreased from 1,365 persons per sq. km of cultivated area to 1,063 persons. The mid-western mountain region had the biggest change and the far-western mountain region had the least change. In the Middle Mountains, the change in density was even greater; it decreased from 1,572 persons per sq. km of cultivated land to 762 persons. The largest change occurred in the central section of the Middle Mountain region and the smallest change occurred in the mid-western section.

On the other hand, the tarai region had an increase of 97 persons per sq. km of cultivated land. The density changed from 371 in 1971 to 468 in 1981. All regions in the tarai had increases in density; the highest increase was in the far-western tarai and the least increase was in the central tarai. These increases reflect the differential rates of change in the population growth and in the acreage of land brought under cultivation in these regions during the last 10 years. This may be due to the loss of population through migration or the increase of deforestation at a faster rate than the population growth rate.

Since none of these regions lost any population between 1971 and 1981, it may be assumed that the decrease in density of population per sq. km of cultivated land must be directly related to the increase in deforestation and/or the increase of marginal land brought under cultivation.

Migration pattern

Although Nepal is a small agricultural country with a rough mountainous terrain, its people have always been mobile. About a quarter of the total population is continually moving, particularly during the dry winter season (Hagen, 1961: 107; Gurung, 1968: 8). The poor agricultural land, low productivity, lack of alternative employment other than agricultural, lack of market, and high population pressure on the land have forced people to make seasonal trips to other parts of Nepal, particularly to the towns near the southern border. Some people even go outside the country as far as Assam and Singapore for trade and/or employment. At present, however, the seasonal migration to Sikkim, Bhutan, and Assam has decreased due to ethnic conflicts in these areas but has increased to Bihar, Uttar Pradesh, West Bengal, Delhi, and Haryana.

Since 1959 trade across the northern border has also been drastically reduced, and the seasonal migration has ceased. Before the 1950s most people either moved within the Middle Mountain region or moved to Tibet or India for trade and service. There was little movement within the country in those days. Because of deadly malaria in the tarai, people from the Middle Mountain region always avoided that area for settlement. Instead, they moved outside the country to Darjeeling, Sikkim, Bhutan, and Assam in India, seeking jobs on tea plantations. Some went to Burma, settling for rice cultivation on newly reclaimed land, or seeking recruitment in the British Army or the Burmese Military Police (Kansakar, 1973–74: 63).

After the political unification of Nepal in the 1790s, the government encouraged the Indians and Tibetans to immigrate to the border areas to increase agricultural production and government revenue from taxes on agriculture land. During the nineteenth century, there was an increased concentration of land ownership and undue oppression of the peasants in the Middle Mountain and tarai areas. Therefore, people left Nepal in search of better jobs in India (Regmi, 1971: 192).

Internal migration

A large-scale lifetime migration really started during the 1950s after malaria was eradicated in the tarai region. In the 1940s less than 14,000 persons were recorded as having changed their residences within Nepal. Two-fifths of these migrants moved to the Kathmandu Valley; less than one-third of them moved to the tarai region. Movement to the eastern tarai was more pronounced than to the central and western tarai. More than 80 per cent of these migrants came from the Middle Mountains, about 10 per cent came from the Kathmandu Valley, and the rest came from the tarai.

A mass exodus of people from the northern and Middle Mountains to the tarai started in the late 1950s. The total life-time migrants increased from 19,000 to 178,000, not including 88,000 in the "origin unstated" category. The major destination for these migrants was the eastern tarai, followed by the central tarai region. The Kathmandu Valley received only 14 per cent of the total out-migrants. Inmigration to the Middle and Great Himalayan regions was limited to 9 per cent.

During the 1960s the number of life-time migrants increased by 2.8 per cent (fig. 16). The Middle Mountain region contributed the largest share of out-migrants – 86 per cent. The Great Himalayan region contributed about 10 per cent and the tarai contributed 4 per cent. The tarai region, including a major portion of the earlier inner tarai region, received 87 per cent of the total migrants. The Middle Mountain region received about 11 per cent, while the Great Himalaya received only about 2 per cent. The eastern and central areas of the Middle Mountains were the largest source of migrants; the eastern and central tarai were the principal destinations. Of the small outmigrant group from the tarai (18,510), 52 per cent moved to the Middle Mountains, 3 per cent went to the high Himalayas, and the remaining 45 per cent moved within the tarai region itself.

In the 1970s more than one million persons, or almost 7 per cent of the total population, were on the move. Part of this unprecedented increase in movement could be attributed to the increase in the number of geographic regions. In the 1971 census, Nepal was divided into 10 regions; in the 1981 census, it was divided into 15 regions. Out-migration from the mountain regions continued to comprise the overwhelming majority of life-time migrants (table 13).

The mountain population (of the Great Himalaya), which comprised less than 9 per cent of the total population of the country,

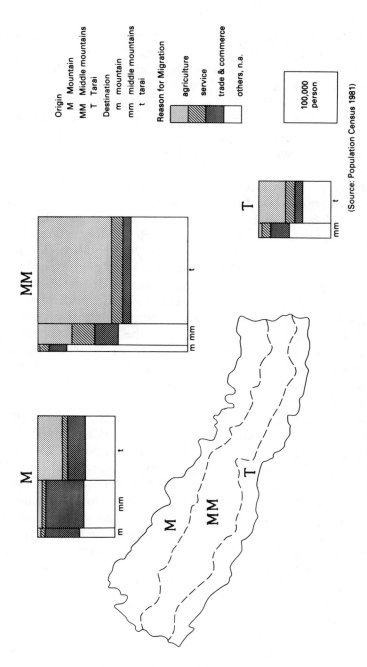

Fig. 16 **Lifetime migration (Source: Population Census, 1981)**

contributed 30 per cent of the total migrants. Of this, 6 per cent moved to high mountain regions, 43 per cent moved to the Middle Mountains, and the remaining 51 per cent moved to the tarai (table 13). The eastern mountain region alone contributed 23 per cent of the total migrants. The Middle Mountain region contributed about 61 per cent of the total life-time migrants. Their major destination was still the eastern tarai (table 14).

However, compared to earlier destinations, there was a very significant shift in the migration pattern this time. More people were moving toward the western, the mid-western, and the far-western tarai regions.

Since birth and death rates across the nation have had little spatial variations during the last four decades, migration has become the most important factor in bringing about changes in population size, structure, and density. A population, which was once concentrated in the Middle Mountain region, began moving south into the tarai region. During the 1950s and 1960s the strongest migration flow was towards the eastern tarai. This is still the major destination, but movement has now started to change toward the mid-western and far-western tarai. This is due to increasing population pressure and the lack of available land for cultivation in the east and central tarai. In comparison, the western part of Nepal still has a larger percentage of land under forest (Kenting Earth Sciences Ltd., 1986). Recent changes in the government's population policy might also account, to some extent, for the shift in destination.

Migration is a selective process with respect to age, sex, and education. More than 70 per cent of the migrants in 1981 were in the 15–59 age group. Children below age 15 constituted nearly 23 per cent, and people over 59 constituted slightly more than 7 per cent. Male migrants constituted more than 51 per cent of the total. The Middle Mountain region as a whole had more male out-migrants than the Great Himalayan and tarai regions. The central, western, and mid-western parts of the high mountain regions and the eastern and central tarai had a slightly higher female out-migration. Most of the females had moved a shorter distance to adjacent regions, whereas the males had moved farther away from their birthplace. Some of these moves by the females may have been related to marriage migration (Central Bureau of Statistics, 1987: 116).

The overall educational levels of both the male and female migrants were higher than those of the non-migrant population. The propensity to migrate increases with educational level and occupation. A person with a postgraduate degree is twice as likely to move from the area than a person with only a primary education.

Among the reasons for leaving their place of birth, the majority of persons cited population pressure, increased family size, declining agricultural production, and floods and/or landslides (Centre for Economic Development and Administration, 1977: 88). The main reasons to move to the tarai were the availability of land, the lower cost of agricultural land, and employment opportunities.

The reasons for migration were collected for the first time in the 1981 census. The largest percentage of males named agriculture (36.27 per cent) as the main reason, while the females stated marriage (30.30 per cent) as the main reason (fig. 17). The Demographic Sample Survey conducted in 1986–1987 had the same findings. Dependency was the single most important reason for leaving among migrants younger than 29, while agriculture was the most important reason for moving into rural areas among men older than 29. Among females, the most important reason for migration was "marriage," followed by "dependency" (Central Bureau of Statistics, 1988: 39).

Migration within Nepal has been basically from rural to rural areas. Rural to urban migration has remained very low compared to rural-urban migration in other developing countries. Urban development in Nepal is still in its infancy. In 1991 only 9.2 per cent of the total population lived in 33 designated urban areas. Over 81 per cent of the population worked in the agricultural sector, which contributed the bulk of the total gross domestic product of the country.

A major shift in the population distribution through migration can be a symptom of an ailing economy and of environmental degradation in the Middle Mountains. If this process continues, a larger percentage of the total population will concentrate in the tarai. Because of the larger population share and higher rate of marginal returns from investments made in the tarai, most of the private and public expenditures will be spent in the tarai, which will cause an even greater economic disparity between the high mountain, Middle Mountains, and the tarai regions. This in turn could create still more social and political unrest in the country.

Circular migration

The 1981 census classifies circular migration, both internal and external, as absentee population. The internal absentee population consists of short-term seasonal migrants who leave the mountains for

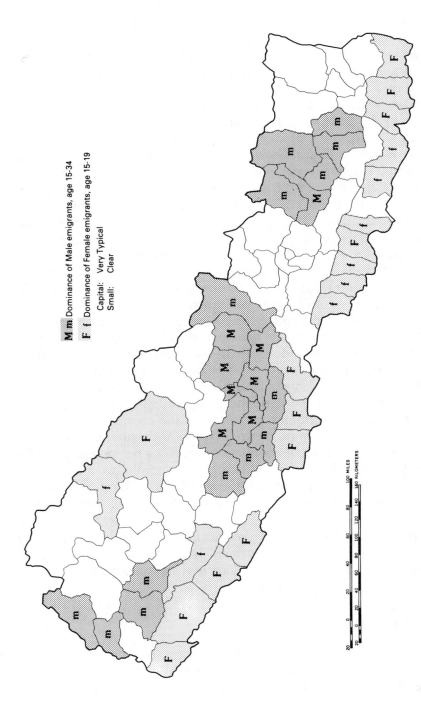

M m Dominance of Male emigrants, age 15-34

F f Dominance of Female emigrants, age 15-19

Capital: Very Typical
Small: Clear

Fig. 17 Dominance of male and female emigrants

116

temporary employment in nearby towns and generally return to villages for farming after the winter is over (fig. 18). The external absentee population comprises long-term migrants, most of whom go to India to work (fig. 19).

As the population pressure increased in Nepal in the 1950s, people began to move to India in search of long-term salaried employment as a *chaukidar* (doorman or guard), to go into the services, or for factory jobs. These circular or absentee migrants normally visit their families or villages in Nepal every year or so. Some of these external circular migrants settled in India, but those who retired from army service returned to Nepal after their discharge. Although Nepalese emigrants are found in South and South-East Asia, Japan, Europe, North America, Fiji, and Guyana (Kansakar, 1973–74: 65), and recently a significant number moved to the Middle East for employment, the largest number of Nepali emigrants are in India, particularly in the northern and north-eastern states.

The 1961 Indian census recorded 493,400 Nepali-born persons (277,200 male and 216,200 female) working in India. In 1971 the figure increased to 526,526. The preliminary 1991 census data and data collected from Parbasi Nepali Sangh (an organization to assist new Nepali immigrants in Indian cities) reveals that over 1.5 million Nepali citizens are working in India alone. Weiner (1973: 621), investigating the pattern of emigration from Nepal to India in 1961, concluded that approximately 82,000 Nepalese migrated annually to India and about 62,000 of them returned after having worked in India from one to five years. Of the 20,000 who remained in India, half were males and half were females. At least half of these females came to India as a result of marriage.

Recent policies in Bhutan have forced many Nepalese who have settled in southern Bhutan since 1920 to return to Nepal. Talks between Bhutan and Nepal about these Nepali migrants from Bhutan were resumed in 1993. Earlier talks had failed because the two countries could not agree on an appropriate term for the 86,000 people who are now living in refugee camps in Jhapa and other areas in Nepal. While Nepal had insisted on calling them "refugees," Bhutan felt that they should be referred to as "displaced persons." Nepal maintains that these groups have fled from "ethnic cleansing" and "cultural persecution" in Bhutan. Bhutan insists that the migrants are being incited to leave the country by elements seeking a greater share in Bhutan's political systems. The Nepali-dominated Bhutan National Democratic Party and the Bhutan People's Party have launched a

117

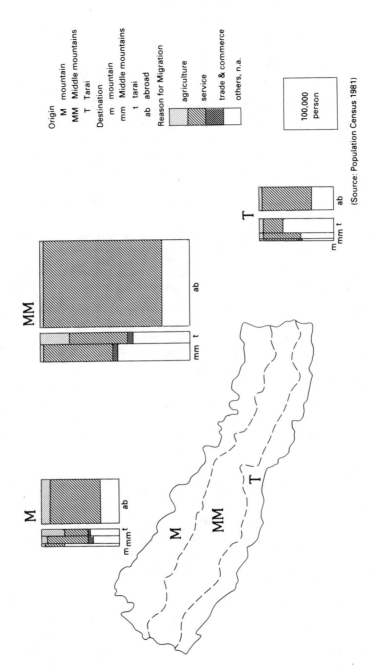

Fig. 18 Circular migration (Source: Population Census, 1981)

(Source: Population Census 1981)

Origin
  M   mountain
  MM   Middle mountains
  T   Tarai
Destination
  m   mountain
  mm   Middle mountains
  t   tarai
  ab   abroad
Reason for Migration
  agriculture
  service
  trade & commerce
  others, n.a.

100,000 person

118

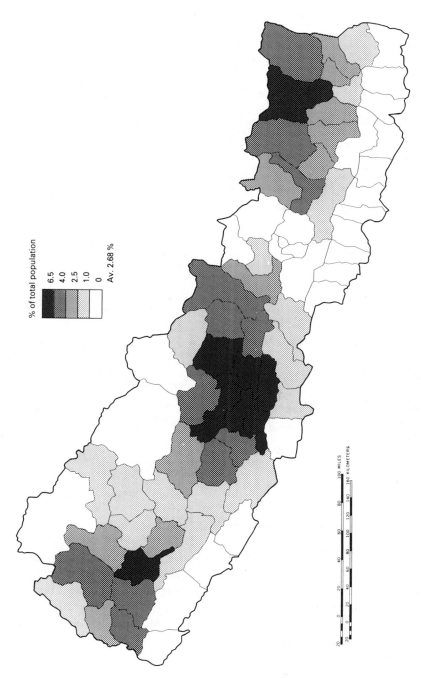

% of total population

6.5
4.0
2.5
1.0
0

Av. 2.68 %

100 MILES
160 KILOMETERS

Fig. 19 **Population working abroad, 1981**

119

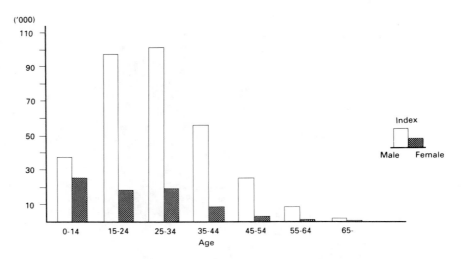

Fig. 20 **Nepalese working abroad by age, 1981**

campaign to destabilize the prosperous southern districts in order to give the ethnic Nepalese greater power and privileges.

The 1952–1954 census reported that 198,120 persons, or 2.3 per cent of the total population, lived outside the country. The mountain regions contributed more than 97 per cent of the total number living abroad. In 1961 the number increased to 328,470 persons, constituting 3.5 per cent of the total population and a 60 per cent increase over the 1952–1954 figure. The 1971 census did not include data on the absentee population. In 1981 the absentee population reached a total of 402,977, which constituted 2.7 per cent of the total population.

India was the main destination of these emigrants. In 1952–1954, 79.4 per cent of the emigrants lived in India; in 1961 the number increased to 92 per cent; in 1981 the number was 93 per cent. The Demographic Sample Survey of 1986–1987 indicated that there were 12 emigrants per 1,000 population – 20 male emigrants per 1,000 male population and 4 females per 1,000 female population. The emigration rate was higher in the rural areas. Most of these emigrants came from the mountain regions. The tarai region had the lowest emigration rate. The absolute majority – 96 per cent of the males and 100 per cent of the females – moved to India.

Migration to India and service in the Gurkha regiments abroad provide relief from the population pressure. The Nepalese who work

120

abroad send money to their families, which makes a substantial contribution to the economy. More than $50 million in hard currency continues to pour into Nepal from soldiers' salaries sent back home, pensions, and other Gurkha-related payments. Of the five Gurkha battalions in the British army, three are in Hongkong, one is in Britain for ceremonial and rapid deployment use, and one is on loan to the Sultan of Brunei. More remittance comes from India, which has an estimated 30,000 Nepalese in its Gurkha units and over 1.5 million Nepalese employed in the country. These remittances and pensions have been invested, for example, in the Khudi village, Lamjung district, and in small restaurants, lodges, and shops. This provides an important source of non-agricultural income in many areas of the Middle Mountain region of Nepal. However, the large-scale migration of the Nepalese to India is not a permanent solution to the increasing population pressure and ailing economy. But, for land-locked and resource-poor Nepal, there are few choices.

Indian and foreign migrants

An open border and close economic and cultural ties with India have facilitated the continuous movement across the India-Nepal border. The 1961 census recorded a total of 337,620 persons (3.6 per cent of the total population) as foreign-born. In 1981 there was a significant drop in both the percentage and the absolute number of immigrants to Nepal. The total number was 234,039, which constituted about 1.5 per cent of Nepal's population. The Demographic Sample Survey on Migration in 1986–1987 found that the migration rate for the country as a whole was 28 immigrants per 1,000 population (Central Bureau of Statistics, 1988: 6). This estimate was much higher than the 16 persons per 1,000 population indicated in the 1981 census. There was a significant difference in the sex composition of migrants into Nepal.

There are more females than males among the migrants into Nepal. In 1981 the males constituted 30.59 per cent of the total in-migrants while the females constituted 69.43 per cent (Central Bureau of Statistics, 1984: 1). Almost 95 per cent of the immigrants were from India, a little more than 1 per cent were from China (Tibet), and the rest were from other countries. In general they were more literate than the native population, and their main reasons for staying other than marital (43.34 per cent) or unstated (30.28 per cent) were agriculture, trade and commerce, and service.

In the 1981 census, the mountain (Great Himalayan) region had the least percentage (0.8 per cent) of the immigrants; the Middle Mountain region had almost 7 per cent; and the tarai region had more than 92 per cent. Within the tarai, the central and eastern regions had the highest concentrations – 39 per cent and 33 per cent respectively. The Demographic Sample Survey showed that there was a difference in the immigration rates between the urban and rural areas. For all of Nepal, the rate of immigration to the urban areas was 47 per 1,000 population, while it was only 26 per 1,000 in the rural areas. Eighty-two per cent of the male immigrants and 67 per cent of the female immigrants in the urban areas came from India. In the rural areas, 34 per cent of the males and 11 per cent of the female immigrants came from other Asian countries, mainly Burma, Bangladesh, Bhutan, China, Pakistan, and Sri Lanka. Most of the Indian immigrants have come during the last five to 14 years.

Efforts were made by Nepal to register Indian immigrants and to require work permits. This was in violation of the 1950 Treaty of Peace and Friendship, which allows Indians to migrate to Nepal, and the Nepalese to migrate freely to India. However, the registration and work permit requirements were dropped because of the threat of India's reciprocal requirement of visas and work permits for the Nepalese who were employed in India.

Private enterprises in Nepal are not willing to spend money to train a relatively unskilled and inefficient Nepalese workforce to replace the Indians who are employed in Nepal. Nevertheless, Indian migrants working in Nepal constitute a source of resentment in the country. In the larger economy and work force in India, there is no resentment against the Nepalese citizens who work in India. For certain types of long-term salaried employment in India, such as the army, doorman or guard service, or factory security services, the Nepalese citizens are preferred over local labour.

Taranagar Village: A case study of population mobility in the Middle Mountain region

Taranagar Village, located in Gorkha district about 150 km from Kathmandu, illustrates some of the major ideas concerning migration (fig. 21). Geographically, the village contains two ecological sub-regions: (1) traditional settlements on the mountainside at 800 to 1,000 m, inhabited by the Magar, Bahun, and Chetri castes; and (2) valley bottom settlements called "Besi" between 450 and 550 m, tra-

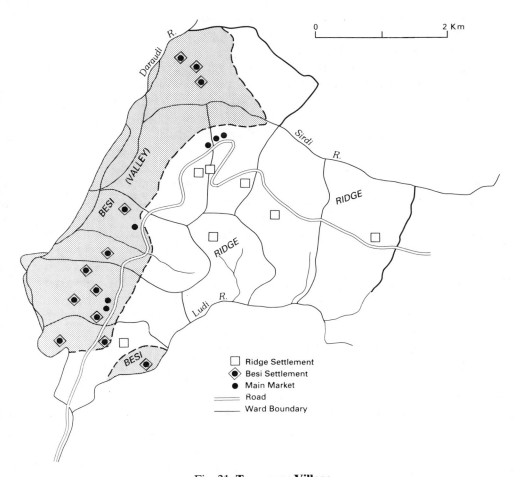

Fig. 21 **Taranagar Village**

ditionally inhabited by the Kumal caste, but recently attracting migrants from other areas in the Middle Mountains.

According to the administrative block, Wards No. 2–7 belong to the hillside area; No. 1 and most of No. 8 and No. 9 are located mainly in the Besi zone. Along the Gorkha-Khalani highway (which passes through the village), some commercial centres have developed; the largest commercial activity is located on the boundary between Wards No. 4 and No. 5.

The population growth rate of the village is about 3 per cent annually (table 15). This is higher than the national average because of the continuing in-migration, which characterizes the Besi area. The village is overpopulated; the average agricultural plot is about 0.7 hectares per household.

In-migration trends into this village can be divided into two main streams: migration as a subsistence farmer, mainly into the Besi zone; and migration as a store-manager into the new bazaar, which developed after the highway was completed in 1980.

The first stream, which comprises mostly local migration from the hillsides to the lower Besi, called "ridge-to-valley" migration (C. B. Shrestha, 1990; Minami, 1990) by subsistence farmers, is common in the Middle Mountains of Nepal. The dominant Nepalese Hindu castes, such as the Bahun, Chetri, and Newar, do not like to live in the lower river basin, even if they own their small paddy fields. Because they prefer to live on the ridge sides, dense settlements characterize the ridges with an intense demand for land and rapidly inflating land prices.

Besi land is owned by the local Kumal caste who, until the early 1980s, sold their land at relatively cheaper prices than in the ridge villages. Due to the difference in land prices, small paddy owners in the ridge settlements were able to enlarge the size of their farms through migration to the Besi. This type of ridge-to-valley migration occurred until the price of Besi land increased after the huge ridge-to-valley migration began. Table 16 indicates the price of farmland, both in the hills and in the Besi in the Taranagar area. Until the early 1980s ridge-to-valley migration was possible in Gorkha district.

But now the land in Besi is also overpopulated, and the price of land is higher than on the ridge slopes. Source villages of in-migrant households are concentrated in a rather small area adjoining the valley (fig. 22). The ridge-to-valley migration, which is on a micro scale, is ignored in the census data because it does not involve intra-district migration. The mountain to tarai migration is also prompted by the great difference in land prices; it is similar to the ridge-to-valley migration (Kobayashi, 1991; 1992).

As well as farmers, other main in-migrants from outside villages to the Taranagar are traders and merchants, who are also common in other Nepalese villages where roads have recently been constructed. In Taranagar this type of migration has continued since the highway was built in 1980.

Most of the recent immigrants into the Besi have bought land from

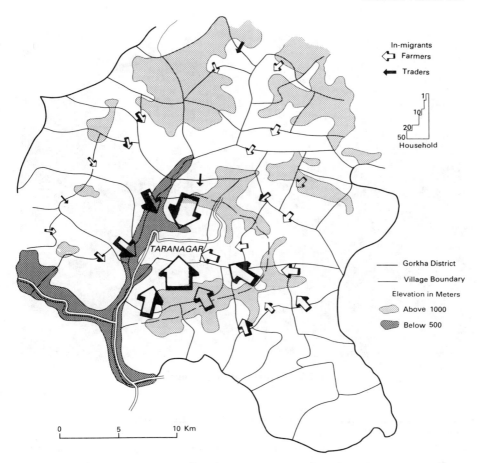

Fig. 22 **Taranagar migration streams**

large-scale landowners who sold their land in the rural areas in order
to purchase land in the Kathmandu Valley as an investment. Land is
more expensive here and the cost is expected to rise more rapidly
than in the rural areas.

In the western part of the Middle Mountains, subsistence economy
is combined with other activities; working outside the villages has
been one of the main methods of earning money. In Taranagar Village the timing and destination of the out-migrants (table 17) reveals
that India is the major destination of out-migrants looking for jobs.
An increased flow to Kathmandu is a new trend that has been
observed.

125

Hillside settlement in Taranagar

Fertility, mortality, and demographic transition

A systematic analysis of trends in fertility and mortality behaviour in Nepal is handicapped by the lack of adequate and reliable data. In the absence of vital registration data, the only source for estimating fertility and mortality are the population censuses and data obtained in the National Sample Surveys. The Nepal Fertility and Family Planning Survey (NFFS) 1986, published by the Ministry of Health, is the most recent national demographic sample survey of the country. The NFFS was undertaken to evaluate the status of the family planning programme and to monitor changes since the 1976 Nepal Fertility Survey (NFS) and the 1981 Nepal Contraceptive Prevalence Survey (NCPS). Using data from the above surveys, Tuladhar (1989) concluded that it was difficult to ascertain accurately the decline in fertility.

Several estimates of fertility and mortality rates have been made, based on various types of demographic methods by Vaidyanathan and Gaige (1973), Gubhaju (1975), and the United States Bureau of

New commercial centre along a newly constructed road, Taranagar

the Census (1979). Their estimated crude birth rates range from 48.7 per thousand in 1954 by Vaidyanathan and Gaige to 42.1 by Gubhaju for 1961, and 43.4 by the United States Bureau of the Census for 1971. The estimates of crude death rates range from 36.7 per thousand by Vaidyanathan and Gaige in 1954, to 34.2 by Gubhaju in 1961, and 24 by the United States Bureau of Census in 1971.

The high fertility levels are attributed to the prevailing social, cultural, and economic conditions which favour large families. These conditions have not changed radically over the last 40 years, so it is unlikely that any dramatic fall in fertility has taken place so far. The high death rates are attributed to the inadequacy of medical and health services, and the low level of economic development. The development of modern medical and health services was started only recently; there was hardly one doctor for a population of 80,000 in 1958. The low level of living associated with the average per capita income of about Rs 260 per month in the rural areas (World Bank, 1991: 5) makes even the minimum standards of nutrition, clothing, and housing beyond the reach of the average person. The high death

127

Indian labourers working in a brick plant in Taranagar

rate is, therefore, not surprising under the socio-economic conditions prevailing in the country.

Since 1951 improvements in health care facilities have led to a decline in the child mortality rate from 297 per 1,000 in 1961 to 147 in 1991. The general death rate has also declined. During the years 1953–1961 the death rate was 27 per 1,000, declining to 21.4 per 1,000 in 1961–1971, and to 13.5 in 1971–1981 (Central Bureau of Statistics, 1987). However, fertility in Nepal remains high, with a crude birth rate of 44 per 1,000 in 1981. Declining mortality and high fertility have accelerated the population growth. With a high birth rate and declining death rate, Nepal is trapped in the second stage of its demographic transition. The living standards in the country are not showing continuous improvement, and its population growth rate is not dropping.

Population policy and family planning

During the years 1956–1965 Nepal's population policy placed emphasis on absorbing the increasing population by reclaiming the tarai forests for resettlement. In the third development plan (1965–1970)

Labourers waiting for work in Kathmandu

there was no mention of the need to formulate and implement a population policy which would influence the size, growth, and distribution of the population, but the section on health services highlighted the importance of family planning in reducing the birth rate. In 1965 family planning services were initiated as part of the maternal and child health programme. Initially, these services were available only in Kathmandu, but later on they were gradually extended to cover the entire valley. In 1968 the Nepal Family Planning and Maternal Child Health Board was formed to provide family planning

129

Numbers of Madesi (people from the tarai and India) have recently been increasing in Kathmandu

services, education, research and training, as well as the maternal and child welfare services in the country.

In the Fourth Plan (1970–1975) the control of the population through a reduction in the birth rate was recognized as a major objective and the government tried, without much success, to make family planning services available throughout the country. The Fifth Plan (1975–1980) placed a greater emphasis on population policy than the previous plans had. One of the objectives of the Fifth Plan was to regulate the rate of population growth through (a) reducing the birth rate from 42 to 38 per 1,000 by the family planning programme, (b) regulating the internal migration from the Middle Mountain to the tarai and from rural to urban areas, (c) controlling immigration, (d) encouraging the development of small urban centres to foster regional development, and (e) promoting an optimal spatial distribution of population in relation to the resource endowments of the different geoecological regions of the country.

Subsequent five-year plans have emphasized population and family planning programmes, but there has not been any substantial achieve-

130

ment. The present Eighth Plan (1992–1997) calls for population control and family planning strategy to reduce the birth rate through both direct and indirect means, such as female literacy and mother and child health care programmes. Specific elements of the population control strategy include: (a) the creation of a social and economic milieu which would favour small families with no more than two children; (b) the promotion of women's development, literacy, and education programmes to improve the status of women and their access to family planning; (c) the integration of a family planning programme with a general health programme to utilize effectively the social and institutional resources; and (d) improvements in the delivery of family planning services at the village level.

Among other factors, improvement in the delivery of family planning services is the critical element in the success of the population policy. Field research in Nepal has revealed that the failure of family planning and modern health care services to reach people in the rural areas can be attributed to: (a) the location of the health centres or clinics, which in most cases were not within the activity space of the villagers; (b) the communication gap between the health service providers and potential clients; and (c) the inefficient management and organization of the Primary Health Centres and clinics. An analysis of the movement patterns of the population in the tarai and in the Middle Mountains for various types of purchases revealed that in general most of the clinics were outside the daily activity space of the people. Nepal's Family Planning and Maternal Child Health Board operates more than 200 clinics to provide family planning services. If these clinics were moved to more central locations, they would have a substantial effect on the adoption of family planning practices in Nepal.

Nepal's demographic target of reducing the current fertility rate of about six children per woman of child-bearing age to 2.5 by the end of the century poses an enormous challenge. In order to reduce the birth rate, the number of contraceptive users must be increased six times from the current figure of about 470,000 to 2.8 million (Thapa and Tsui, 1990). In addition to the projected cost for delivery of family planning services, the target may have to be re-evaluated and set at realistic levels consistent with the resources available to achieve results.

Shrestha, Stoeckel, and Tuladhar (1991) have identified the reasons for non-use of family planning among the women in Nepal who want to space their children or limit the number of births; this is based on a sample survey of 5,152 women. Most of the reasons given by respondents for non-use of family planning methods indicated a lack of information, education, and communication. There is a need to integrate the information on method-specific reasons for non-use into the training programme for health workers. The achievements of the family planning programme in terms of acceptors have not been very encouraging. While the number of new acceptors has increased, acceptances are heavily weighted towards less effective birth control methods, such as the condom. Over time, there has been a shift in acceptance from IUDs, which have a high continuation rate, to condoms. Acceptances are mostly confined to older (32–35 years) wives with a high parity (4–5 children), a pattern which would not make a significant demographic impact.

Although Nepal has developed a policy to moderate the rate of population growth, it faces several difficulties in expanding family planning activities to reduce the fertility rate. In addition to the specific problems noted above, the mountainous terrain makes it difficult to deliver family planning services and information to potential acceptors. There is an acute shortage of trained medical personnel to implement family planning activities. The relatively less significant role of women in various decision-making processes and their relatively small participation in the newly emerging economic activities also hinder the promotion and expansion of family planning activities.

Health care, literacy, and human development

Through their influence on mortality, fertility, and migration, health services and literacy affect the development of Nepal. Despite substantial improvements during the past 40 years, health conditions in Nepal remain far from satisfactory. Large numbers of babies and young children die, and many who survive are burdened with illness and malnutrition. Deprivation during the vulnerable years of childhood has lifelong consequences, and children grow to adulthood with their health already compromised. For the predominantly rural population, their adult life is physically gruelling and their life expectancy, estimated at 52 years, is one of the lowest in Asia. The life expectancy for females is even lower.

Hygiene, sanitation, and nutritional status are poor. In rural areas the proximity of animals such as cows, goats, and buffalo to the family living quarters encourages the spread of disease through faeces and insect vectors, and the incidence of diarrhoea is widespread. Over half the children under five years suffer from moderate to severe malnutrition (Savada, 1993: 100). Nutritional health is further weakened by the lack of various micronutrients in the diet. Iodine is deficient in landlocked Nepal, and goitre and cretinism are consequently common. Visual disabilities or other systemic problems may be related to the traditional diets of the various ethnic groups.

Gender disparities in health care, nutrition, and literacy are quite significant for females. After the first year of life, the mortality for females is higher than for males. During the period 1980–1987, for every 100,000 live births, 850 women died as a result of pregnancy or childbirth (UNICEF, 1987; 1989). A striking feature of Nepal's social poverty is the low level of literacy among women. The literacy rate was recorded at 39.6 per cent in the 1991 census. Literacy among women was only one-third of the above figure. The low level of female literacy and the widening gap between male and female literacy are major constraints to the effectiveness of both the economic and social development programmes.

In the 1950s and 1960s the major focus of the health programme was in the area of malaria control and the development of infrastructure and manpower. During these early years the United States was the single largest donor in the health area and is largely credited with controlling malaria in the tarai, which opened this previously almost uninhabitable region to agriculture. Today, almost 50 per cent of the population, much of the country's food production, and most of its industrial activities are concentrated in the tarai.

During the 1970s the focus of health care moved toward integrating the various programmes under a single service delivery model. Integrated service delivery and decentralized management characterize Nepal's current health strategy. The Eighth Plan (1992–1997) embodies several themes, which place emphasis on health services for women by women and village-level health services, especially the control of diarrhoeal diseases, immunization, and family planning.

The decentralization policy is based on the recognition that as Nepal develops, it becomes increasingly difficult to manage programmes from the centre. Although this is a conceptually sound idea, decentralization is more formal than real. The district-level staff have very little authority over the budget or personnel. The system remains highly centralized and control-oriented and is not responsive to local conditions. Nevertheless, continued centralized control is justified by officials in Kathmandu in the name of programme quality and accountability.

133

Today as much as 70–80 per cent of Nepal's development budget in health is funded by foreign aid with the largest contributions coming from multilateral organizations such as UNICEF, WHO, and UNFPA. In the 1950s and 1960s the United States was the largest donor. The government of Nepal is extremely adept at courting donors. The World Bank and Japan International Cooperation Agency (JICA) are willing to invest in Nepal's health and family planning programmes. Large resources from these donors could overwhelm the absorptive capacity of the public health system and may actually undermine the policy reforms.

The Nepalese people use both traditional and modern medicine. For most illnesses they first use home care, including herbal remedies and dietary regimes. If illness persists, the next resort is usually a traditional healer such as a *jhankri* and a *dhami*. Health clinics and hospitals are often the last resort and sought only for serious or persistent illnesses. Ayurvedic and Indian herbal medicine are used, and practitioners are also consulted where available. Except for diseases believed to be caused by spirits, patients appear to be comfortable mixing their treatments and using whatever they perceive to be effective. As pointed out earlier, the people in the rural areas do use public and private health family planning services if these are accessible and if staff and medicine are available. The location of the health facilities must be carefully selected to maximize their use. The attitude of the health workers towards patients, in addition to their caste and ethnic background, language group, and social status, influences the effectiveness of the health care delivery.

Nepal ranked 152nd among 173 nations according to a 1993 Human Development Report prepared by the UN Development Programme. The advent of a new democratic government affords an opportunity for Nepal to undertake a re-examination of its human resource development policies, programmes, and organization. Sufficient progress has been made in laying down a basic infrastructure for human resource development. Now the focus should be on the quality, efficiency, and financial sustainability of the various human resource development programmes, particularly in removing gender and rural-urban disparities in regard to the access to social services such as health, education, and economic opportunities.

6

Cultural patterns

The diversity of cultural patterns is interesting from the standpoint of the social organization of Nepal, but the ramifications of cultural diversities in the development of the country are the important considerations in this study. The relationship between culture and change has yet to be explored in detail in Nepal. However, it seems that ethnic diversity and linguistic regionalism have intensified the problems of creating a national orientation. Some degree of unification in terms of social interaction as well as political integration are prime requisites for Nepalese development. Small as it is, the tendency is strong to consider the country as a homogeneous unit for purposes of development planning. However, the evidence of heterogeneity is too strong for this assumption to be realistic. Nepal's diversity can be a source of strength in providing a range of options for change; it can also complicate the task of modernization and development.

Language groups

Language is an important aspect of culture and serves to differentiate Nepal's ethnic groups. The names of many ethnic groups coincide with the language they speak. Nepal lies in a region where people who speak the Indo-European language and people who speak the Tibeto-Burman language come into contact (fig. 23). The Indo-European languages are dominant in the south and west, and the Tibeto-Burman languages are conspicuous in the north and east. These two major groups are further divided into subgroups.

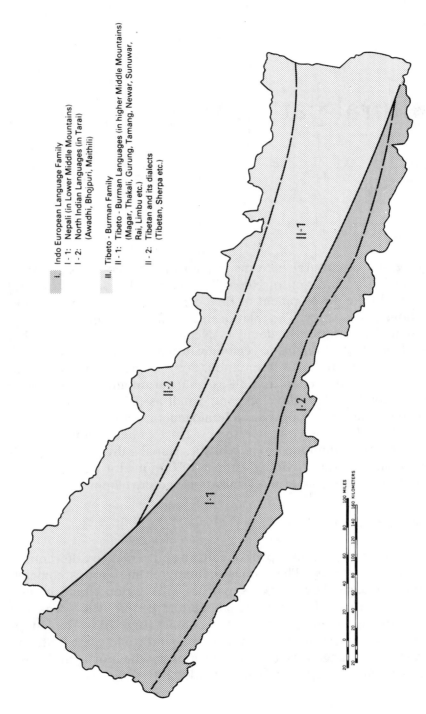

I. Indo European Language Family
 I - 1: Nepali (in Lower Middle Mountains)
 I - 2: North Indian Languages (in Tarai)
         (Awadhi, Bhojpuri, Maithili)

II. Tibeto - Burman Family
 II - 1: Tibeto - Burman Languages (in higher Middle Mountains)
          (Magar, Thakali, Gurung, Tamang, Newar, Sunuwar,
          Rai, Limbu etc.)
 II - 2: Tibetan and its dialects
          (Tibetan, Sherpa etc.)

II-1

II-2

I-2

I-1

100 MILES

160 KILOMETERS

Fig. 23 **Linguistic regions**

136

The Indo-European language subgroup

A major group in the Indo-European family is Nepali, the national language of Nepal, which was formerly called Gorkhali (Gurkhali) or Khaskura. There is no agreement on the generic name for this group of people as a whole, but here they are referred to as Parbate (or Parbatiya) Hindus (meaning "Hindus of the mountains"), a word sometimes used by Nepali scholars (Sharma, 1978: 2).

The second group in the Indo-European family are those languages spoken in the tarai: Maithili, Bhojpuri, and Awadhi, from east to west respectively. These languages are closely related to Hindi and Bengali. The Tharus, Danuwars, Majhis, and a few other groups who are regarded as indigenous residents of the tarai also speak languages that belong to the Indo-European family.

The Tibeto-Burman language subgroup

Representative among these, from east to west, are: Limbu, Rai, Tamang, Newar, Gurung, Thakali, and Magar. A distinct subgroup in the Tibeto-Burman family is the Tibetan language and its dialects, spoken by the Tibetans in Nepal. The Sherpas, who live in the southern part of the Great Himalaya and not on the Tibetan plateau, are a part of this group since their language is a Tibetan dialect.

Most of the language names in the Tibeto-Burman family are also used as ethnic names. For example, the Gurungs use the Gurung language as their mother tongue, and the Magars use the Magar language. No similar situation exists in the Indo-European family, mainly because people speaking the Indo-European languages tend to use their caste names to express their group identity.

Apart from the above main groups there are some minor language groups found in the tarai – Satar, which belongs to the Munda family, and Dhangar, which belongs to the Dravidian family.

Table 18 shows the population breakdown of Nepal by the mother tongue. More than half of the total population speaks Nepali, about one-fifth speaks North Indian, one-sixth speaks the Tibeto-Burman languages in the Middle Mountains, and less than 1 per cent speaks Tibetan and its dialects. The population of each ethnic group in the Tibeto-Burman family does not exceed 600,000, whereas the numerical strength of each Indo-European language is much larger. Data from 1952–1954 to 1991 (table 18) indicate large increases in the Nepali-speaking population, substantial growth among the speakers of the tarai languages, and a small increase or even a decline among the Tibeto-Burman groups.

Several factors are responsible for the difference in population growth of the various groups. First of all, because of the government policy of encouraging the use of Nepali for educational and official purposes, many people stopped using their mother tongue and switched to Nepali (especially when speaking to their children). This contributed to the increase of the population registered as Nepali-speaking in the census though their ethnic affiliation may be different.

In the census of 1991, the population of Tibeto-Burman groups and the Tharus increased substantially; the number of Magars more than doubled, the Rai and Limbu populations nearly doubled, and many other groups increased by more than 50 per cent. On the other hand, the rate of increase in the Nepali-speaking population slowed down; their proportion in the total population decreased from 58.4 per cent in 1981 to 50.3 per cent in 1991. These figures do not reflect a drastic change in the language composition of the population. Rather, they should be interpreted in terms of the change of attitude of the respondents and census enumerators. As discussed later in this chapter, there was a movement for democracy in 1989–1990 that gave birth to the new constitution of 1990, which characterized Nepal as a multi-lingual and multi-ethnic kingdom. Since the 1991 census was carried out just after its promulgation, it is very probable that people who had responded to the previous censuses as Nepali-speaking felt free to respond this time as speakers of their own mother tongues and that census enumerators were also willing to accept the response. If the 1991 census figures are interpreted in this way, they may be closer to the actual number of speakers of various languages. It can also be presumed that (1) the actual population of each ethnic group is greater than the number of speakers of the corresponding languages, and (2) that the Parbate Hindu population is much smaller than that of the Nepali-speaking population.

Secondly, there might have been a real difference in the rate of population increase among the Indo-European and the Tibeto-Burman groups. Though data on ethnic affiliation to substantiate this point are absent, the Parbate Hindu kinship custom to assimilate into their group those offspring born of a Parbate Hindu father and a mother of other ethnic origin (Fürer-Haimendorf, 1956b: 529; 1960: 23) supports the point. The Hindu ideology (a moral obligation for every householder to have at least one son) may also contribute to the increased number of speakers of the Indo-European family of languages. The Parbate Hindus' rapid spread throughout Nepal since the eighteenth century offers indirect evidence of this.

There is a problem with classification regarding the number of speakers of the tarai languages. Many people who are listed as speaking "other languages" in 1952–1954 are classified in later censuses as speaking Maithili, Bhojpuri, or Awadhi (Abadhi). Avoidance of the word "Hindi" (which might as well be applied to Awadhi) is a notable feature in the censuses. The decrease of Awadhi speakers in 1981 most probably reflects the change of classification and not the change of language of the speakers.

Society, culture, and the economy of ethnic groups

Parbate and tarai Hindus

The Parbate Hindus of the Middle Mountains and the tarai Hindus share many customs. Both believe in the great Hindu deities (Shiva, Vishnu, Saraswati, Lakshmi, and Durga) as well as local gods and other supernatural beings, which may differ from place to place. The Parbate and tarai Hindus live in caste societies; their ideal patrilineal joint family is headed by a senior male, though in actual practice the nuclear type of household is the most common. Also, their dietary habits are similar in that rice with lentil soup (*dal*) and side dishes (such as *tarkari*) constitute their meals, though unleavened bread (*roti*) increases in importance along with rice in the western tarai.

There are major differences in the lifestyles of the Parbate and tarai Hindus. People generalize and simplify some obvious differences and make them into stereotypical notions to distinguish the different groups. For example, people of the Middle Mountains often refer to the tarai Hindus as Madesi, but they sometimes use the expression *"dhotiwala"* (those who wear a *dhoti* or a man's waistcloth) also, contrasting with those who wear a *suruwal* (Nepali style trousers) and *topi* (a cap with no brim).

Settlements of tarai Hindus are agglomerated in the level piedmont plain; they live in one-storey houses with a small courtyard in the middle. In contrast, Parbate Hindus live in two or three-storey houses with a front court; their settlements are dispersed on terraces or hilltops. However, Parbate Hindus in the north-western corner of Nepal live in agglomerated villages with flat-roofed houses and have different beliefs and customs from other Parbate Hindus of Nepal.

In everyday life, Parbate Hindu women not only do domestic work but may also engage in agricultural work, while high-caste Hindu women in the tarai seldom engage in farm work. Socially, women in the tarai are more secluded from their senior male kin and from out-siders. However, their lives are busy with participation in rituals, which include singing and painting.

There are considerable differences in the way they perform various rituals and festivals such as weddings, initiations, and funerals, as well as seasonal festivals. A typical example of the latter is *Durga puja*, or the festival of the goddess Durga. It is called Dasain in Nepali and celebrated on a national scale by the government, and on the family and lineage level by most people of the Middle Mountains, including the Parbate Hindus and Tibeto-Burman speaking people. In the tarai, however, the festival is called *Durga puja*, and it is accompanied by decorated images of Durga and other goddesses displayed outdoors.

Though most of the life-cycle rituals of both groups contain vedic rites as core elements, they accompany many other rituals unique to each group. Among these are: the Parbate Hindu custom of *goddhuwa* (foot washing) at weddings in which the parents (and rela-tives) of the bride wash the feet of the newly wed couple and give them presents; the two stages of the tarai Hindu wedding ceremony (separate from a betrothal ritual): (1) the bride stays in her parents house for many years, and (2) the female kin and neighbours on the bride's side participate in the ritual examination of the bridegroom and other rituals for promoting fertility and prosperity.

A full comparison of festivals and rituals is not feasible because of space limitations, but it can be pointed out that rituals are often resorted to by people to differentiate cultural groups because of the frequency, visibility, and importance attached to them. So, in many respects the Parbate and tarai Hindus are clearly distinguishable from each other even though they share the common background of the great Hindu tradition.

The Parbate Hindus and tarai Hindus identify themselves by their caste names. The name "Brahman" can also be used for "Bahun" of the Parbate Hindus.

Tarai castes are the same as those in north India, including the Brahman (priest), Rajput (warrior), Kayastha (scribe), Baniya (mer-chant), and many artisan castes such as Lohar (blacksmith), Kumhar (potter), and the "untouchables." The Parbate Hindu caste system is characterized by the lack of middle-rank artisan castes and the numerical strength of the two topmost castes – Bahun (Brahman) and Chetri (Kshatriya – warrior). There are small numbers of lower castes such as the Kami (blacksmith), including the Sunar (goldsmith), Sarki (cobbler) and Damai (tailor). Some of them engage in their traditional caste-specific occupations, but many are farmers, including tenants and landless agricultural labourers.

Among the Parbate and tarai Hindus, the farmers are inclined to grow rice paddy wherever possible. However, in the Middle Mountain areas, in spite of their aspirations, people are prevented from practising extensive paddy farming. Their main crops – on the terraced mountainsides – are maize, dry-land rice, wheat, barley, potato, pulse, and some vegetables. Crop rotation is practised to some extent, but many fields are left fallow during the dry (winter) season. Though mostly dependent on agriculture, some of the people, especially in the urban areas, work for the government, are in the army, or are white-collar workers, shopkeepers, etc.

A Rai churning in a house in east Nepal (courtesy M. Tamura)

Tharu woman of the tarai with tattoos (courtesy M. Tamura)

The tarai Hindus depend heavily on rice. Where irrigation in the dry season is possible, they can grow two or three crops a year, but there are still many places where farmers leave the fields fallow in the dry season. Along with rice, the main crops are wheat, pulse, potato, vegetables, mustard, sugarcane, and jute. Mangoes, papayas, and bananas are also popular. There are still many comparatively large-scale landholders and landless labourers in the tarai. In some urban areas, tobacco, jute, sugar, and match factories offer employment, as do transport and commerce.

The tarai Hindus are closely related to the people in the northern part of the Ganges plain in India. There are many marriage ties as well as commercial relations. Movement across the border is frequent; people cross the border in search of work, go on pilgrimages to renowned religious places, and sometimes send their children to schools in India if they can afford to. For a long while, the border was not a barrier for people living close to it, but the situation has changed under the new Nepalese policy. For people coming from India it has become more difficult to acquire land or other property, to find a job in the government, or to obtain a licence for commercial and industrial activities, unless they are registered as Nepali citizens. In recent years more and more people from the Middle Mountains have settled in the tarai because of malaria eradication and the government's resettlement policy. But they have tended to settle in the northern tarai and have not mixed with the tarai Hindus except in the urban areas.

Tibeto-Burman groups

Among the Tibeto-Burman speaking population, the Tibetans, Sherpas, and a considerable number of Tamangs are Buddhists. There are also a few Tibetans who follow Bonism, which is thought to be an older religion in Tibet but shows some similarity to Tibetan Buddhism. An old sect of Tibetan Buddhism, characterized by the absence of a centralized network of monasteries, has been preserved and is popular in the northern part of Nepal. The Magars, Gurungs, Thakalis, Rais, and Limbus have been "Hinduized," but still retain their indigenous beliefs in shamanism and animism.

The Tibeto-Burman ethnic groups are mostly patrilineally organized, but this principle is not as clear among the Tibetans. Though none of these (except the Newars) are organized by the caste system, some show internal stratification. On the other hand, cross-cousin marriages are preferred among such groups as the Tamangs and the Gurungs, and the principle of reciprocity is important even within stratified societies. The women are more outgoing, actively engage in domestic, agricultural, and forestry work, and even work as porters. Households are mostly of a nuclear family type, but some of the ethnic groups have joint or stem family types. Research is needed

143

to ascertain whether or not the existence of the joint family is related to the Hinduization of these groups.

House types vary depending upon family structure, environmental conditions, and tradition. In the Middle Mountains, one or two-storeyed houses stand alone. Stone, timber, thatch, and slate are popular building materials. In the northern dry area, roofs are flat; in the north-western area houses on the slopes share walls and roofs. The *golghar* house (with an oval plan) of the Gurungs seems to be on the wane. There are both compact and scattered settlements. The Magars, Gurungs, Thakalis, Tamangs, and Newars have agglom-erated settlements. Most of the Rai and Limbu settlements are scat-tered on the mountain slopes.

Many of these people depend on a combination of agriculture and animal husbandry. In the Middle Mountains, people grow dry-land crops (wheat, maize, barley, potato, and pulse) on terraced, unirri-gated fields. They raise cattle, sheep, goats, fowls and, in some areas, hogs. Some have paddy fields below 1,800 m, but they usually practise agriculture at higher altitudes than the Parbate Hindus. Maize, potato, meat, and beer made of maize and millet are impor-tant in their diet.

In the past, trade has been popular among these people. The Thakalis of the upper Kali Gandaki are known for their success in trade; this is discussed later. Some groups have resorted to other occupations, most notably military service, which includes those in the Nepali army and mercenary services under Britain and India. The Gurungs and Magars and later the Rais and Limbus joined the Brit-ish and Indian armies most actively, but many of the higher officers came from the Chetri caste. Until recently remittances by merce-naries formed a major source of foreign currency for Nepal.

The Tibetan people cultivate the high land around 4,000 m north of the Himalayas. They grow such dry-land crops as barley, buckwheat, and potato during the summer on irrigated fields. They graze yak, sheep, and goats in the higher altitudes in the summer and descend to the lower areas in the winter. Also in the wintertime, men descend to the Middle Mountain areas and the tarai with animals, carrying goods such as wool, cloth, and (in the past) salt, which are traded for cereals, sugar, and small industrial commodities. Salt must now be imported from India because since 1959 there has been a ban on trade by the Chinese across the Nepal-Tibet border. Milk, milk products, and meat are very important to their diet, and barley flour and beer are

Tibetan novice spinning in north-west Nepal (courtesy M. Tamura)

quite popular. Trade activities, in which the men are absent from home for months, are closely related to their custom of polyandry.

The Newars in the Kathmandu Valley occupy a unique position among the Tibeto-Burman speaking groups. They include both Hindus and Buddhists, have their own caste system, which includes many castes of totally different names from other caste societies, and have maintained their urban civilization for many years. Even their villages look quite urban with brick buildings of three or more storeys

145

Newar woman washing in a village in the Kathmandu Valley

built in rows. Their Buddhism, being brought from India directly, differs from Tibetan Buddhism in that it lacks celibate monks and coexists with the caste system. There are many socio-religious organizations (called *guthi*) among both the Hindus and Buddhists, and their social life is rife with festivals and rituals.

In the Kathmandu Valley the Newars depend mainly on agriculture (rice, wheat, potato, and vegetables), commerce and crafts (bronze casting, and gold and silver work). Like most of the Hindus in Nepal, rice with lentil soup and side dishes (such as *tarkari*) are the staple food but buffalo meat, beer, and liquor are quite popular.

Government offices, private companies, and construction and transport sectors are attracting workers not only from among the Newars but also from various groups in and outside of the Valley. Developing as a cosmopolitan capital, Kathmandu has been absorbing many migrants in recent years. On the other hand, about half the Newars now live in the trading and administrative centres of Nepal, engaged mainly in commercial activities and partly in agriculture and clerical jobs. The Newars, though not large in population, have been an important group in Nepal for many years, with their civilization based on the Indian influence and their wealth acquired through trade with India and Tibet. They have maintained their cultural identity in the Kathmandu Valley despite the large inflow of people in the Valley, including the politically dominant Parbate Hindus.

Environmental attitudes of cultural groups

Tibeto-Burman groups of the Middle Mountains

As stated above, the livelihood of the groups in the various ecological zones differs considerably. Accordingly, there exists a diverse relationship between man and nature. If the relationship between livelihood and forest is considered, it stands out for the Tibeto-Burman groups in the Middle Mountains: the forest is indispensable for their subsistence, and agriculture is intricately combined with animal husbandry. This combination arises from the fact that their farmlands, most of which are not irrigated, need to be fertilized; for this they depend on animals that feed to a great extent on forest products.

For the farmers in the Middle Mountain area in Nepal, where the land is mostly on the rugged mountainsides and generates little cash income, the scope of using chemical fertilizers and tilling machines is small. Here, livestock is important not only for milk, meat, and wool, but also for energy (for ploughing) and dung. The dung is made into compost by mixing it with straw, grass, tree leaves, and other plant residue. During the fallow season cattle are driven into the fields to graze and enrich the soil with their dung and urine. In some places, human manure is also used as fertilizer. Animals are grazed in forests as well as in pastures, especially in the summer; in other seasons, they feed on grass and fodder. Tree fodder is very important since large pasture lands are not available. Thus the forest is not only important for the acquisition of timber, firewood, fruits, and other products but it is also deeply connected with agriculture through animal husbandry.

Studying the Magar villages, Kawakita (1984: 12) points out that "the Magars are very knowledgeable about the ecological functions of the forest ... they feel an affection and exhibit a sort of pious atti-

147

tude towards jangal [jungle]," and they enjoy their unrestrained life in the forest and high altitude pastures. Kawakita contrasts these Magar attitudes with the rather pragmatic attitude of the Hindus in the same area whose interest in the forest, he asserts, is mainly economic.

Special characteristics of landscapes and agriculture prevail in the Middle Mountains. A typical rural landscape consists of stone walls to prevent animals from entering croplands; a special kind of slanted terraced field, called "network terraces" by Kawakita, in which upper and lower terraces are joined at either end so that oxen and ploughs can ascend several terraces without interruption (Kawakita, 1974: 6); fallow fields in the dry season; and the forest above the farmlands, which is utilized for multiple purposes. Agricultural practices include crop rotation and the long-term leasing of livestock.

When farmers do not have enough domestic animals, they lease cattle, buffalo, goats and/or sheep from their neighbours. By leasing, they use the animal products (milk and dung) and the neighbours receive half of the calves or lambs which the leased animals bear. This kind of arrangement can be found not only between neighbours but also across ethnic boundaries and between households of different villages. Animals are so important for the owners of dry fields that they try their best to get access to them.

Some of the Tibeto-Burman groups still practise slash-and-burn agriculture, usually in combination with other modes of cultivation. Using this method, people clear forests, plant crops for a few years, then abandon them for natural recovery. They are thus more dependent on and confident of the regenerating power of nature than are ordinary farmers. Since the resultant ashes following the clearing and burning of trees can serve as fertilizer, it is not imperative to combine animal husbandry organically with this form of agriculture. It is reported that animal husbandry is seldom practised among the Chepangs in Pandrung, even though their basis of economic subsistence is agriculture (Rai, 1985: 29). Today they also cultivate paddy fields and terraced dry fields with minimum fertilization (Rai, 1985), probably reflecting their past, when they depended more on slash-and-burn agriculture. Hunting, food gathering, and fishing also play important roles in their subsistence economy. For them, the forest is a place where almost every necessity of life can be obtained.

Some authors have noted the villagers' recalling the existence of thick forests in the Middle Mountain areas (Macfarlane, 1976: 44; Coburn, 1982: 28). Although villagers have been participating more in activities for the recovery and control of the forests, people in the Middle Mountains have only recently become conscious of the deteriorating environment. However, the idea of nature preservation has not caught on among the Nepalese (Numata, 1987: 34) except for a limited number of people. Most other people's centuries-old attitude of dependence on nature seems to persist.

There have been systems to control the use of the forests and other resources (Fürer-Haimendorf, 1964: 110–113; McDougal, 1969: 37; 1979: 49; and Gilmour and Fisher, 1991: 39-56). But Gilmour and Fisher point out (1991: 48–49) that most systems are quite new, are based on local administrative bodies, and are directly related to the difficulties people face in obtaining forest products. Gilmour and Fisher (1991: 41) also note that where products are relatively accessible, it is unlikely that people will actively participate in organizations to protect and manage the forests. But we have to keep in mind that people do not automatically become active in conservation until products become scarce. Customary notions and practices might be followed even when they are no longer functional if proper stimulation and education is lacking.

Other groups

The combination of agriculture and animal husbandry is less intricate among the non-Tibeto-Burman ethnic groups and a few Tibeto-Burman groups in Nepal. To consider this point, we first note the average number of livestock per household in villages in different areas (table 19). The figures in table 19 show that the Tibetans own the largest number of livestock per household, followed by the Sherpas. The figure for the Tharus in the tarai area is almost the same as for the Sherpas. On the other hand, the Maithili speakers in the tarai and the Newars show remarkably small figures. Numbers for the Parbate Hindus and Gurungs of the Middle Mountains fall in between. These figures indicate that cultural differences in the same or similar ecological conditions bring about different livelihood structures and different relationships between nature and life, though they occur only within the limit of ecological possibility.

Tibetans who live under the harshest ecological conditions in Nepal depend heavily on animals. They raise their livestock in pastures and do not depend on tree fodder since it is not available at the high altitude where they live. They are by no means "forest people," but are foremost pastoralists as the above figures show; they are more oriented toward the nomadic lifestyle. Among the Tibetan groups, however, those who live on the southern flank of the Himalaya – where the altitude is relatively lower and there is more precipitation – depend more on the forest. Still, the altitude of this area has not allowed them to exploit the environment in a random way. Because of the scarcity of wood, the Sherpas used to control the utilization of the forest through forest guards acting on behalf of the village community before responsibility was transferred to the formal district administration (Fürer-Haimendorf, 1975: 11–12; Fisher, 1986: 54). Here, the scarcity of resources made concerted measures necessary.

The Newars in the Kathmandu Valley are exceptional among the Tibeto-Burman groups; their degree of dependence on cattle and the forest is among the lowest in Nepal. This applies not only to the urban Newars, but also to the Newars in rural areas. Unlike other people in the Middle Mountains, most of the Newar farmers use hoes instead of ploughs to till the soil, and they have their own method of fertilizing. Some also use hand tractors. Along with compost, the use of human waste and soil dressing to utilize the fertile soil dug from underground was popular before the introduction of chemical fertilizers in the 1960s.

Milk and milk products are used to a limited extent, and the Newars eat buffalo meat and chicken. It is quite usual for immigrants from the surrounding mountain areas to complain about the lack of milk in the Kathmandu Valley, which is due not only to the population increase, but also to the traditional lifestyle of the Newars. Their low degree of dependence on livestock can also be seen in transport, since they do not let the animals carry loads on their backs or pull carts. They feed their livestock (buffalo, cattle, goats, and sheep) grass and straw, and graze them on small fields.

The Kathmandu Valley lost most of its forests except for the ones in the hills which form the rim of the Valley and those which were preserved for religious reasons. The Newars, who are remote from the forest life, acquire forest products from people of other ethnic groups. Most of the Newars are either urban dwellers or farmers oriented toward paddy cultivation; their contact with the natural forest environment has been considerably diluted. Some of their habits, including the limited use of milk products, are reminiscent of those in East Asia.

The Parbate Hindus who live in the lower Middle Mountains have a combination of agriculture and animal husbandry similar to the majority of the Tibeto-Burman people, especially if they depend heavily on upland farming. They are strongly inclined toward paddy cultivation and try to maximize irrigated fields if possible. On the other hand, they do not cooperate with people of different ethnic groups in distant villages. This makes it difficult for them to carry out large irrigation projects, so only small-scale irrigation along the rivers is realized in this area.

Where farmers cultivate rice paddy, there is a lower degree of dependence on livestock for fertilizer since water for irrigation usually contains some fertilizing elements. Still, they keep livestock for ploughing, nutrition, and other purposes. Though there are less forests in the lower altitudes of the mountain areas, they manage to feed their livestock with rice straw, grass, and tree fodder, which can be acquired either from the meagre remaining forests or from fodder trees planted along the edge of the dry fields. The use of fodder on these private trees is controlled by individual households so that they need not go far to collect it during busy crop seasons. On the other hand, some farmers do not usually plant fodder trees in their paddy fields since more sunshine is needed there. In this case rice straw can be used for feeding the animals. Also, paddy fields are often located in areas far from the settlements.

When the low valleys were infected with malaria, it was common for the farmers who had land in the lower river beds to live in houses at a higher altitude and commute to the lower, irrigated farms. These days, more people are going down not only to the tarai and to the towns but also to lower cultivated areas. A yearning for more income and also for paddy production lies behind this movement. Similar movements can also be seen among the Tibeto-Burman groups of the Middle Mountains, who seem to prefer rice cultivation these days. In general, a lower degree of interdependence on agriculture and forest prevails among the Parbate Hindus compared with the Tibeto-Burman groups, and the former are less emotionally attached to the forest than the latter.

The Hindus of north Indian origin in the tarai show a very low degree of animal husbandry, as do the Newars. But the way they use animals is by no means the same as that of the Newars; ploughs and bullock carts not usually seen among the Newars are commonplace in the tarai. Their average number of livestock is low because of the low consumption of meat, the need for agricultural land, and the existence of many poor households without livestock. Pasture land is scarce and the use of tree fodder for livestock is minimal. Forests have been cleared in many areas, leaving only sparsely wooded areas which can be utilized for fuelwood or fruit. Among them, mango trees are given economic and ritual importance, since they are used on various occasions, such as marriage ceremonies or cremations. Though more remote from the forest life than the mountain people, they have a deep attachment to plants.

The indigenous populations of the tarai or the Tharus are closely related to forest and animal husbandry. Their settlements are found in the middle of or near to the forest. Some of them own large herds of cattle, but many have fallen to the status of tenant or agricultural labourer and have found it difficult to preserve their traditional way of life.

Many people have migrated to the tarai and inner tarai. Some are old settlers, but many are newcomers whose movement was stimulated by the Nepali government's policy following the Rana period. In particular, the resettlement projects introduced from the mid-1960s, together with malaria eradication, induced many people in the mountains under population pressure to come down. Among them were both the Parbate Hindus and Tibeto-Burman groups. They established their farms and houses by clearing the forest. Their settlements are separate from the other tarai residents, and they have largely retained their own lifestyles and values.

Initially, the new settlers were given forest land to clear and other facilities by the government. As time passed, the amount of land given to the individual settlers decreased; finally, in the early 1980s, the government stopped releasing new forest land for resettlement purposes (Ghimire 1992: 171–173). This did not stop the flow of population from the mountains to the tarai. Many settlers (called *sukumbasi*) arrived, with no legal right to the land on which they lived. Conflicts arose between them and other residents or government agents, which grew to be one of the serious political issues of the country in the 1980s. Since many of them lived on the edge of the forest, the government considered this a threat to the forest conservation policy and tried to evict them in some areas. This problem will remain unless the government takes effective measures to resettle these people and provide them with employment.

Historical context of ethnic interaction and change

The mountainous area constituting present-day Nepal has been a buffer between China and India. Though there were some isolated instances in which foreign forces subjugated this area, it was not absorbed by the Indian, Chinese, or British political entities. Independence of this kind, which was made possible by Nepal's geo-topographical condition, is a rare phenomenon among Asian countries. However, the same condition brought about Nepal's landlockedness.

Though Nepal emerged in history before the Christian era, it was only in the eighteenth century that Nepal emerged as a country. Previously the word "Nepal" had been applied solely to the Kathmandu Valley. Chronicles written after the fourteenth century list three old dynasties – Gopala, Mahishapala, and Kirata. The first two are legendary; the Kirata dynasty, although some scholars have said it existed, is not well documented. What is commonly accepted is that the Kathmandu Valley was (and has been) inhabited by people who spoke the language which belonged to the Tibeto-Burman family, which most probably developed to become the Newari language today. This suggests that the original inhabitants of the Valley inmigrated from the east or the north; shortly after there may have been immigrants from other directions, including the Ganges plain. What kind of socio-political organization prevailed at that time is open to question.

The earliest Nepali dynasty whose existence is undisputed is the Licchavi dynasty, evidenced by a Manadeva inscription dated 464 A.D. and about 200 other inscriptions that followed. Centred in the Kathmandu Valley, the dynasty most probably expanded its sphere of influence to the Kali Gandaki River in the west and the Kosi River in the east during its peak period. Some scholars think that Nepal's current size was already attained in this period (Vajracarya, 1973: 28). However, it is misleading to think that Licchavi Nepal had a clearly demarcated border, which is characteristic of the modern nation state.

The history of the Licchavi period, as well as the Malla period after that, is deeply coloured by Indic culture, though most of the ordinary inhabitants seem to have spoken a Tibeto-Burman language. Historical documents, relics, and other facts attest to this. For example, the very names "Licchavi" and "Malla," the letters and language (Sanskrit) used in inscriptions, and the names and styles of old religious statues are mostly Indic. Both Hinduism and Buddhism, which have survived until today, came from India. Even in its socio-political set-up and city planning, early Nepal owed much to the Indian civilization. Some scholars think that the Licchavi rulers of Nepal descended from the Licchavis of Vaishali in India, but this has not been proven.

The Licchavi dynasty prospered in the seventh century with a high level of temple and palace architecture and arts and crafts, whose inspiration came largely from a religious culture already characterized by the coexistence of and tolerance between Hinduism and Buddhism. Socio-economic and administrative structures were established to support the prosperity of the Licchavi dynasty; agriculture with irrigation, water conduits, and the road system, and the local administrative bodies and organizations functioned.

Nepal served as an entrepot of commodities and culture (including Buddhism) between India and Tibet. There were political, military, and other relations also. Some historians assert that the royal Nepalese families intermarried with those of Tibet as well as those of India, and Nepal was politically dependent on Tibet at one time. Nepal even had contact with T'ang China. In T'ang annals and in other records, mention is made of Nepali and Tibetan armies, led by a Chinese envoy, attacking Magadha in North India just after the demise of King Harshavardhana.

Whether Nepal's subjugation to other countries really occurred or not, Nepal was surrounded by mountainous terrain too rugged to allow a long-standing foreign occupation. However, the distance and the ruggedness did not play a prohibitive role as far as cultural and economic relations were concerned; Nepal absorbed enough foreign elements to enrich its culture and to trade across the Himalayan passes and malarial tarai plain. In the latter aspect, the landlockedness was not so detrimental nor was the difference between the efficiency of transport by land and by sea as great as it is today. The location of Nepal in the past was not so unfavourable and it enjoyed comparative prosperity.

However prosperous as it was from time to time, we should not be misled into thinking that the population of Nepal was as large as or even close to its present size. Assuming the Kathmandu Valley population to be around 1,200,000 in 1991, and about 400,000 (nearly one-third that of 1991) in 1952, and the fact that the population of the Valley increased sharply because of the in-migrants from the Middle Mountain areas from the late eighteenth century, it is reasonable to assume that the Valley population in the Licchavi period was rather small (presumably below 100,000). The Middle Mountain areas, into which Licchavi Nepal extended, must have been sparsely populated, too.

The Licchavi dynasty (or the ancient period of Nepal) came to an end in the late ninth century and was followed by the medieval period, according to popular view. The early medieval period, which was unstable and poorly documented, culminated in the Malla period (1200 to 1769), in which the valley was divided into three kingdoms in the late fifteenth century, which were eventually conquered by the Gorkhas in 1769. The territory of the Malla dynasty, as in the Licchavi period, was limited to the Kathmandu Valley and surrounding area, though there were times when its territory expanded.

The Malla period was different from the preceding era in that it had contesting powers in the Middle Mountain areas and in the Tarai, and there were Muslims in the Ganges plain to the south. There were instances of Muslim invasion in the Valley in the fourteenth century in which cities were destroyed and plundered. The Valley was also invaded from time to time by powers in the western Middle Mountains and in the tarai. Natural calamities such as earthquakes and famines were also prevalent.

The culture of the Valley under the Malla dynasty flourished in such fields as architecture, arts and crafts, literature (in Newari and Sanskrit), and in religious and ritual practices including various festivals and rites, a good part of which has been handed down to the Newars and exists today. Production and earnings from paddy agriculture, Indo-Tibetan trade, and handicrafts were the main sources of livelihood. The cultural influence of Mithila to the south was strongly felt. On the other hand, Nepal exerted some economic influence on Tibet, where Nepalese coins circulated. There was also a colony of Nepali traders there. Diplomatic relations with China were exemplified by the exchange of gifts between Nepal and Ming China.

The disappearance of Buddhism in India under the Muslims and the flight of the Brahmans into the Himalayan foothills were other important events during this period. The Brahmans contributed greatly to the Hinduization of these areas. For example, Jayasthiti Malla, who reigned in the late fourteenth century, is known to have systematized the society with the help of Brahmans from India through such means as the legalization of the caste system and the standardization of weights and measures. On the other hand, Buddhism survived but began to follow its own path as the Buddhists became absorbed in the caste system. The two religions came close to each other, accelerated by the proliferation of tantrism at the time. Waves of Hindu migrants reached the Middle Mountain areas also, which not only contributed to the population increase and Hinduization of the area, but also contributed to the political consolidation of various areas influenced by Hinduism.

As the power of the Malla dynasty decreased after its division into three kingdoms during the fifteenth century, there were active political and military movements in the western Middle Mountain areas, where scores of small rival political entities were wrestling for control of respective areas after the downfall of the Khas Mallas of the Karnali area in the late fourteenth century. The Gorkhas, led by King Prithvi Narayan Shah, eventually emerged successful in the power struggle. After a long military campaign, the Gorkhas conquered the kingdoms in the Kathmandu Valley in 1769 and expanded their territory rapidly.

The success of the Gorkhas was deeply related to their (or to Prithvi Narayan and his predecessors') understanding of the geography, economy, and administrative and judicial situation of the country. The Gorkhas controlled important trade routes and succeeded in raising taxes. They were aware of the economic importance of the tarai and incorporated the area into their territory. In the utilization of land revenue, they resorted to the *jagir* system (in which government employees kept the collected revenue from the land in lieu of salary). Even lower-ranked soldiers were given direct access to this revenue. Internally, the administration was carried out by a principle which was already in existence at the time of Ram Shah in Gorkha during the seventeenth century. These combined elements contributed greatly to the successful consolidation of modern Nepal.

Under the Gorkhas, Nepal continued its expansion. By the second decade of the nineteenth century, its area was twice as large as that of present-day Nepal. It continued to have economic relations with Tibet and also tried to extend its power to the north. In 1788 there was a dispute concerning Nepal's claim for a new exchange rate of its coins in Tibet. Before the issue was settled, Nepal went to war with Tibet, but because of China's strong military support of Tibet, Nepal could not succeed in its campaign and had to sign a treaty with China and send tributes.

In the south, Nepal's expansion resulted in a clash with the British East India Company, which was claiming its right to the tarai and, at the same time, was interested in trade with Tibet. The Anglo-Nepal War of 1814–1916 reduced the country to its current size and allowed British diplomats to reside in Kathmandu. But Nepal kept her independence.

The Rana autocracy, which followed the *kot* massacre in 1846, continued about a century after Jang Bahadur. During that time the kings were only nominal rulers. One of the important policies during this period was the promulgation of Muluki Ain (the legal code) of 1854, which – by consolidating various castes and ethnic groups of Nepal – strengthened the caste order (Höfer, 1979).

During this period, Nepal closed its doors to other countries except India and Britain and had a minimum inflow of foreign cultural elements. There were, however, some attempts at modernization as seen in the policies of Chandra Shamsher (1901–1929), who introduced such institutions and facilities as a college, hospital, hydro-electric power plant, etc. He also abolished slavery and the custom of *sati* (a woman's suicide on the bier of her husband).

The Rana autocracy collapsed in 1951 when it faced the anti-Rana movement in which King Tribhuvan, the Nepali Congress party and others, including the Ranas of the lower strata, cooperated. The 1950s were a period of trial and error. Governments organized by various parties followed each other without being able to carry out any effective policies. Dissatisfied with this condition, King Mahendra seized absolute control of the government in 1961, arresting the prime minister and other ministers.

King Mahendra tried to unify the country through the partyless panchayat system (stipulated in the constitution of 1962), which prohibited discrimination by caste and created assemblies and councils (panchayats) on various politico-administrative layers. There were village, town, and district panchayats and the national panchayat, or the parliament. Representatives of these panchayats were elected by indirect vote except for the lowest layer, in which they were elected by direct vote.

Under this system, which was led by the king, political parties were banned and the administrative chiefs nominated by the central government were sent to districts and zones. Though called the panchayat democracy, the system was under strong control from the palace, which germinated popular dissatisfaction.

This system continued under King Birendra, who succeeded to the throne in 1972. But in 1979–1980 the panchayat democracy faced a crisis, which was evaded by a referendum in which the panchayat side won by a narrow majority over multi-party votes. Finally, it came to an end in 1990 through the mass movement of the people for democracy along with the economic dislocation that resulted from the lapse of the trade and transit agreement with India in March 1989.

After severe clashes, a united front of the Nepali National Congress and communist parties succeeded in letting the cabinet resign and in having negotiations with India on the one hand and with the palace on the other. The trade and transit agreements with India were resolved and King Birendra agreed to the promulgation of the new constitution in November 1990, in which political parties were made legal, the panchayat was abolished, the King was made a symbol of the nation, and Nepal was defined as a multi-ethnic and multilingual nation. However, the introduction of democracy did not assure economic improvement. Rather, Nepal has been suffering from economic hardships that have been amplified by natural calamities.

Interaction between cultural groups

The ethnic groups in Nepal are by no means isolated from each other. They have been interacting with other groups over many years, even in remote mountain areas. Though the Himalayas and Middle Mountains have certainly been an obstacle for communication and movement, people have overcome a myriad difficulties and have had contact with the outside world through trade, migration, pilgrimages, conquests, and other movements. Movements and contacts are motivated by various factors – economic, political, social, and religious. In this context it is important to keep in mind the following geopolitical and cultural aspects:

1. The existence of two great civilizations, namely those of India and Tibet, which wedge and influence Nepal.
2. The development of political entities (or a political entity in the modern period) independent of India and Tibet.
3. The existence of many ethnic groups and castes, which we will call "cultural groups" here.

These cultural groups not only interact with each other but also undergo such changes as aggrandizement, fusion, fission, and identity switches. They are not static if seen from a diachronical perspective. Rather, their group borders and structures are constantly changing, according to the kind of interaction they experience. Since the population size, culture, and geographical background of each group differs from the others, the mode of interaction between the groups and the resulting pictures are diverse. We will consider this point, bringing into focus the period after the inception of the Shah (Gorkha) dynasty. First, we will deal with the dominant position and influence of the Parbate Hindus, showing that the cultural changes have not been one-sided but multifarious.

Parbate Hindu dominance and influence

Modern Nepal was formed as a result of the expansion of the Gorkhas (Gurkhas). The name "Gorkha," which was derived from the name of a small settlement about 100 km west of Kathmandu, should not be taken as the name of an ethnic group. Rather, it denotes a political and military power led by Nepali-speaking (Parbate Hindu) high castes and including several ethnic groups such as the Magars, Gurungs, Rais, and Limbus, who joined the army after King Prithvi Narayan Shah started his expedition from Gorkha to conquer the area which is now called Nepal. The king was of Nepali-speaking Thakuri origin. The high caste Parbate Hindus occupied most of the important positions, and people of other ethnic origins were recruited into the lower strata of the government and the army. As such, the Indo-European (in this case Parbate Hindu) and Tibeto-Burman elements were already combined. This composite characteristic of the Nepali society was intensified as the Gorkha conquest proceeded to more remote areas.

To give order to such a complex society, the Shah dynasty resorted to the caste system. Though most of the Tibeto-Burman ethnic groups (except for the Newars) were originally foreign to the caste order, they were ranked in the middle of the caste hierarchy, which was unoccupied by Parbate Hindus. A typical example of the legalization of such a rule was the Muluki Ain of 1854, a written legal code which conceptualized Nepali society as a caste society and gave a detailed description of the position and proper conduct to be observed by each "caste" under the Gorkha rule (Höfer, 1979). (Newar castes were given various ranks based on their own caste hierarchy.) This code remained in effect for over 100 years with modifications, and during this time there occurred cases in which originally non-caste ethnic groups adopted caste-like customs. Behind this lay the idiom that not only the government but also lay people contributed to the dissemination of caste ideology.

The penetration of the caste system, however, did not proceed so far as to involve every group in the intricate division of labour according to caste at the local level, but was characterized more by social ordering through categorization and hierarchization. However, because of the penetration of the Parbate Hindus, more and more

Tibeto-Burman people have resorted to the services of the lower castes such as blacksmiths (Kami), cobblers (Sarki), and tailors (Damai, also musicians). Some Hinduized people have also become dependent upon Hindu priests (Bahun) on occasions.

On the other hand, a stereotyped notion developed that equated some ethnic groups with certain occupations. For example the Newars, though they engage in various occupations, are known to others as *sahu* or shopkeepers, and Musalman (Muslims) as bangle vendors. More vaguely, the Gurungs, Magars, and later the Rais and Limbus were regarded as suitable for military occupation.

Many Tibeto-Burman-speaking people underwent Sanskritization as seen in the suspension of beef eating among the Gurungs and the adoption of Hindu deities, rituals, and festivals such as Dasain, Tihar, and Swasthani-puja. But it is also necessary to keep in mind that they have kept their traditional customs and rituals, such as the dependence on Shamans for healing, to a considerable extent. It is a notable characteristic of the caste system that it can absorb foreign groups as different castes even though they continue to keep their inner structures and traditions intact.

As the Nepali term *"jat"* connotes both "caste" and "ethnic group," it has been quite common in Nepal not to distinguish between these two concepts and to treat various ethnic groups as castes. Such a usage made the emergence of pseudo-castes easier.

There were people who quickly changed themselves in response to government policies and the sociocultural orientation of the leading group. One example is provided by the Thakalis of the Kali Gandaki Valley. They successfully carried out trade in Tibetan salt and grain from the south by acquiring a monopoly from the Rana government in the nineteenth century, and tried to "Nepalize" their customs and separate them from the indigenous and Tibetanized ones. They abandoned Tibetan costumes, yak meat (regarded as beef by the Hindus), and Tibetan beer, discouraged the use of the Thakali language in front of others, tried to reinterpret their pantheon with Hindu idioms, and claimed their Thakuri ancestry by changing their myths (Iijima 1963: 43–52, 1977: 82–90, 1982: 24–26).

This movement can also be interpreted as an example of the efforts made towards the formation of a new ethnic group. Seen from a linguistic point of view, the Thakali language belongs to a language group (Tamang group) to which the Tamang and Gurung languages also belong. Before the Thakali core groups began their Nepalization, the former ethnic condition there was more nebulous; their

Flat-roof Thakuri houses in Simikot in north-west Nepal (courtesy M. Tamura)

customs, religion, and language were less distinct than those of the surrounding people. Led by able leaders, four core clans tried to make themselves more distinct from others by trying to keep the appellation "Thakali" to themselves. The movement was collective, multifaceted, and targeted towards exclusivity. But people of other clans also claimed the same appellation, probably because the name became more prestigious. As is often seen in other cases, the ambiguity of a group border prevailed and still remains. Yet this case is a

161

notable example of an attempt at ethnic reformation and enhancement. We can point out a paradoxical aspect in passing – they adopted the Nepali language and failed to reinforce their own language in this move towards a distinct identity.

The Thakali case by no means stands alone as an example of ethnic reformation. It is now known that certain other ethnic groups took their present form under the Shah dynasty. For example, the term "Tamang" was officially introduced only in 1932 before which the Tamangs were not distinguished from the Tibetans (Höfer, 1979: 147–148, Holmberg, 1989: 30). No doubt other groups' demarcation lines were also made clearer under the policy of the Shah (and Rana) government in upholding the caste system.

Ways of coping with the Parbate Hindu dominance were quite diverse. The Limbus in the east, although they had been assured of their right to ancestral land in return for their support of Prithvi Narayan, were not successful in keeping their land. Many alienated Hindu (in this case Brahman or Bahun) immigrants who were better at handling official matters and money-lending, and freer from expensive social expenditures succeeded in acquiring land from Limbu peasants (Caplan, 1970: 4–5). Together with government legislation and the migration of lay people – including the dispatch of officials (and teachers nowadays) from the centre – the Parbate Hindu influence has extended to every corner of Nepal. In rural areas, there appeared many cases in which Parbate Hindu landlords and farmers who were latecomers hired indigenous people as agricultural labourers. In the case of Brahman landlords, this was inevitable since, like most of the Brahmans in South Asia, they were (and still are) prohibited by caste rule to handle ploughs. Moreover, it has become part of the lifestyle of high-caste Parbate Hindus to hire other people for physical labour whenever possible. Here, labour relationships imbued with the caste ideology have become integrated into a multi-ethnic situation.

Mutual interaction between cultural groups

Contact among cultural groups has not always been one-sided. The Middle Mountain people, including the Parbate Hindus, have associated with and exerted influence on each other. There have been cases where minor groups tried to assimilate themselves with more prominent groups nearby but not necessarily with the Parbate Hindus. In the north-west there are people who have begun to claim their

Gurung ancestry, and in the north-east some Tamangs and Tibetans who live among the Sherpas have been assimilated into the latter. There are Parbate Hindu low-caste people who wear Sherpa-style clothes and are bilingual in the Sherpa and Nepali languages in that region.

A tolerance for inter-caste (inter-ethnic) marriages characterizes Nepali society and makes the cultural differences between groups smaller. It was an advantage for the Parbate Hindus that they were not strictly endogamous, since they could marry into such ethnic groups as the Gurungs, Magars, and Newars even during the course of their military expansion and still keep their offspring within their group due to their strong patrilineal principles. This contributed to the expansion of their population and hence their military and social power.

Inter-caste (inter-ethnic) marriages are now more common in ur-ban areas, where a more uniform culture is observed among the different castes and ethnic groups than in the rural areas (Fürer-Hai-mendorf, 1960: 16–31, Caplan, 1975: 138–148, Yamamoto, 1983: 1–38). Thus, in each named group whose boundary is kept distinct, there are many people who have been brought up by mothers from different groups. It is a matter of course for people of such birth to inherit their mother's habits and ways of thinking, though socially they remain members (sometimes secondary members) of their father's group.

The existence of the custom of *mit* (fictive kin, ritual brotherhood, or ceremonial friend) in Nepal is well known (Okada, 1957; Fürer-Haimendorf, 1975: 282). This relationship is often made between people of the same ethnic group, but there are also instances of cross-ethnic bonds. These may be contracted for the purpose of facilitating trade and other movements or for sheer friendship. There is no doubt that the custom has contributed not only to commercial transactions but also to the mutual understanding and accommodation of different groups.

In north-western Nepal, we find instances in which economic motives induced the Parbate Hindus to make cultural changes. High castes (Brahmans, Chetris, and Thakuris) engaged in trans-Hima-layan trade in salt and grain side-by-side with the Bhotias. In practice, they emulated the local (Bhotia) pattern of trade, intricately combined with continuous movement in the search for pastures and markets. Some people entered into a relationship of ceremonial friendship with the Bhotias. There were even cases in which the ritual of donning the *janai* (sacred thread) was postponed or given up in order to facilitate an association with the Bhotias (Fürer-Haimendorf, 1975: 261, 281–282).

The Parbate Hindus' adaptation to other group's customs can be seen even in religious matters. In the Middle Mountain areas some Hindus consult with Shamans of the Tibeto-Burman-speaking population. In this case both parties share common features since shamanic practices are not totally absent among the Hindus, and a shaman possessed is temporarily equated with the possessing deity.

On the other hand, a Bahun woman in a village in central Nepal expressed her awe of the supernatural ability of Tibetan Buddhist monks, saying that they were more powerful than Brahman (Bahun) priests. This was a comment based on hearsay, but it reflects the ambivalent attitude of the Hindus of the Middle Mountains towards the Tibetan people, whom they usually refer to by the derogatory term "Bhote" (or Bhotia). This is an example in which some enigmatic power is accorded to the marginal element of one's conceptual world.

The Tibetan civilization with Buddhism at its core has been a great source of inspiration to the people in northern Nepal. The Tibetans and Sherpas who are established Buddhists have been more immune to the penetration of Hindu civilization and have not changed their identity as Buddhists under 200 years of Hindu rule, which contrasts sharply with the Thakali.

The case of the Sherpas, who have come into frequent contact with Hindus and foreigners in the recent wave of tourism, illustrates this point. According to Fisher, "Rather than Westernization or nationalization ... there has been an intensification of Sherpa culture" and "Sherpas have not only maintained their cultural identity and intensified it, but they have also contributed to making Tibetan life-styles generally respectable in Nepal." It is also "significant that Khumbu Sherpas wear either Sherpa clothes or Western dress, but never the Nepali national dress" (Fisher, 1986: 51–52). This is an example of the resilience of one civilization against another civilization; even when facing Hindu practices and logic, the Tibetan Buddhist had a system strong enough to cope with them. Marginal as they are in the eyes of the Hindus in Nepal, these Buddhists are not so marginal in as far as the distance from civilization is concerned.

Among the people sandwiched between the Hindu and Buddhist civilizations, there are some who opt to strengthen their Buddhist orientation in the course of culture change rather than adopting

Hinduism. Among such groups are the Nyish
Nyishang Valley of Manang district. They enga
ities earlier in Assam, later in South-East Asi
Calcutta, and rose to wealth through more r
Kong and Singapore. Some of them even estab
idences in Kathmandu. But, unlike the Thaka
of the Nyishang people has been associated
Buddhist practice, at least in its outward a..
tions" (Cooke, 1985: 47–53). True, as Cooke points ou,..
ment they face is different from that of the Ranas, which was heavny
inclined towards Hindu conformity with which they had to cope. But
it should also be remembered how deeply the Nyishang people had
been involved in Tibetan Buddhism prior to their economic growth
and social expansion.

Transformation of a Newar village

During the latter half of the twentieth century Nepal has experienced
significant changes approximately every 10 years: the fall of the Rana
regime in 1951; the seizure of power by King Mahendra in 1961; the
subsequent introduction of the panchayat system and the closure of
the Tibet-Nepal border by the Chinese government in 1959; the
demise of King Mahendra in 1972, which activated the anti-panchayat
groups; the anti-government movement in 1979, which led to the referendum in 1980; and the movement for democracy from 1989, which
put an end to the panchayat system and gave birth to the new constitution of 1990.

To show how the national-level politico-economic change affected
local societies during this period, we will briefly trace the transformation of a Newar village in the Kathmandu Valley. The village
(Satungal), which is situated about 7 km west of Kathmandu, includes eight Newar castes and some new in-migrants. Among them
the Syesyas (Shresthas) and Jyapus (Maharjans) are numerically
strong and have been competing in village politics. The Syesya caste,
whose stereotypical occupation is not very clear-cut though they are
sometimes said to be the officer and merchant caste, engage in agriculture and other jobs and have been dominant in socio-ritual and
political matters in the village. The Jyapus (agricultural caste) are
numerous and a little more inclined towards agriculture than the
Syesyas, though most of them also combine this with various other
jobs.

...ace of change quickened from the mid-1960s, when the pan-
...t system began to function with development policies. Among
...main events of this period – which influenced village society and
...ccelerated its change – are: the inflow of modern goods and technologies, the abolition of old types of land ownership, the introduction of high-yielding varieties of crops, and the development of
transportation and communication.

Electricity was first brought to this village in 1971. Since then all
houses have electric lamps. Electric heaters have been introduced for
cooking and/or heating. Some people set up mills which were run by
electricity and began to earn money by husking rice, grinding wheat,
and making flattened rice (*chiura*). Radios became common, though
a few transistor radios were there before the introduction of electricity. TV broadcasting began in the 1980s, and now several houses
have TV sets. A health post, which only existed as a building in 1970,
began to function from the late 1970s. Toilets, which did not exist in
the village in the 1970s, began to be made by some villagers from the
early 1980s, but the public toilets which were built at about the same
time ceased to be used after a few years because of the difficulty of
maintenance.

There have also been improvements in the village schools (grades
1–5), both in terms of buildings and the number of students enrolled.
Among students and other young people, western-style costumes
have become ordinary, but traditional clothes are commonly worn by
older people and married women.

There has been a general increase of production and in income
since the 1960s. Among many laws which changed the forms of land
ownership, two measures were especially relevant to this village: the
abolition of the *rakam* (the obligation to offer a stipulated number of
labourers to the government), and the *birta* form of tenure – land
grants made by the state to individuals, usually on an inheritable and
tax-exempt basis (Regmi, 1976: 16–19, 233–235).

The introduction of improved varieties of paddy, wheat, and maize
from the mid-1960s contributed greatly to their increased production.
Their yield nearly doubled initially, but declined to some extent later.
Villagers were able to sell more crops but also faced the need for cash
to purchase chemical fertilizers and other necessities to keep the crop
production level.

The development of roads, transportation, and communication
(including increased bus services to Kathmandu, which was growing
as the national capital), induced many villagers to commute to Kath-

mandu as white-collar workers, merchants, and labourers. As a result, fewer villagers (except for women and old people) tended to engage in agricultural work themselves and hired labourers from outside for farm work, which also increased the need for cash.

The village's growth in population size (1,121 in 1970 to 1,550 in 1984) was due to natural increases and the inflow of people seeking jobs in the village as well as in Kathmandu. Needless to say, the expanding production and job opportunities have been supporting the increased population.

The increasing dependence on a wider-scale economy significantly transformed the traditional socio-ritual structure of the village. Many of the ritual groups began to economize on their ritual expenses, simplifying and decreasing the number of feasts. Intra-village cooperation and inter-caste dependence greatly declined. The lower castes, stimulated by education and modern ideas brought from the capital, began to regard their traditional subordination to the higher castes as demeaning and then as a burden. The middle castes resented the higher castes because of the latter's behaviour in the newly introduced political situation and form of election and withdrew some of their caste-specific ritual services in the village festival (the Vishnudevi festival), which was regarded by Syesyas as a serious threat to the integration of the village.

The local administrative unit became the arena of contest for political power. Some of the village elders and others who aspired to influential positions began to compete in elections for the new politico-administrative offices created by the panchayat system. The rationale for the acquisition of power changed from that of ascription, based on caste and kinship, to the number of votes. People began to manoeuvre their affiliation to caste and kin with the logic of numbers, resulting in the fission and fusion of various groups, together with quarrels, which sometimes escalated into fights and lawsuits. In daily activities the villagers' mutual cooperation declined, as seen in agricultural activities in which they grew more dependent on hired labourers from outside.

Thus, village integration in terms of inter-caste and intra-village dependence decreased, and more antagonism between castes prevailed. Still, it is a notable fact in this village that many villagers aspire to celebrate the village festival in a grandiose way so that they are assured of the favour of the goddess and the ritual integration of the village. So, in 1993 the village festival was held on a different date from usual, celebrating the restoration of some of the images stolen

Palanquin being carried in a village festival in Satungal, Kathmandu Valley

from the village temple several years before. This shows that traditional symbolic order is still valued by the villagers but it does not
necessarily lead to the restoration of all the traditional village's socio-
political order, since villagers have become more and more dependent on the outside world, leaving the village integration partial and
nominal.

Since the late 1980s, several large factories have been built within
the jurisdiction of this village by outsiders, including the Marwaris,
who chose this area because of its flat plots, closeness to the capital,
and comparatively low land prices. Many villagers sold their fields to
the factories, but there were only a few who were employed by them.
From among about 70 employees in one factory, only four were from
this village. The other employees were from other areas, including
India. Among those villagers who sold land, some purchased land
in the tarai, others bought cars and mini-buses and began earning
money with them, and some invested money in trade and other

activities. Unfortunately, the lapse of the trade and transit treaty in 1989 soon followed and many of the villagers suffered from economic hardships. Many young people sought employment abroad; India and other South Asian countries, South-East Asia, and even East Asian countries were included in their destinations.

Though the economic effect of the political upheaval of 1989–1990 was detrimental to the village as it was to the nation as a whole, the influence of the democratization of the same period seems to have been felt less here than on the national level. As far as the new local politico-administrative structure was concerned, it was not so different from the previous system; the election system was already there and the newly introduced "village development committee" (*gaun vikas samiti*) was almost a renamed equivalent of the village panchayat.

This Newar village in the Kathmandu Valley has experienced a green revolution and monetization and is still experiencing various forms of modernization. A transformation of the traditional village structure has resulted, and people's thoughts and behaviour have also changed considerably.

Recent sociocultural changes

The influence of the rapidly changing national political system has been felt in every corner of Nepal. Compared to other areas of Nepal, the above example of the Kathmandu Valley is rather exceptional since most of the villages in the mountains and in the tarai are not electrified and many mountain villages are not connected to motorable roads. The green revolution has not been successful except in the Kathmandu Valley and in part of the tarai. Even in those places where it was successful, it was overshadowed by a heavy population increase. The cash economy has spread during these 40 years. In urban areas and places visited frequently by tourists, the economy has been greatly monetized. In general, modernization has been slow, though it cannot be denied that it has been taking place.

Studying the remote isolated village of Magars (whose villagers speak Kaike) in Tichurong in the mountains of north-west Nepal, Fisher cites an interesting case in which villagers settled a private quarrel by voting to change their own marriage rules and merge the two highest classes of marriage into a single intermarrying group. According to Fisher, "Two of the compelling arguments leading to this decision were (1) that people in other, more progressive (i.e.,

169

Hindu) parts of Nepal do not have such cumbersome and backward marriage rules; and (2) that under the new laws everyone is supposed to be equal anyway." This happened as early as in the late 1960s when "ideas of democracy and equality" had already been absorbed by the village people "along with concepts of caste ranking" (Fisher, 1986: 186–189).

This village and the Newar village provide two extreme examples of local societies: one is remote, secluded, and based on kinship; the other is close to the capital and has castes. With all their differences, both have been exposed to outside influences, including that from central government, and have responded to them in their respective ways. It is notable that the direction towards more freedom of choice and egalitarianism can be seen in both of these examples, though some temporary confusion was inevitable.

The abolition of discrimination based on caste was already included in the constitution of 1962. Though the government was not very active in enforcing its anti-discrimination laws, a situation quite different from that in the previous era prevailed and people were no longer forced to abide by the caste order. As far as the legal aspect was concerned, a more amicable condition was there for those who wished to change or be free from traditional social settings. Some of the changes have been made voluntarily and comparatively easily, but some have included struggles with privileged groups.

Among the societies which have had castes (namely the Parbate and tarai Hindus and the Newars), the caste consciousness – or sense of the hierarchical ordering of named social categories (*jat*) – has not disappeared, though there has been a general decline of inter-caste dependence based on the division of labour. *Jats* (castes) among them have become separate entities from one another because of the disappearance of the intricate web of services.

On the other hand, the dependence structure within each caste has for the most part persisted. In-group dependence is sometimes strengthened and enlarged, as seen when group confrontation occurs. Factions with their cores based on traditional ties but including other people with the same interests have become instrumental in the pursuance of goals. Within those groups are perpetuated what Bista (1991: 4, 97–100) calls the collectivism of one's own people (*afno* or *aphno manche*).

In the new constitution of 1990 egalitarian ideas were strengthened. The constitution defined Nepal as a multi-ethnic and multi-

170

lingual country. In democratization movements, not only political groups but also cultural groups were organized among various Tibeto-Burman speaking groups. They demanded that the government and public take the necessary measures to preserve and promote their own languages and cultures. In many cases those demands were written in Nepali in pamphlets, but in some cases indigenous languages written in *devanagari* script were used. Group consciousness was manifest. In those cases they still referred to their own and other groups as *jat*. But here the use of the term has been altered considerably since the connotation "caste" was virtually lost when used by Tibeto-Burman speaking people to claim an equal footing with other groups, including the Hindus. They depart from their pseudo-caste standing and strengthen their characteristics as ethnic groups. It should be noted that they have continued as separate groups, or rather clarified their identities in the course of recent democratic movements.

Urbanism, caste, and ethnic groups

People of different ethnic groups have been mingling more and more in many places in Nepal. Needless to say, it is in the urban areas that this has been taking place extensively. But are they forming a melting pot with cultural uniformity or a salad bowl with different cultures? Though the discussion above seems readily to point to the latter case, the actual situation does not allow such simplistic treatment.

In a 1969 study of an administrative town in far-western Nepal, Caplan argues that there is no cultural plurality of castes (Caplan, 1975: 145). Not only the castes of the Parbate Hindus but also the Tibeto-Burman ethnic groups such as the Magars, Gurungs, and Newars (Newars are considered as one single caste in this area) have been assimitated.

"Interaction between these groups is clearly anything but restricted and the result is a broadly uniform set of customary practices. All speak Nepali as a first language (including Newars), wear the same dress, celebrate the same festivals and household rites, utilize the same category of ritual specialists and so on. Still, despite this uniformity, perhaps because of it, there is a sense in which we may speak of cultural distinctiveness. It is not the fruit of separation, as Berreman suggests, but rather arises from a common belief in and perception of difference imposed by a system founded on hierarchy"

171

(Caplan, 1975: 145). Perceived differences based on hierarchy rather than differences resulting from the restriction of intermarriage and interaction are responsible for cultural distinctiveness.

We do not know the present condition of the town studied by Caplan, but it certainly offers a typical example of the urban situation in Nepal. A system founded on hierarchy is considerably diluted and is gradually being replaced by the notion of "separate but equal." What Caplan points out seems to apply to many small towns in the Middle Mountains, including the new settlements springing up along motorable roads. These settlements are melting pots, but they have retained their people's identities.

The situation is different in large urban centres like Kathmandu. True, there has been cultural interaction and mingling between groups, but as far as the interaction of traditional cultures is concerned they have not produced a uniform set of customary practices in the Kathmandu Valley. Though the Newars have absorbed the Nepali language to a considerable extent, and some of them have intermarried with Parbate Hindus, they have retained their own customs, festivals, residential styles, dress, and diet. On the other hand, some in-migrants, including the dominant Parbate Hindus, have adopted Newar-style houses but those who have done so are few in number and the majority live separately and with their own distinct customs.

The cultures of some of the later in-migrants are clearly different from both the Parbate Hindus and the Newars. The Tibetan, Sherpa, and Nyishang people have been observing Tibetan Buddhism, keeping their own diets and other customs, including women's costumes. It has been noted that the Thakalis in Kathmandu have resumed their traditional rituals based on "native animism called *dhom* or *jhankri*" (Iijima, 1982: 32). The existence of these characteristics indicate that the identity of these groups is kept not only in name but also in practice.

Towns in the tarai area have absorbed many people from the Middle Mountains. Many of the earlier residents are people of north Indian origin who keep to their own way of life. There are also those who have come down from the Middle Mountains, namely the Parbate Hindus and Tibeto-Burman groups. They have not absorbed the rituals, clothes, language, and other customs of the tarai people and have continued as distinct groups.

The ethnic situation in the large cities as well as in the towns in the tarai is of a salad-bowl type in which different ethnic groups keep

Krishna mandir (temple), Patan, Kathmandu Valley

their identities and their cultures. This contrasts rather sharply with the typical small town in the Middle Mountain area, of which an example was given by Caplan. Thus, from the present perspective we have two types of urban settlement in Nepal: (1) a salad bowl, and (2) a melting pot in practice but salad bowl in name. The present national trend towards cultural pluralism will strengthen the salad-bowl aspect, but we need to keep in mind that other modern forces are working to equalize different cultures and ways of thinking.

Universalism, education, language, and foreign influences

Education not only contributes to the enhancement of literacy but also to the penetration of the educator's ideology and way of think-ing. In the 1970s the Nepali government prepared all the lower and secondary grade textbooks in the Nepali language. They included

An image of goddess Saraswati being carried to a river at the end of her festival in the tarai

various kinds of scientific knowledge as well as ideas about the Nepali government, which was headed by the king. Education became compulsory in Nepali and textbooks were used all over the country, irrespective of the students' cultural background and mother tongue. This will no doubt give rise to a uniformity of knowledge and ideas among the younger generation with a formal education and a cleavage between different generations. To what extent this takes place should be ascertained by using a broad-scale survey.

The policy of making Nepali the national language of Nepal and to use it as the main medium in government as well as in education has been exerting a deep influence over all Nepal. The Nepali language had already been used to some extent in Kathmandu and in eastern Nepal during the Malla period, and it spread rapidly under the Gorkha rule to become a second language to many people in the

Middle Mountains. It has now penetrated into every corner of Nepal. In a sense it can be taken as a continuation of the trend from the previous period, but the penetration has accelerated recently since the advent of foreign assistance.

A long association with the Parbate Hindus made Nepali the first language of some of the Middle Mountain people. In large cities, there have been families in which the children are spoken to by parents in the Nepali language even though their mother tongue is not the same. Clearly, socio-economic reasons for looking on the Nepali language as advantageous lie behind this change. However, tarai residents whose second language is Hindi have been more reluctant in this respect. Some of them have sent their children to boarding schools in India, and some classes have not gone smoothly because of a lack of fluency accompanied by an eagerness to speak Nepali among both the teachers and the students. However, it is a fact that it has been getting easier to communicate in Nepali in the tarai area.

During and after the democratic movement of 1990, demands were made for the use of languages other than Nepali for education and mass communication. In broadcasting, Newari, Maithili, Hindi, Bhojpuri, Magar, Tamang and Gurung began to be used (though to a very limited extent), and in schools the use of minority languages in teaching was resumed. But progress in this direction has been limited because of the absence of a writing system in many languages, the lack of administrative efficiency, and a conflict of interest among the concerned parties. It remains to be seen to what extent ethnic languages are preserved and become instrumental in promoting the different cultures.

Foreign influences should also be mentioned as an important factor in generating uniformity. There has been no ethnic barrier to adopting foreign goods and ideas. Modern technological machines, new-style clothing and houses, etc., can be used irrespective of the ethnic group, though the degree of acceptance will vary according to the generation, gender, or economic class of the people. Contacts with foreigners and foreign commodities have been increasing under growing tourism and foreign aid projects. The mass media can reach everyone with information on new, as well as traditional, ideas.

Ideas such as development, equality, and freedom are shared by many people though there are many problems to be solved before these can be realized and implemented. It may be that the acceptance of these elements may blur the demarcation of ethnic groups in some

175

respects. But today, the ideas of development, equality, and freedom are combined with a new desire to enhance ethnic identities and cultures. Therefore, a sense of separateness will persist among groups in spite of the penetration of universalism or other ideologies. How the latter will change the internal structure of groups as well as their mode of interaction is a problem to be investigated in the future.

7

Settlement patterns and urbanization

The vast majority of Nepal's population lives in small rural settlements. In the 1952–1954 census, 28,780 localities, with populations ranging from less than 500 to more than 100,000, were identified. A little more than 99 per cent of these localities had populations of less than 2,000; almost 85 per cent of the localities had a population of 500 or less. Eighty-nine per cent of the total population lived in localities that had a population of less than 2,000. There was no significant change in their number in 1961.

After the introduction of the panchayat system of government in 1962, these small hamlets and villages were regrouped to form a village panchayat, so that in the 1971 census, these localities were grouped into 3,931 village panchayats. After another restructuring of these panchayat boundaries in the 1970s, the number was reduced to 2,935, but they reverted to their former size in 1982.

The 1971 and 1981 censuses indicated a higher proportion of settlements with populations of 2,000 to 4,999 (68.71 and 55.71 per cent in 1971 and 1981 respectively). In 1971, 82.96 per cent of the total population lived in settlements with less than 5,000 population. In 1981, the proportion of the population living in settlements of the same size decreased to 40.55 per cent (P. Sharma, 1989: 16). This decrease might have been the result of the increased population of the settlement size as a whole and/or from the rise of spontaneous new settlements in the tarai through the internal migration of the Middle Mountain population (Ojha, 1982: 32). The data on settlement sizes and numbers as reported in 1971 and 1981 are not compatible with the 1952–

1954 and 1961 data. Information on settlements from the 1991 census has not yet been published.

Geography and social traditions have strongly influenced the size, shape, and distribution of settlements and house styles. The last 20 years have witnessed a major expansion of settlements, which are fairly large and nucleated in the tarai. Proximity to India and access to Indian railheads and roads have contributed to this growth. The growth of settlements is closely related to the location, access, and quality of the transportation network.

In the eastern tarai, the villages, which are comparatively large, are generally located above the flood plains. In the drier parts of the mid-western and far-western tarai, the villages are smaller and less widely separated. The dominant house type in this region is rectangular and gabled, constructed of wooden posts and bamboo, and has a steep thatched roof. Walls are made of wattle-grass, plastered with mud. The wealthier people build their houses similarly, but with brick walls and tiled roofs.

In the Middle Mountains, settlements are usually dispersed. Houses within the settlement are widely scattered and usually located on the southern slopes of the mountains in order to receive most of the sun's rays throughout the year. Since productive land is limited and water is scarce, settlements are usually located on higher ground so that the flat valleys close to a source of water can be used for cultivation.

A typical house in this region is two-storeyed and set on a raised foundation about three feet from the ground. Walls are made of stones or slate and plastered with red lateritic soil. Usually, the houses are double-roofed and thatched with rice straw. In front of the main door there is an open veranda called a Pindhi, which plays a big part in the social life of the people. This is where neighbours sit and socialize. People from outside the village can even stay overnight on the Pindhi.

Since these houses are free standing, they can face in any direction. There is usually some open space in the front, which can be used for drying grains or as a kitchen garden. The ground floor contains a kitchen, which is separated from the dining section by a low wall. Beside the door there might be a small narrow raised bed and a staircase to the first floor. These houses lack adequate windows, and people do not build chimneys because they fear a fire might start in the thatched roof. Hence, the ground floor is usually dark and smokey while cooking is taking place. The first floor usually contains the bedrooms. Cattle and goats are accommodated in outbuildings, where there is also space for storage.

In the western part of Nepal, some of the Gurungs still live in round houses of stone with thatched roofs. A house on a platform has walls plastered by clay sometimes painted in white and brown and with simple colour drawings.

In the west-central part, even some Brahmans build round houses with a brightly painted circular platform raised about three to four feet above the ground. If they contain a *tulasi* plant (a herbaceous plant), it is a sure sign of a Brahman house. This *tulasi* plant is considered to be holy according to Hindu scriptures.

Other ethnic groups have slightly different house types and floor plans; a Newar settlement is significantly different. Newar houses – both in the rural and urban areas – are built in continuous rows which face the street. The settlements are more compact, and the rows of houses are separated only by a narrow lane. It is common to have a courtyard surrounded by buildings on all sides. This enclosed courtyard becomes a centre for family activities and for social interaction (M. N. Shrestha, 1981: 30).

The houses are usually three or four storeys high and made of bricks, mud, wood, and tiles. The ground floor, which usually does not get enough sunlight, is continually damp, so it is used for storing farm implements, cattle, poultry, manure, etc. The first floor contains bedrooms and a storage area. The second floor is an open room without partitions; it is used as a visiting place, work room, or living area. A kitchen and dining area are on the third floor. This type of settlement and house type is found in the Kathmandu Valley and in areas where the Newars of the Kathmandu Valley have settled for trade and commerce.

Settlements in the Great Himalaya are usually small and clustered on more or less level ground near the cultivated land. Houses are made of stone or slate; the flat roofs are covered with slate or thick boards. The houses are usually two-storeyed. The ground floor is used for storage and as a stable, whereas the first floor is used as the living quarters. A flat roof holds a thick covering of snow, providing a somewhat insulating effect in the winter. In the humid eastern part of the region, the roofs are gabled, but the slope is low enough to hold snow in the wintertime (Karan, 1960: 56–58).

The dispersion of the population in small settlements over the large and rugged mountainous terrain has far-reaching consequences in the delivery of services, economic development, and administrative facilities. The excessive cost of constructing roads and the longer travel time on foot presents obstacles to the movement of goods

Settlement with flat-roof houses and *kot* (old fort with a temple) in north-west Nepal (courtesy M. Tamura)

Magar village in west Nepal

and services from one part of the country to another. Providing even the basic necessities – food, water, electricity, schools, and clinics – is difficult.

180

Gurung golghar (oval plan house) in the Pokhara Valley (courtesy M. Tamura)

Due to this inaccessibility, these villages have maintained a subsistence agricultural economy without any other alternative employment opportunities. Rural settlements have remained underdeveloped and isolated from the many social and economic changes that are taking place in Nepal's capital and other large cities. Despite 40 years of economic development efforts, the people in the rural areas of the country remain poor, except for some wealthy farmers in the tarai.

Urban settlements and urbanization trends

Urbanization is a process of both quantitative and qualitative changes in population characteristics. With an increase in population size and density, a settlement becomes a centre for commercial and industrial development, and a focal point for cultural change. In Western coun-

181

Tharu village in Chitwan in the inner tarai (courtesy K. Tachibana)

tries, urbanization has been associated with industrialization and economic growth (McGee, 1971).

In developing countries such as Nepal, the number of urban centres has increased significantly but without much industrialization.
Many large settlements still keep their rural environment and rural
economy. The high growth rates of urban population in developing
countries should not be taken as a sign of urbanization, nor should
they be taken as an indication of a significant shift in the country's
economic base. A distinction, therefore, should be made between the
growth of the urban population per se and the urbanization associated with changes in the economy and in people's lifestyles (Conway and Shrestha, 1980: 480).

The meaning of "urban" in Nepal

The lack of specific information and the lack of continuity of common
definitions are major problems in the analysis of Nepalis settlements.
The alteration of boundaries of the urban settlements, change in basic
definitions, change in the data format, and the exclusion of certain data
from subsequent census publications make it impossible to conduct
any meaningful spatial time-series analysis of urban development.

In the first census of 1952–1954, 10 urban centres, known as Shahar, were identified, but no formal definition of an urban area was given. The 1961 census provided a formal definition of an urban area for the first time. An urban area was defined as a locality inhabited by not less than 5,000 people, which must have schools, government offices, legal courts, and marketing facilities. With the change in the political system the following year, the nomenclature of an urban area was also changed from a Shahar to a Nagar Panchayat (Town Panchayat).

The Nagar Panchayat Act of 1962 defined a Nagar Panchayat as "an area having not less than 10,000 population." It did not specify any other attributes. In 1976 the population requirement of a Town Panchayat was reduced to 9,000. However, this population criterion was not strictly followed. Some settlements, such as Illam, Bhadrapur, Rajbiraj, and Tansen, were classified as urban areas even though they did not have the required population size and were functioning only as lower-order market centres. Other areas, such as Sivaganj (17,891), Hatiya (12,939), Rajghat (10,049), and nine other centres that had larger populations and were functioning as higher-order market centres were excluded from the urban category.

The designation of urban status – Nagar Panchayat – was not made by Nepal's Central Bureau of Statistics, but by the Ministry of Panchayat. Thus, it was based on political and administrative decisions rather than on any objective functional grounds. This system seriously underestimates the actual number of urban centres and urban populations in the country. Now, after the third change in the political system in 1990, these Nagar Panchayats are simply called "municipalities."

Patterns of urban growth

Nepal is among the less urbanized countries of the world. With the exception of the Kathmandu Valley, urbanization in other parts of the country was almost non-existent until recently. In the 1952–1954 census there were only 10 urban centres and only 238,275 persons (2.8 per cent of the total population) living in urban centres. One-half of these urban centres, with more than three-quarters of the urban population, were located in the Kathmandu Valley (table 20). In 1961 six more centres were added, and the urban population increased to 336,222, or 41 per cent of the 1952–1954 urban population. In 1971, some of these centres were dropped from the list and new centres were added. The total urban population increased by 37 per cent between 1961 and 1971.

In 1976 seven new centres were incorporated into the Nagar Panchayat. Hence, the urban population in 1981 increased to 956,721, twice the urban population of 1971. The urban population reached 6.4 per cent of the total population of the country in 1981. Ten more centres were incorporated in 1987. This increased the total number of Nagar Panchayats to 33. In the 1991 census, these 33 designated urban centres comprised about 9.2 per cent (or 1.7 million persons) of Nepal's population (fig. 24). Although the rate of urban population growth during the past four decades has been faster than the rate of total population growth in the country, the total urban population has still remained rather low when compared to other South Asian neighbours.

The urban population growth has not been uniform in all cities and geographic areas of Nepal. In the 1950s the eastern and central tarai had the highest growth. The population of Biratnagar (eastern tarai) increased its 1952–1954 population more than three times, followed by Nepalganj (46.28 per cent) and Janakpur (27.0 per cent). In the 1960s Pokhara had the highest (280 per cent) increase, followed by Janakpur (60.10 per cent) and Rajbiraj (49.69 per cent). In the 1970s Nepal's urban population growth was more widespread and also reached its highest point (107.11 per cent) within the past 40 years (table 21). Birganj had the highest growth followed by Janakpur, Pokhara, Hetauda, and Biratnagar.

The urban growth rate in the 1980s was 77.24 per cent. The highest increase of population was in Pokhara (104.29 per cent), followed by Bharatpur (98.07 per cent) and Butawal (96.04 per cent). From 1950–1990 the Kathmandu Valley gained only a modest increase in urban population; it no longer holds the large share of the total urban population that it did in the 1950s. At present, the valley contains only 35.32 per cent of the nation's urban population.

In addition to the natural increase in the urban population, population increases through the reclassification of new places as urban centres, migration, and the annexation of rural areas into urban territories have contributed to the growth in Nepal's urban population. The fertility rate, infant mortality rate, and crude death rate are all lower in the urban areas (Central Bureau of Statistics, 1987: 198).

If all other variables are held constant, the urban population should increase at a slower rate than the rural population. For estimating the annual urban population growth rates, only the localities that were

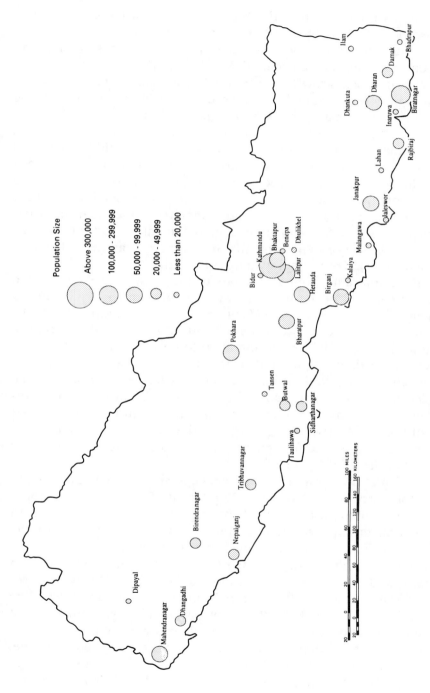

Population Size

Above 300,000

100,000 - 299,999

50,000 - 99,999

20,000 - 49,999

Less than 20,000

Ilam

Bhadrapur

Damak

Dharan

Dhankuta

Inaruwa

Biratnagar

Lahan

Rajbiraj

Janakpur

Jaleswor

Malangawa

Kalaiya

Birganj

Hetauda

Bidur

Kathmandu

Bhaktapur

Benepa

Dhulikhel

Lalitpur

Bharatpur

Pokhara

Tansen

Butwal

Sidharthanagar

Taulihawa

Tribhuvannagar

Birendranagar

Nepalganj

Dipayal

Mahendranagar

Dhangadhi

100 MILES

KILOMETERS

Fig. 24 **Urban settlements**

classified as urban in all of the censuses were considered. Although the growth rate has increased in recent years, how much of this can be attributed to natural increase, migration, and changes in the urban boundaries cannot be determined. P. Sharma (1989: 59) suggests that the overall urban growth in the 1960s was caused largely by the addition of new towns, and that migration contributed the least to the growth of older urban centres during that period.

Migration in Nepal has remained greatest in rural to rural areas, but its impact on urban growth cannot be underestimated. Compared to other Asian countries, rural to urban migration in Nepal has been low. The reason for such a low rural-urban migration could be due to the economic structure of the cities. The basic functions of these urban centres have been trade and commerce rather than industry, and hence, they offer very limited employment opportunities. Furthermore, the majority of poor migrants coming from the villages do not have any skills for employment in the cities.

Lifetime migrants from all regions to the urban areas constituted about 12 per cent of the total migrants in 1971, and a large majority of them came from the Middle Mountain region (P. Sharma, 1989: 61). The urban centres in the tarai were the destination of 58 per cent of the total interregional urban migrants, followed by the Kathmandu Valley. More than 42 per cent of the urban population in the tarai urban centres were lifetime migrants either from other parts of Nepal or from foreign countries, particularly India. The proportion of foreign-born and native-born migrants together constitutes only 9.5 per cent of the Valley and 16.5 per cent of the Middle Mountains. Over 84 per cent of the total foreign-born population living in urban areas is found in the tarai (table 22).

In 1981 lifetime rural-urban migrants constituted about 20 per cent of the total urban population and 27 per cent of the tarai urban population. More than 50 per cent of the migrants from all regions went to the tarai urban centres, contributing almost 20 per cent of the increase in the tarai urban population. This rural-urban migration contributed the largest share to the total urban population growth in the tarai and the lowest in the Kathmandu Valley. Newly incorporated urban centres and the centres located along the foothills – like Dharan, Hetauda, and Butwal – show a relatively high percentage of migrant population compared to other older urban centres.

The foreign-born population in the 1981 census showed a decline. However, a survey conducted by the National Commission on Population (1983) found that both the internal and international migrations in the tarai urban centres were on the rise. This study also revealed that the foreign-born population in the tarai was rising at an annual rate of 4.2 per cent, and the destination of almost 50 per cent of these immigrants was the tarai urban centres.

The reclassification or addition of new urban centres is another important variable in the urban population growth. The population of reclassified urban centres constituted 8.9, 13.2, 16.8, and 46.9 per cent of the total urban population in 1961, 1971, 1981, and 1991 respectively. Many of these urban centres cover large areas, but only a fraction of their territories are built up as urban areas. This could change the size of the urban population and also influence the density of population in some of the urban centres (table 23).

Mahendra Nagar, for example, has a total area of 192 sq. km, and less than 4 per cent of this area is built up. If we take the total area, the density of population in Mahendra Nagar will be 322 persons per sq. km. On the other hand, if we take only the built-up urban area, the density will increase to 8,949 persons per sq. km.

Since the information on the changes in urban boundaries and the built-up areas over time is not available, it is difficult to estimate how many people living in the rural areas have become a part of the urban population. However, it is obvious that migration and reclassification or the addition of new urban centres in the 1970s and 1980s contributed most to the growth of the urban population in Nepal.

The present distribution of the urban population is a direct result of the differential growth rate of the economy, initiated and maintained by national planning policies and projects. After the successful eradication of malaria, land development, and resettlement programmes initiated by the government in the 1950s, the tarai region became a haven for landless farmers from the Middle Mountains. This new opportunity in the tarai produced an impetus for a mass exodus, particularly to the central and eastern parts. Many of the new urban centres that developed after 1960 are therefore located in the tarai.

The Great Himalayan region has no urban population. Only small villages and trading centres fulfil the functions of a centre. It is customary for the people in this region and also in the Middle Mountains to move to the south during the winter months to buy and sell goods and services for the entire year. Of the 33 urban centres listed, only 13 are located in the Middle Mountains; the remaining 20 urban centres are in the tarai.

In terms of the total urban population and the urbanization level, the Middle Mountain region has a slight edge over the tarai (table 24). If these geographic areas are further subdivided, the central part of the Middle Mountain region (25.88 per cent) has the highest level of urbanization, followed by the far-western tarai (15.80 per cent) and the eastern tarai (11.82 per cent). Within the Middle Mountain region, the least urbanization is found in the far-western and mid-western areas. These variations in the levels of urbanization are due to the availability of employment opportunities and the centrality and productivity of the hinterland.

The principal settlements of the tarai serve as "land ports," and their respective growths are related to the proximity of the Indian transportation infrastructure. Tarai cities serve primarily as marketing and distribution centres for the Middle Mountain region. Urbanization in the tarai began swiftly when trade with India expanded. This initiated the growth of urban centres such as Biratnagar, Birganj, Nepalganj, and Janakpur – all border points at Indian railheads. Increasing north-south trade led to the growing importance of these tarai urban centres. At a breakpoint between the Middle Mountains and the tarai, urban settlements such as Butwal and Dharan emerged.

Spatial organization of urban centres

The dominance of subsistence agriculture in the economy and the mountain barriers has produced a loosely integrated urban network in Nepal. Both the movement of people and goods in the country are seasonal and are basically oriented towards India in the south. Surplus agricultural products are sold in India, and all necessary manufactured goods are imported from India. Thus, the major growth of the urban centres has taken place in the southern plains near the Indian border or along the foothills of the Himalayas at the break-of-bulk points (M. N. Shrestha, 1985; P. Sharma, 1989: 118).

During the last 40 years the focus of urbanization has shifted to the tarai, the eastern tarai in particular. Urbanization in the Middle Mountains is proceeding at a much lower rate due to the poor resource base, problems of access and transportation, and limited potential for generating off-farm employment.

On the basis of the circulation pattern of the people, trade, and the transportation network, the whole urban system in Nepal can be divided into six separate regional urban networks. In the east, the regional urban network is dominated by Biratnagar. Dharan, the second largest town in the area, is located at the breakpoint between the mountains and the plain. Other towns and trading centres, such as Dhankuta, Illam, Bhojpur, and Taplegunj, are located further up in the mountains.

Janakpur is the hub of another urban network. It has a large tobacco and cigarette factory that employs several hundred workers. As the district headquarters and regional service centre, it is one of the fastest growing tarai cities. It is located near, but not directly adjacent to, the Indian border. It has a small airfield and access to the Indian railway and the East-West Highway. Janakpur's economic and commercial integration with the mountain region in the north is limited because of the difficulty of north-south movements. Thus, its trade area has remained small. Recent developments in transportation have improved accessibility to the north.

The third urban network is headed by Kathmandu, the capital. It is the largest city and its hinterland extends from Ramechhap in the east to Gorkha in the west. All urban centres in this network, including Birganj and Hetauda, are located along the major highways. Shrestha (1975) recognizes Birganj-Hetauda as a separate network. The heavy traffic and commerce generated here are primarily due to the dense population of the region. Kathmandu is the major urban market for manufactured goods. The economic base of this urban system is strengthened by its fertile valley.

The network west of Kathmandu is dominated by Pokhara, which has grown significantly since the completion of two major highways, which connect the city with Siddhartha Nagar near the Indian border and Kathmandu in the east. Butwal is located at the break-of-bulk point between the Middle Mountains and the tarai regions. Siddhartha Nagar–Butwal is identified as a separate regional network by Shrestha (1975). Tansen and Syanja (unincorporated settlements) are other important central places located along the highway north of Butwal. It has become the gateway to other parts of western Nepal, including the Mustang area in the north.

Nepalganj (in the mid-western tarai), which has a large tributary area, is the focus of another regional urban network. Birendra Nagar and Tribhuvan Nagar, which developed only in recent years, are within Nepalganj's hinterland. Nepalganj is served by the Indian rail facilities. It is an administrative and regional service centre for its agricultural hinterland and contains a number of agro-industries.

Mahendra Nagar, Dhangadhi, and Dipayal, in the far-western

189

Houses in a Kami (blacksmith) settlement in Dhading district, central Nepal

region, form another small regional urban network in an embryonic state. Two of these cities are in the tarai region and one is in the mountains. Before these urban centres developed to their current sizes, most of the trade of the area was carried on directly with India across the border. The commercial linkage with the hinterland in this area is poor, and both trade and commerce are limited in scope.

This urban system suffers from its isolation from the rest of the country. The completion of the East-West Highway will facilitate its economic and commercial linkage with the rest of the country. Mahendra Nagar is located in one of the few areas in the tarai that has remained forested. However, lumbering and the subsequent spread of cultivation have led to the development of the area.

On the basis of the foregoing discussion, it is obvious that Nepal's urbanization has hardly begun. The initial impetus for urban growth was first brought about by large-scale regional and international migration after malarial eradication in the tarai. Many of these urban centres still have rural characteristics, and the majority of the people in these cities are still engaged in primary activities and commerce.

190

These cities have yet to play a significant role in bringing about the expected economic and social changes in the country.

Kathmandu Valley towns: A cross-section of Nepal's cultural history

Kathmandu City is one of three cities located in the Kathmandu Valley. Though the valley is physically isolated from other parts of the region, it has been one of the centres of political, social, and religious activity for the past two millenniums. Buddhism and Hinduism coexisted and complemented each other. People frequently shared each other's temples, shrines, and deities. The ancient folk religions, rituals, and deities were also integrated into the broad conceptual framework of these religions. With this unusual mixture of people and different cultures, a unique Newar culture evolved.

The present urban landscape of the Kathmandu Valley is largely a product of planning and reconstruction that took place during the Malla period (1200–1769). The architectural design and method of construction actually dates back to the earlier Licchavi period. Significant changes in many sections of Kathmandu City occurred after the 1934 earthquake.

A city, according to Hindu cosmology, is a microcosm of the universe, and it should, therefore, be in perfect harmony with the subtle laws of the universe (Acharya, 1920; Dutt, 1977). On this basis, several scholars have tried to show that the cities of the Kathmandu Valley – Kathmandu, Lalitpur, and Bhaktapur – were planned in accordance with the basic Mandala principles as described in the town-planning treaties of the Manasara (Pieper, 1975; Gutschow and Kölver, 1975; Levy, 1990).

However, a visual comparison of the street patterns of Kathmandu, Lalitpur, and Bhaktapur, with eight basic designs of Mandala, indicates no close relationships. The orientation of the major streets in all three cities do not follow the due north-south or east-west direction, and the gates are not located on the four cardinal points (Shrestha, 1984).

Local legends and chronicles, however, indicate that these cities were planned to resemble specific religious objects to ensure constant protection by the gods and goddesses, and to insure the health, wealth, and prosperity of the cities' inhabitants. The late chronicles tell that Kathmandu City was founded and consecrated around the second half of the tenth century A.D. by King Gunakama Deva. However this lacks inscriptional evidence. Kathmandu was known as Yen (north) in Newari and was also called Kantipur. The city was planned to resemble the sword of Mahalakshmi. The southern part of the city toward the confluence of the Bagmati and Vishnumati rivers represents the handle, while its apex is thought to have extended as far north as present-day Thamel (Malla, 1978: 34).

The location and distribution pattern of the various castes within the cities can be observed. Wealthy people of high social status usually lived near the centre of the city, while the poor and low-caste people occupied the space outside the city (Gutschow and Kölver, 1975). At present, the wealthier people have started moving outside the city into suburban houses, and the traditional spatial characteristics of the localities are rapidly vanishing.

The basic layout of the streets in Kathmandu City followed the main trade routes. The central areas remained open spaces; all major arteries converged there. The major temples, monuments, palaces, rest houses (*sataa*), retail shops, water ponds, and wells were all centrally located. Secondary roads and narrow alleys (*galli*) passed through compact high buildings, which enclosed small quadrangles known as Baha (*vihara*), which were at one time Buddhist monasteries and learning centres. The scale and arrangement of the open spaces, the distribution of the temples, rest-houses, water fountains, and gates all indicate an excellent understanding of visual response to urban design and principles of social interaction.

The physical environment, economic feasibility, and existing settlements were the subtle forces that actually seemed to determine the site and shape of present-day Kathmandu City. During the consecration and formal naming of the city, some symbolic form must have been thought of in accordance with the religious predilection of the king, who consolidated the smaller settlements into a larger urban centre. The symbolic form, however, was never translated into urban space; it remained only as a "symbolic awareness" that transformed the profane space into a sacred space suitable for human settlement.

During the Malla period (1200–1769) the three cities of the Valley were separate city kingdoms. Many of the buildings and temples were built during that time. After the unification of the kingdoms and principalities that existed at that time in the Middle Mountain by King Prithvi Narayan Shah, Kathmandu City became the capital of unified Nepal. For a long time, the Kathmandu Valley was the only urbanized area in the country.

Kathmandu: The primate city

Since the 1950s the population of Kathmandu City has been increasing in absolute terms, but its size in relation to the total urban population has declined consistently. In 1961 the Kathmandu population constituted only about 36 per cent of the total urban population. In the 1971 and 1981 censuses, it declined further, to about 33 and 25 per cent of the total urban population. In the 1980s it was holding its position at the same level as in 1981. Whether it is going to remain stable at this relative size, or change in the future, depends on the addition of new urban centres and on the relative economic development in the Kathmandu Valley and in other regions of the country.

One of the factors that could impose some limits to urban growth is the physical environment. Since the city is located in a valley, there are inherent limits of available space and a resource base. The tremendous danger of air and water pollution may discourage any further physical development in the future. With the increase in urban population, the open space that used to separate Kathmandu and Patan (Lalitpur) does not exist any more. Kathmandu and Patan form a Twin Cities urban system with one single built-up area (Karan, 1973).

The inner cores of Kathmandu and Patan contain a high population density with compact housing (fig. 25). The density of some inner-city blocks in Kathmandu is as high as 1,200 persons per hectare (Khanal and Chitrakar, 1987: 4). The streets in the inner core are mere passageways between crowded buildings. There is a rigid social segregation, and wards are occupied by specific social or caste groups. In the centre of both Kathmandu and Patan stands the palace of former Malla kings. Brick-paved streets radiate from the palace, or Darbar Square. In close proximity to the palace lived high-ranking officials; traders, artisans, and craftsmen occupied the outer ring; and low-caste scavengers and sweepers lived in the dwellings beyond this area. In Kathmandu-Patan each neighbourhood, or "*tol,*" delineates a specific ethnic or occupational group living in the urban area. Although changes are constantly taking place, the above-mentioned spatial arrangement of the social classes in the inner core of the Twin Cities can still be observed (Karan and Bladen, 1982).

Surrounding the crowded, densely-built inner core lies an outer zone which was developed during the Rana rule between 1847 and 1950. The Rana families built numerous palaces with extensive grounds outside the inner city. Housing for servants and palace em-

Fig. 25 **Growth of Kathmandu**

ployees sprang up around the Rana palaces, and roads were built
to link the palaces with the city centre and with other palaces. These
roads attracted businesses as well as residential developments. Between 1950 and 1990 residential developments accelerated greatly,
filling most of the vacant land. The Rana palaces are now used for
public or institutional purposes such as schools, colleges, embassies,
hospitals, and government offices.

Beyond the outer zone lies the urban fringe of the Kathmandu-

194

Newly built houses on a hillside in a Kathmandu suburb

Patan Twin Cities. Until the 1970s this area was an open spacious belt with rural characteristics. During the last 20 years most of this rural area on both the eastern and western fringes of the Twin Cities has been absorbed by new housing developments. New housing construction has taken place in areas such as Baneshwar, Battisputali, Chabhil, Tahachal, and Kalimati without planning, zoning, or other land development regulations (Joshi, 1973; PADCO, 1986: 133). Over the years several proposals for land use regulations have been formulated to guide urban development in the Valley, but they have been largely ineffective.

Income levels and ethnic characteristics within the three zones of the city – inner core, outer city, and urban fringe – differ greatly.

195

Newar houses in Kathmandu

Families in the inner core consist of: (a) low-income, unskilled workers of various ethnic groups living in the worst housing and providing cheap labour and services for the core's commercial establishments; and (b) some upper and middle-class Newars, educated professionals, well-paid civil servants, businessmen, and semi-skilled wage earners. The outer city, dominated by the former Rana palaces, which are now in public or institutional use, are interspersed with the houses of respectable, status-conscious, upper and middle-class people of the Brahman and Kshatriya castes. The urban fringe is occupied mostly by imposing houses owned by wealthy Newars and Parbate groups. Some upper and middle-class professionals from the inner core are now moving to these new residential areas.

City sizes, primacy, and rank–size relationship

An index of the extent to which the urban settlements form a national system is provided by the rank–size distribution – that is, the populations of the urban centres ranked in the decreasing order of size and plotted on a graph that has logarithm of population on the ordinate and logarithm of rank on abscissa. A number of scholars, notably Zipf (1941), have argued that if the plot of observations in such a graph forms an approximate straight line with a slope of −1, an integrated national system of cities is indicated.

At roughly the same time that Zipf advanced the concept of rank–size regularity to describe the distribution of city sizes, Mark Jefferson (1939) introduced the concept of the "primate city." Primacy is present when the largest city is several times the population of the one that is second in rank. Later authors have applied the term to the whole distribution of cities of different sizes. Primacy, they say, exists when a stratum of small towns and cities is dominated by one or more very large cities, and there are fewer cities of intermediate size than would be expected from the rank–size rule.

Rank–size regularities in the distribution of city sizes are generally associated with economically advanced countries. Small developing countries such as Nepal exhibit primacy. The gradient of the regression line is steep in the case of Nepal, indicating the lack of medium and small-sized cities (fig. 26).

The changes in the urban rank hierarchy in Nepal indicate the rapid changes that are taking place in the distribution of population through migration and economic development in various regions. The addition of new urban centres from time to time has kept the middle and lower ranked centres in perpetual flux (table 25). Within the last four decades, only two cities – Biratnagar and Pokhara – have consistently moved upward in the ranks. In 1981 Lalitpur (Patan) dropped to third place, and Biratnagar took over in second place, rising from seventh place, in 1952–1954. Bhaktapur and Nepalganj dropped significantly from their third and fourth places in 1952–1954. In 1991 Bhaktapur was in eighth position and Nepalganj was in twelfth position. Pokhara became the fourth city in the rank hierarchy.

Kathmandu City, however, kept its primacy throughout these four decades. The relative size of Kathmandu in relation to the second and third-ranked cities remained stable until 1981 (P. Sharma, 1989: 55). In the 1980s its relative population size in relation to the second largest

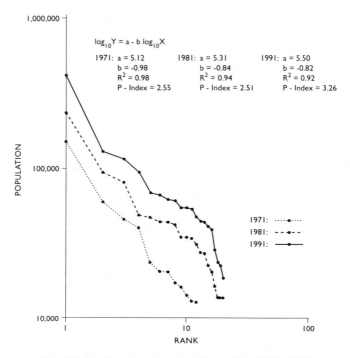

Fig. 26 **Rank order of urban hierarchy, 1971–1991**

city increased from 2.5 to 3.5 times. This indicates a 30 per cent increase in the level of primacy of Kathmandu City. Whether this is an indication of a transitional period in the economic development of the country (El-Shakhs, 1972: 30) or only over urbanization (Clark, 1983: 14), cannot be identified with certainty with the data available at this time.

Medium and small towns, and balanced regional development

The role of small and medium-sized towns in national development has received considerable attention. The case for the development of small towns and market centres has been made on the premise of the central place theory, which states that a hierarchically ordered and integrated system of settlements provides the most rational and efficient spatial system for the organization of population, economic activities, services, and marketing networks.

Small towns also play an important role in the agricultural and rural development of Nepal as effective and generative links between the larger towns and the rural hinterlands. There is a need for government investment in public services and infrastructure, and in programmes for expanding private enterprise, designed to stimulate and strengthen the economic and physical linkages between the market towns and rural areas. Development programmes for market towns that improve urban-rural linkages and strengthen regional marketing systems can make important contributions to the national development efforts in Nepal.

The ever-increasing pressure of population in the Middle Himalaya has resulted in a large-scale migration from the rural highlands to the rural lowlands. Small towns, which could become potential centres for the creation of off-farm employment for poor and marginal households, could become counter magnets to absorb some of the migrant population. Based on the circulation patterns in the country, a number of regional centres and growth points were identified for development as marketing and service centres (Karan and Iijima, 1983; Karan and Iijima, 1984). Nepal's Fourth Plan (1970–1975), Seventh Plan (1985–1090), and the current Eighth Plan (1992–1997) have emphasized the need to develop small towns as development service centres to link each region with higher-order towns as well as lower-order service centres. These official development policies in the five-year plans have not been implemented.

In Nepal small towns can perform an effective role in development if their growth is linked with economic strategies for increasing agricultural production and with operational programmes to ensure access for the poorest households to new opportunities for production, marketing, and employment. The role of small towns in bringing about balanced regional development will be limited until policies are developed to deal with structural problems such as monopolized marketing structures, unfavourable agricultural pricing, and with issues relating to access, control, and the participation of people in resource use (Blaikie, 1981).

Regional research is required to select those settlements for investment that perform important economic functions with growth potential and that can serve as strong linkages with their rural hinterlands. C. B. Shrestha (1973–1974) has made a major contribution to the understanding of the nature of market centres along the Kathmandu-Kodari road, or Arniko Rajmarga. He found that the ruggedness of the terrain and the significance of the locality with respect to long-distance trade often determined the number and order of the central places. In his study area covering 4,350 sq. km, the distribution of 33 different central places in five different orders were conditioned more by transportation than by the marketing principle. Blaikie's (1976; 1980) research in the mid-1970s in west-central Nepal revealed that the expansion of bureaucracy, increase in trade, and construction of highways were major factors in the growth of the market centres. Blaikie found that advantages from the growth of small towns in his study area were largely concentrated among the few entrenched merchant classes, and that the market towns were not able to transform the economic base of the surrounding rural area.

Research is also needed to understand fully the social and economic changes that result from expanding markets. Some of the changes can have an adverse impact on the poorest of rural households. The extension of roads in Nepal among the market towns has resulted in the growth of some towns in the tarai, and a decline of others in the Middle Mountains. In some areas the completion of roads which link towns and cities has led to the decline of local cottage and small-scale industries and increasing dependence on imports. Messerschmidt (1980) has noted the decline of Bandipur, an historic town, which resulted from the construction of the Kathmandu-Pokhara road (Prithvi Rajmarga), which bypassed the town. Bandipur lost its gateway function to the northern hinterland to Dumre on the Prithvi Rajmarga, and the new road also contributed to the demise of the textile/handicraft industry in Bandipur. Often the growth and expansion of market towns benefit the middle and upper-income groups, or outsiders, who have disposable income and investment capital, more than the local poor. Further research is needed to highlight the spatial, economic, and other impediments which must be taken into consideration in an operational strategy to enhance the effectiveness of small towns in the development of Nepal.

Aspects of urbanization and the environment

Generally speaking, there tends to be a strong association between large urban concentrations and environmental degradation. The marked spatial concentration of population and economic activity in a few large centres in Nepal have resulted in the more intense problems of human settlement and the environment (Bhattarai, 1988). Improvements in the urban environment and prospects for sustained development are possible with urban management policies that address specific problems such as air and water pollution, sanitation and housing, and the provision of essential social services such as education, health, and family planning, especially to the poor.

Access to a safe, piped water supply for drinking is a major problem in Kathmandu (Joshi and Shrestha, 1988). Even the chlorinated water of Kathmandu was found heavily contaminated with faecal material, due to the mixing of sewage and leaks in the water pipes (Sharma, 1989).

The Nepal Water Supply Corporation has received several loans from the International Development Association, the World Bank affiliate, to improve the water supply by installing a functional water distribution system in the capital. The Corporation has only two water treatment plants – one at Sundarijal and the other at Maharajganj – while the water is collected from a variety of physically separate sources. The problem is compounded by leaking sewers laid along the water mains. In addition, illegal connections and leaky old pipes account for as much as a 70 per cent water loss from some neighbourhood taps (Dixit, 1992). Despite enormous amounts of foreign aid expenditure on the Valley's drinking water supply, the situation has not improved because of managerial and political problems. In order to improve the water supply, the Corporation must strengthen the operation and maintenance capability, carefully monitor the rehabilitation of the urban water network, and involve the users in the management of water resources. To augment the Valley's water supply, there is a proposal to divert the flow of Melamchi Khola of Helambu, north-east of Kathmandu, through a 27-km-long tunnel into a storage reservoir at Sundarijal.

The main rivers of the Kathmandu Valley – the Bagmati and Vishnumati – also serve as a source of water for drinking, washing, bathing, and irrigation. The Bagmati also receives raw sewage from the metropolitan area, untreated effluents from industrial estates, hospital wastes, toxic chemicals and acid from carpet washing plants, pesticides and chemical fertilizers washed by rainwater from the fields, and the detritus of cremation. It is estimated that Kathmandu produces 150 tons of waste each day, nearly half of which is dumped into the river. About 4,000 persons in Kathmandu's inner city use the Vishnumati, mostly in the mornings, for their daily ablutions. With a winter-time flow of 2.04 cubic metres per second, the Bagmati is unable to cope with the effluents.

The Bagmati River water was relatively clean until recently, when it began to receive sewage from Kathmandu City. Today the Bagmati water is polluted by washings from the upstream carpet factories, from leachings from solid waste landfills, and from the faecal inflow from open sewage outlets even before it reaches Kathmandu's metropolitan area at Gokarna. An Italian firm, DISVI, which studied Bagmati water in 1988, found that the pollution levels rise considerably after the untreated waters of the Dhobi Khola, Tukucha, and Vishnumati, and the sewage from the Kathmandu-Patan Twin Cities drain into the river.

Industrial effluents are not treated in Nepal. The industries of Kathmandu, Patan, and Bhaktapur discharge significant amounts of toxic compounds into the river system. The Bansbari Shoe Factory, for example, discharges high concentrations of chromium directly into the Dhobi Khola (Khanal and Chitrakar, 1987: 5). Inadequate waste management is becoming a more visible problem in the urban centres of Nepal.

The large numbers of poorly maintained motor vehicles, unplanned growth, temperature inversion in the Valley during the winter months, and emissions from factories such as the cement plant (four km from the city centre), have contributed to the air pollution problem in the Kathmandu Valley. The Himal Cement plant at Chobar, built in 1974, emits five to six tons of dust each day, which could be prevented from being spewed into the valley atmosphere if emissions were controlled. The Himal Cement's silica dust, ash, and smoke is spread in a thin haze throughout the Valley and hugs the base of the surrounding mountains. The two Chinese-built brick and tile factories and many brick kiln chimneys that dot the valley use coal and firewood and produce smoke emissions into the air. The domestic use of traditional biomass fuels, which include firewood, animal dung, and crop residues, also produces smoke, which is a major source of air pollution.

Air pollution levels have increased as the average age of both public and private motor vehicles tends to be overextended and proper maintenance becomes more difficult. The number of vehicles has also increased four times during the last decade. In 1987, there were 13,460 cars and jeeps, 6,150 motorcycles, 4,510 buses and trucks, 900 power tillers and tractors, and 620 autorickshaws (Khanal and Chitrakar, 1987: 7). Many of these vehicles were poorly maintained and emitted excessive amounts of carbon, sulphur, and lead. The promotion of a mass transit system and regulations of emission standards may ease the air pollution problem. Apart from being more advantageous to the poor, mass transit is less energy-intensive and less polluting on a per passenger basis, and thus is more in keeping with sustainable development strategy.

A serious problem arising from urbanization in the Kathmandu Valley is the loss of agricultural land to urban use. The built-up area of the Kathmandu-Patan Twin Cities increased by 88 per cent between 1971 and 1981 (PADCO, 1986: 34). During this period the urban growth resulted in the loss of about 1,500 hectares of agricultural land. At this rate, no prime agricultural land will exist in the Valley in the year 2020. At present the conversion of agricultural land to urban use is profitable due to the high price of land on the urban fringe. But the conversion conceals other costs such as pollution, congestion, the loss of green space, and rising costs for urban management and services. The implementation of a land use plan for the Valley would help guide urbanization and preserve prime agricultural land.

In Nepal, environmental problems that were hardly understood in the 1960s and 1970s have become increasingly palpable in the 1990s in the wake of accelerating industrialization and urbanization. Water and air pollution insidiously harm the health and productivity of the urban residents. In the countryside population growth and poverty exert pressure on natural resources. This is in addition to pressure from the requirements of the construction industry in cities, as well as exports, all of which entail the rapid exploitation of forests at the same time that reafforestation efforts are slow. The fast thinning of forest cover in Nepal exemplifies the cumulative environmental decay. Nepal has enunciated an environmental policy to protect the environment and conserve natural resources for sustainable development. The importance given to this policy goal is exemplified by the establishment of ministries, departments, agencies, or councils to deal with environmental matters. But despite these high-level environmental offices, the policy instruments to achieve environmental goals remain largely equivocal, incoherent, and ineffective. This situation may be explained by an insufficient appreciation of the problem, and the conflict of interest among players in both the public and private sectors, and in the vested interest groups. While urbanization, population pressure, and poverty may be the proximate causes of environmental degradation, policy failures to formulate and implement appropriate environmental regulations are frequently the underlying cause. Closely related to environmental policies in Nepal are population policies that have not given much thought to the population-environment nexus as a concern. Even less well-defined is a human settlement policy, either in spatial or urbanization terms. A human settlement policy would integrate the physical structure of a city, town, or village with all human activity processes – residence, work, education, health, culture, and leisure – which support them. This would require policy instruments from all government ministries. If that were possible, the benefits to the environment of well-planned human settlements would undoubtedly be substantial.

8

Industrial development

The overall economic development of Nepal is primarily dependent on the success of its programmes in agriculture and forestry, but a pragmatic consideration of the development of an industrial sector also enters the scale of priorities. For Nepal, a country with limited resources and markets, the commitment to industrial growth and the nature of that commitment are important factors. The policy of balanced growth within the industrial sector has been articulated, but a viable development programme, which will implement the policy and result in real growth, has not been formulated.

During the first third of the twentieth century the Rana regime did little either to regulate or to promote industrial activity (Regmi, 1958: 162). The first step towards encouraging industry occurred in 1935 with the establishment of the Udyog Parishad (Development Board) to promote crafts and expedite the use of indigenous raw materials. The large-scale organization of industrial enterprise was facilitated for the first time with the Nepal Companies Act of 1936.

Subsequently, the first joint stock company – the Biratnagar Jute Mills – was incorporated by Indian entrepreneurs with a capital of Rs 1,500,000. The pre-war and wartime world market for jute was such that even with limited finances and relatively untrained labour, the Biratnagar Mills were almost immediately a financial success. An important element in the success of the mills was the favourable tax position in Nepal; unlike Indian producers, the Biratnagar Mills were exempt from taxation on capital equipment and supplies for seven years from the date of incorporation. The disruption of the jute economy in India as a result of Partition further enhanced the position of Nepalese enterprise.

While other joint stock ventures were floated during these years, only the Juddha Match Factory survived the initial stages of development. The post-war scarcity of essential goods on the Indian market encouraged a plethora of Nepalese manufacturing concerns to take advantage of the favourable conditions. During the period 1945–1946 to 1950–1951, 35 public companies were incorporated (Shrestha, 1967: 164). In many cases the concerns were liquidated before actually moving into production as the realities of the industrial process were explored. The growth and decline of early industrial establishments are summarized in table 26.

The liquidation represented a loss to the economy of capital resources that otherwise could have been productive in Nepal. The psychological effect on the public mind of failure as a deterrent to greater participation in capital investment was also a negative factor. Furthermore, the flight of Rana capital to Indian investment markets further diminished the potential for capital investment with Nepalese sources.

In 1951 the Companies Act was revised to provide for the establishment of private limited companies. As a result, the number of private limited companies increased markedly, although the majority of them were established with very modest authorized capital. In 1963 there were 92 private limited companies as compared with 18 public limited companies (Shrestha, 1967: 166–170). The 1966 edition of the US Department of Commerce's publication *Business Firms in Nepal* listed seven public limited companies and 72 private limited companies.

Nepal took a number of steps to stimulate industrial investment. In 1957 a statement of industrial policy established principles for the encouragement of private and foreign enterprise: suitable tax relief for new ventures and a repatriation of profits by foreign investors. The government also provided the necessary infrastructure to facilitate production: suitable labour legislation, the procurement of land, the provision of foreign exchange, tariff protection from foreign competition, power at the lowest possible rates, and raw materials at concessional prices (Nepal Trading Corporation, 1959: 118–120).

The Industrial Enterprises Act of 1961 was more explicit in offering a 10-year tax "holiday" on new industries, a 30 per cent allowance on foreign currency earned for importing capital goods, lumber for construction discounted at 15 per cent of the auction price, the allowance of foreign capitalists to withdraw 25 per cent of their investments in foreign exchange each year, and the repatriation of profits to 10 per cent each year. The document further promised that there would be no discrimination between Nepalese and foreign nationals or organizations if they cooperated with the terms of the Act (Industrial Promotion and Productivity Centre, 1961). In 1963 legislation was enacted that permitted foreign nationals to be full owners of enterprises in Nepal.

The Nepal Industrial Development Corporation (NIDC) was established in 1959 with a paid-up share capital of Rs 10 million ($1,335,000), funded entirely with American aid. NIDC was formed to assist technically and economically sound private enterprises, to provide credit facilities and guaranteed loans for individual concerns, to act as a consultant in training, market analysis, and credit investigations, to stimulate industrial activity by trading in shares and stocks of individual concerns, and to help establish new industrial concerns (International Cooperation Administration, 1958).

To ensure a standardization of products, the Industrial Development Board was established in 1960. The State Trading Corporation followed two years later as a semi-official agency to facilitate trade within the country and to oversee Nepalese trading problems in Calcutta.

To provide a favourable environment for the establishment of new industries, three industrial estates were inaugurated: Balaju, to the north-west of Kathmandu; Hetauda, in the mid-tarai; and Patan, south-east of Kathmandu. All three estates were established with foreign aid. The Balaju Estate, which began operations in 1961, was initially supported by financial aid from the United States, Switzerland, and New Zealand. It comprised a machine shop, wool spinning mill, furniture and soap factories, and a printing press, among other enterprises. The Hetauda Estate opened in 1965 with similar enterprises. The Patan Estate, financed primarily with Indian aid, produced plastics, textiles, furniture, storage batteries, and curios. The original conception of the Patan Estate was for small industries owned by home craftsmen since Patan has traditionally been a centre for family-organized enterprises.

In 1962 the Indo-Nepal Industrial Corporation Act was passed, establishing a new enterprise and a new relationship with the Birla industrial organization of India for the production of textiles and for other industrial and commercial enterprises. An official connection with the Birla group was designed to open up additional possibilities for industrial growth. Thus, the foundation was laid for a comprehensive approach to the process of stimulating industrial development. However, the policy did not provide all the requisite conditions for industrialization.

The desire for rapid industrial development and the perceived inability of the private sector to meet the goal of industrial growth adequately led to the emergence of public enterprises in Nepal. Between 1956 and 1985 the number of public enterprises grew from just one, prior to 1956, to 55 in 1985 (Kanesalingam, 1991). Of these, 25 were manufacturing businesses established between 1964 and 1985. The oldest public sector industrial enterprise – Raghupati Jute Mills, Ltd. – was established in 1946.

These public enterprises have been dominant in products such as sugar, cement, cigarettes, leather, agricultural tools, petroleum products, and all utilities. Their financial performance has been less than satisfactory (Pradhan, 1982). The return on capital employed was minus 2.6 per cent in 1984–1985. Because of poor financial performance, the government has been providing financial aid (equities, loans, and subsidies), which formed almost 13 per cent (Rs 1.8 billion) of the total development budget in 1988–1989. The failure of public enterprises to achieve the efficiency of the private sector has led to a growing demand for their privatization.

The government has promoted privatization, but there are very few foreign or domestic private entrepreneurs willing to take over existing public sector enterprises as they are. So far only a few public enterprises have been privatized. The Nepal Cheuri Ghee Industry was sold to the private sector in 1985–1986; the Nepal Orient Magnesite Company's ownership was transferred in 1987; and the Nepal Metal Company was sold to a lone individual in 1987. Because of legalities and other problems, efforts to privatize Royal Drug Ltd. (established with grants from international agencies), and the Janakpur Cigarette Factory and Birganj Sugar Factory (developed with Russian aid) failed. Due to the lack of a comprehensive privatization policy and lack of determination, the process of privatization has been slow in Nepal.

Industrial growth since 1950

Since 1950 numbers employed in manufacturing increased from 20,000 to 41,367 in 1972–1973, and to 161,736 in 1990–1991. Despite the significant growth in manufacturing, the contribution of the industrial

sector to Nepal's economy remains low. In 1974–1975 the manufacturing sector provided 4.2 per cent of the gross domestic product,
in 1984–1985 its share was 4.4 per cent, and in 1989–1990 it stood at
4.8 per cent. Limited domestic markets, the cumbersome licensing
and registration system, and excessive regulations and control have
acted as disincentives for private investment in Nepal's manufacturing sector.

Most manufacturing is of a small-scale or cottage nature: of the
2,387 manufacturing enterprises listed in the 1990–1991 *Annual Survey of Manufacturing Establishments*, less than 300 had fixed assets
worth more than Rs 500,000, or $15,000. More than half of these
enterprises were light industries such as carpet, rug, and furniture
manufacturers, or grain and sawmills. More than 25 per cent (567
in 1990–1991) made structural clay products such as bricks and
tiles. Intermediate and capital goods manufacturing activities have
made very limited progress in Nepal during the last 40 years. Light
consumer goods industries continue to dominate the structure of
manufacturing.

Geographical distribution of industries

The bulk of Nepal's manufacturing enterprises are located in the
Kathmandu area and in the eastern tarai (fig. 27). In 1990–1991
there were 2,387 manufacturing establishments employing 161,738
persons (Central Bureau of Statistics, 1992). Of these only about
400 units had investments of more than Rs 200,000 in machinery.
These larger-scale enterprises were concentrated in the Kathmandu
Valley, Hetauda, Birganj, Janakpur, Biratnagar, and Jhapa. Dhangarhi, Nepalganj, and Bhairawa in the western tarai had a few small
enterprises. Most of the industries in the tarai are close to the Indian
border. The proximity to domestic and Indian markets and the relatively superior infrastructure in the eastern tarai and Kathmandu
Valley are major locational determinants of manufacturing in Nepal.

The Birganj-Hetauda corridor in the eastern tarai and its extension into the Kathmandu Valley contains over three-quarters of
the nation's larger-scale manufacturing. Birganj has sugar, cigarette,
match, and metal works. Hetauda has timber and forest-based industries. Kathmandu has textiles, engineering, construction, and food
processing industries. Biratnagar, near the Indian border, has a number of food processing industries and textile and engineering works.
There is a cigarette factory in Janakpur, a sugar factory in Bhairawa,

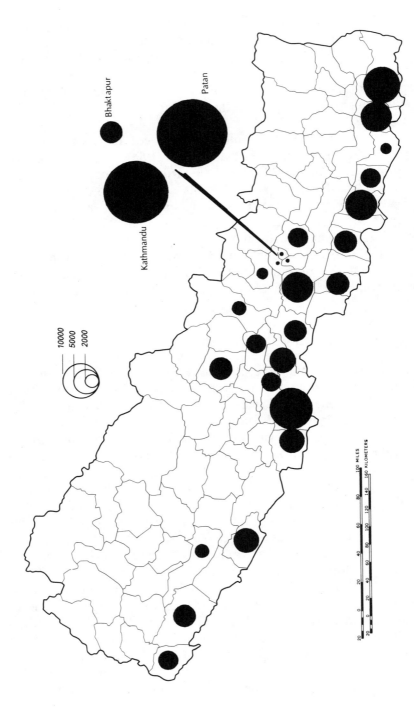

Fig. 27 **Growth of employment in manufacturing, 1981–1986**

210

and a match factory in Nepalganj. Birganj, Biratnagar, Janakpur, Bhairawa, and Nepalganj are located close to the Indian railheads, which provide easy access to Calcutta's seaport and the large Indian market.

The geographical pattern of the distribution of industries has not changed very much during the last 40 years despite Nepal's policy of promoting industries in other areas to bring about a more balanced regional development. Biratnagar, Birganj, Janakpur, and the Kathmandu area continue to dominate the industrial pattern as they did four decades ago. Only Hetauda, located at the junction of two major highways, has developed into a major industrial centre in recent decades.

Major industries

Nepal's most important modern industries include the manufacture of brick and tile, construction materials, and paper; the processing of food grains and vegetable oil extraction; sugar refining; and breweries. Nepal's traditional cottage industries such as basket making, the weaving of cotton fabrics, the manufacture of floor coverings, and ghee-making employ around 1 million workers. These cottage industries will be discussed later.

Cotton garments became Nepal's chief export item when Indian manufacturers redeployed operations to Nepal in 1985. To reduce the large influx of Indian workers – totalling around 60,000 in 1985 – the government instituted a registration policy for garment manufacturers. Within the textile sector, jute and cotton manufacturing are important; carpets became important in the late 1980s but recently their exports have declined. Saw milling, furniture-making and printing are major activities in the wood, paper, and allied industries. Among the mineral-based industries, nine organized units are significant: Himal Cement, Hetauda Cement, two other small cement production units in the private sector, the Agriculture and Lime Industry, the Godavari Marble Industry, the Iron Foundry, and the Orinol Magnesite and the Ganesh Lead industries.

Rice and oil mills dominate the food processing industry. Waste materials, especially husks from rice, wheat and maize, can be further processed to derive a number of other products. Small rice mills are based on the old technology, which results in inefficient milling and wastage.

An important segment of the food industry is fruit processing. A wide variety of fruits are grown in Nepal in each of the major geo-ecological zones of the country. Due to the perishability of fruit after harvesting, it is difficult to link all the fruit-growing areas in the mountains and in the tarai to a major fruit processing facility.

A new plant – Nepal Beverages and Food Products, Ltd. – a joint venture with the Kissan group of India, has been established to process fruits into squash, juice, jelly, and jams. The Sarlahi Fruit Processing plant commenced operations in 1985 with a capacity of 418 tons of processed fruit per year. The total fruit production in Nepal during the 1990s was estimated at about 460,000 tons, and there is considerable scope for expanding the fruit processing industry. There is also scope for the development of vegetable processing in Nepal.

Developing both fruit and vegetable processing would require a close collaboration with the grower, good technical management, a high degree of quality control and grading, entrepreneurial skills, and a knowledge of export market opportunities. The coordination of these skills and factors are the main constraints to the expansion of fruit and vegetable processing.

Potential for industrial development

The expansion of the industrial sector for increasing employment opportunities, generating economic growth, and achieving sustainable growth in the export sector has been an important aspect of Nepal's development policy. In recent years, the government has made a commitment to adopt a liberal, private sector oriented industrial investment policy. Over the years several institutions – such as the Ministry of Industry, the Industrial Promotion Division, the Foreign Investment Promotion Division, the Industrial Planning and Evaluation Division, the Department of Industry, and the Industrial Services Centre – were established to facilitate industrial growth.

The Ministry of Industry is the main agency responsible for the planning, monitoring, coordination, and policy formulation of Nepal's industrial development. The Industrial Promotion Division is principally concerned with policy matters relating to the development of small, medium, and large industries. The Foreign Investment Promotion Division is concerned exclusively with promoting foreign investment in the industrial sector. Apart from providing information to foreign entrepreneurs on prospects for industrial development, it brings together Nepalese and foreign entrepreneurs for joint ventures. This Division acts as a single window for the granting of various permits for starting industrial enterprises with foreign investment. The Industrial Planning and Evaluation Division has two branches – one for planning and evaluation and another concerned with technology transfers and manpower development.

The Department of Industry has the overall responsibility for the development and implementation of Nepal's industrial policy. It is responsible for the licensing, registration, and recommendations for facilities and incentives. An Industrial Promotion Board was constituted recently with representatives from the Ministry of Industry, the National Planning Commission, the Nepal Rastra Bank, the Ministry of Finance, the Ministry of Commerce, and other agencies. The Board functions as a coordinating link between the different agencies involved in industrial policy and administration. The Industrial Services Centre provides non-banking services for local and foreign entrepreneurs by disseminating information on investment opportunities, policies, and procedures for industrial investments. It also conducts techno-economic feasibility studies on industrial ventures.

The effectiveness of the industrial policy cannot be judged on the nature of the institutions established for industrial promotion, but on the ability of the institutions to attract and generate capital from within the economy or to attract external investment interests. As yet, this ability is an unknown quantity. It appears that excessive bureaucratic regulations and control, a cumbersome licensing and registration system, and management practices that hinder industrial growth have not been directly attacked by the government.

Capital formation and investment

The lack of a psychological climate in which risk capital is forthcoming for industrial investment is a major handicap for further industrialization. The relatively small aristocracy, including the multi-dimensional Rana family organization, as well as the royal family, have had their financial security rooted in land ownership, but also and more importantly, in investments abroad. These groups did not have the motivation or the resources to become holders of wealth in forms other than land. The extent to which land is still considered to be the prime store of wealth was demonstrated in a study of leadership on panchayats (Shumshere and Mohsin, 1967).

The reluctance of the wealthy classes to surrender some of their financial security for investment in the domestic economy is demonstrated by the pattern of sources of capital for industries. Most of the large-scale, privately owned industrial enterprises derive their capital from foreign sources, particularly India. It is clear that the industrial sector has not attracted large-scale Nepalese investments, but this must not be interpreted as indicating that resources that could be channelled into investments are not available. For example, the extent of deposits in foreign countries held by wealthy Nepalese is not known; however, the deposits are assumed to be "considerable." It is also well known that the traditional pattern of holding wealth in gems and gold is still widely practised, even among the most modern and "westernized" groups in Nepal.

In recent years nearly 58 per cent of industrial credit has been provided by commercial banks. The Nepal Industrial Development Corporation accounted for around 34 per cent of industrial loans sanctioned in 1985. Nearly 77 per cent of industrial loans in 1986 were made to manufacturing industries. Textiles, food, and chemical industries were the major recipients of industrial loans.

The problems of attracting foreign investments are great. Despite a liberal incentive programme and a source of cheap but unskilled labour, the flow of private foreign capital into the country has been meagre. The number of enterprises owned or partly owned by the government and by foreign investors is small. Many of the larger establishments are joint ventures; partners in the largest ventures generally come from India and other Asian countries. Large Indian concerns, such as the Birla organization (Asbestos and Cement Products, Ltd.) and Camphor and Allied Products (Nepal Resin and Turpentine Industries, Ltd.), have been active on the industrial scene. Additional Indian investments exist extensively on the level of single or small group entrepreneurships, but these are relatively small.

External assistance is an important contributor to the development of Nepalese industries. In the 1980s capital assistance, both in grants and loans, amounted to about $180 million annually. The major bilateral aid donors are Australia, Canada, China, Germany, India, Japan, Kuwait, Saudi Arabia, Switzerland, the United Kingdom, and the United States. The principal multilateral sources include the World Bank, the Asian Development Bank, the European Community, the International Fund for Agricultural Development, and the Organization of Petroleum Exporting Countries Fund, as well as a number of United Nations agencies.

An assessment of the contribution of these bilateral and multilateral agencies to the progress of industry in Nepal reveals an unsatisfactory linkage of many industrial projects with broader national development objectives. In general, emphasis has not yet been placed on developing the capabilities of the public and private institutions responsible for small-scale industrial development, particularly in the rural areas; on upgrading the quality of industrial products; on providing industrial support and information services; on improving credit facilities and incentives; and on promoting import substitutions and export opportunities. Support for these types of activity, particularly in the Middle Mountain region, is particularly desirable in external assistance programmes.

The problem of stimulating capital formation will not be solved easily. Until the isolated areas of the interior can be opened to regular trade traffic, the expansion of markets will be limited. Furthermore, the geographic problems, which will not be solved readily, dictate that the pattern of concentration of industrial investments in the tarai will continue, with an inevitable market orientation towards India rather than towards Nepal. The lack of a skilled labour pool increases the initial cost, since training must be provided before efficient production can be maintained. The history of business failures in the past certainly has had a psychological impact, and some measures must be taken to make investments more attractive than holding wealth in traditional forms. For the foreseeable future, investment resources will probably be generated mostly from the government and foreign private aid sources.

Resources and labour

The natural endowment of the country has been discussed in chapter 2. Certainly the full range of Nepal's resources has not been completely explored, and much could be gained from a full exploitation of the potential resources. Nevertheless, within the limits of national boundaries and the limits imposed by topography, the resource development of much of the country will be difficult for decades to come. It is conceivable that in the future technological advances will make it economically feasible to exploit some mineral resources which are now locked in inaccessible areas, but such exploitation cannot form the foundation for current economic development.

As a result of these factors, the resource base of industrialization will continue to be in agriculture and forestry. The expansion of the industrial possibilities will be tied in closely with an expansion in agricultural productivity, particularly in the western tarai areas, the central tarai, and the Pokhara Valley. In the latter case, the Sunauli-Pokhara Road provides a market outlet for medium-altitude agricultural production and could provide an opportunity for expansion of the food processing industry.

The expansion and improvement of agricultural processing can help use Nepal's resources more efficiently and raise the domestic value added. For example, diffusion of the rice-milling technology could raise the recovery rate by 5 per cent. In the absence of a domestic mill within economic distance, part of the sugar output in central Nepal is exported to mills in India. Excellent fruit is grown in the country, but part of it goes to waste as a consequence of the poor performance of the fruit processing industry (low manufacturing standards, marketing, and transport problems). In the absence of a sufficient domestic milling capacity, some 30,000 tons of raw jute are exported each year. Most tanned hides are exported, while at the same time much of the footwear is imported and the domestic shoe production capacity is underutilized.

The long-range development of the forestry potential will depend on the implementation of sound principles of forest management practices. The development of forest products industries beyond current levels will therefore be minimal and slow for the immediate future. Even though the scarcity of wood resources inhibits the further growth of the wood products industry, increased production of parquet blocks for export appears feasible.

Nepal does possess one great asset for industrial expansion – its relatively large labour force, arising from both its population and its economy, which are underutilized. The size of the labour force or economically active population is about half the population, which is estimated at 9.6 million, and is based on projected statistics pertaining to the structure of the labour force in Nepal's Seventh Plan, 1985–1990. Only 3.30 per cent of the economically active population is engaged in industry, and only 3.8 per cent is employed in the services sector.

During the past four decades the distribution of the labour force has changed very little in Nepal. The 1952–1954 census listed 3.3 per cent employed in manufacturing, reflecting little change in its structure. Nepal's excessive dependence on agriculture for employment has continued over the decades. A major obstacle to the absorption of the labour force in the manufacturing industry is the low level of literacy and the shortage of qualified personnel.

Although primary school enrolment in the 6 to 10-year-old age group had risen to 78 per cent by 1984, the overall literacy rate was estimated in 1991 to be about 39 per cent. The demand for engineering personnel (all levels) during the Seventh Plan period (1985–1990) was estimated to be 7,880 persons, of which the country could supply only 4,800. In the 1980s only about 6 per cent of university students took courses in agriculture or engineering related subjects. Unemployment among university graduates is well over 10 per cent. There is also a shortage of facilities for medium and basic-level vocational training.

Some Nepalese industries, especially the garment industry, have to rely on skilled immigrant labour from India. A significant aspect of the labour profile is the predominance of Indian workers in the industrial sector. The proximity of the industrial establishments in Biratnagar to the Indian border town of Jogbani makes daily crossings of the border the rule rather than the exception (fig. 28).

Earlier studies of mobility among agricultural workers have revealed that as much as 40 per cent of the labour in the agricultural sector may be surplus (Ministry of Economic Planning, 1967). This pool of labour can be tapped for the expansion of the industrial sector. The distribution of surplus labour has significant implications for the location of any industrial activity. A field study in the tarai revealed that workers who are moving to areas where industrial jobs are available are uneducated and untrained. The majority of these migrants indicated their intention to return to their agricultural employment when the construction projects on which they were working were completed. In short, a large segment of the labour force as it exists now is not yet committed to the idea of non-agricultural employment.

Another element in the process of the all-round development of Nepalese society is the integration of women into manufacturing activities. Female employment in the manufacturing sector is predominantly found in the textile and food industries. Even in these industries, however, women are underrepresented when compared with other countries. It is clear that the majority of women are unskilled despite the faster growth rates recorded by female, rather than male, participation in manufacturing and education in recent years. Special programmes designed for women could be linked more intensively to the needs of the industrial sector. Also, an effective enforcement of equal opportunity legislation could lead to a higher percentage of women participating in manufacturing activities.

A review of the limited data suggests that the expansion of indus-

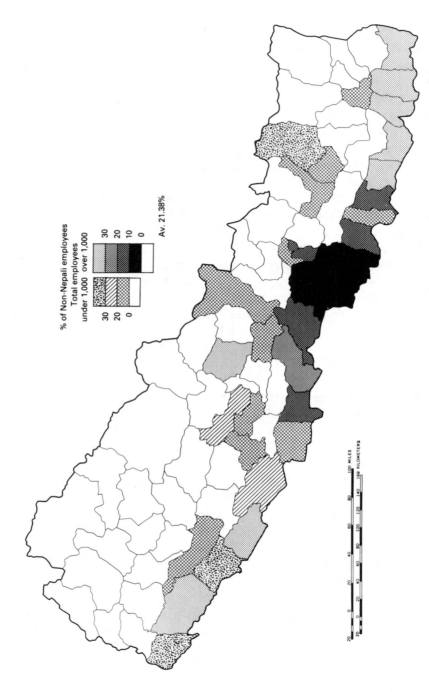

% of Non-Nepali employees
Total employees
under 1,000 over 1,000

30
20
10
0

30
20
0

Av. 21.38%

Fig. 28 **Non-Nepalese employees in manufacturing, 1981**

20 0 20 40 60 80 100 120 MILES

20 0 20 40 60 80 100 120 140 160 KILOMETERS

try will not depend solely on the process of capital accumulation, resources, and labour. The continued and expanding access to markets in India and other countries will be of the utmost importance. A second requisite to accompany the expansion of employment opportunities will be the extension of educational opportunities at all levels.

Energy resources

Energy is essential for industrial development. Nepal's major renewable energy resource is water. Nepal has frequently been compared to Switzerland in its potential for hydropower resources. However, the capacity of the rivers, especially the great transverse rivers, has yet to be fully assessed. General estimates of the potential for power development have been made over the years. Informal estimates range as high as 83 million kw. In 1962 a report based on a survey of selected rivers placed the hydroelectric potential capacity in excess of 1.5 million kw (Scharff and Leerberger, 1962: 4–10). In 1991 the exploitable hydropotential for Nepal was estimated to be 144 twh/year (Weller, 1991: 93–6). These figures should be considered as estimates of potential capacity and not of proven capacity or economic feasibility.

Despite the large potential, Nepal is heavily reliant on imported non-renewable sources of power, such as oil and kerosene. The country is rapidly destroying its forests for firewood. Hydropower can be a key factor in Nepal's development. Aside from forming the basis for industrial growth, the development of hydropower could be a major industry in itself. The mountainous topography provides the opportunity to construct a series of high dams that could form multi-purpose storage reservoirs to augment dry-season flows. In addition, the peak flooding in downstream reaches caused by the monsoon rains could be substantially reduced.

Nepal has so far harnessed only 161 MW, representing about 0.2 per cent of its estimated hydropower potential (C. K. Sharma, 1989: 83). Projects which have been completed are: Sun Kosi, 10.5 mw, Trisuli, 21 mw, Kulekhani-I, 60 mw, Devighat, 14.1 mw, Gandak (on an irrigation canal), 15 mw, and Kulekhani-II, 32 mw. Of all the hydro projects in operation, only Kulekhani-I has a storage element; the others are all run-of-river types. Other schemes, such as the 69 mw Marsyandi project and the 5.1 mw Andihi Khola project, are also run-of-river developments (fig. 6).

219

Transformer substation in Patan, Kathmandu Valley (courtesy K. Tachibana)

Feasibility studies indicate that relatively low-cost hydropower could be generated from many projects in Nepal. Energy generated could be connected with the national grids of neighbouring countries for the supply of energy. In this connection, the potential for selling power to India could generate additional revenue for Nepal, which could develop joint projects with India to harness the hydropower resources (Upreti, 1993). While it is clear that hydropower is one of the great natural resources of Nepal, it is also clear that the extensive exploitation of this resource would require a capital investment far beyond the present conceivable sources. However, a long-range investment in the power sector for industrial purposes offers the potential for expanded employment, but the dimension of that potential is unknown.

Foreign trade and industrialization

In addition to capital, labour, and energy, the absence of an efficient transportation system is perhaps one of the major constraints on the growth of Nepalese manufacturing. Movement and transport patterns are discussed in the following chapter. A related matter concerns the market for manufactured goods. Although most of the manufacturing in Nepal is domestic-demand oriented, a large proportion is also exported. However, the export structure – consisting of textiles, garments, and a small range of manufactured products – is not diversified. The scope for export diversification is small and Nepalese exporters have not benefited from the relatively unrestricted trade policy that India has adopted vis-à-vis Nepal. Nepal usually has a very large deficit in the balance of manufacturing trade.

There exists a very high level of import dependence – industrial policies have not yet sufficiently exploited the scope for import substitutions. Competitive import substitutions can contribute toward the development of a better balance in the regional distribution of large and medium-scale enterprises, but the crucial constraint in this respect is once again the relatively weak infrastructural support for manufacturing enterprises outside the eastern tarai and the Kathmandu Valley.

India remains Nepal's main trading partner, but a significantly larger proportion of Nepalese manufactured imports are obtained from India than the proportion of Nepalese exports to India. India's share in Nepal's manufactured exports – about 30 per cent in recent years – is considerably lower than its share in total Nepalese exports. The main manufactured goods purchased by India from Nepal consist of jute products, polished rice, and timber. Major textile exports are destined for the developed market economies, but the expansion of textile exports is restricted by the operations of the multi-fibre agreement. The United States decided to impose quota restrictions on textile imports from Nepal in 1986.

Entrepreneurial resources

The absence of entrepreneurial and technical skills for modern industries is a major constraint on development. During the period of the Rana rule, the encouragement of activity that could conceivably draw economic power away from the regime was not encouraged. It was only during the trend towards liberalization in the 1930s that any scope was given for extensive local participation or entrepreneurship in economic activity aside from trade. It has been pointed out that entrepreneurs are essential to the creation of new patterns and traditions as a necessary concomitant for economic progress (Schumpeter, 1961).

Nepal has yet to develop its own indigenous entrepreneurial insti-

Machine workshop in Patan

tutions. Limited commercial entrepreneurial activity has existed in Nepal for many decades. Even in remote areas, often several day's journey from sources of supply, shops that deal in manufactured necessities have been engaged in trading for generations. In a sense, the talukdar and other revenue agents have acted as entrepreneurs in the agricultural sector. Nepalese traders have wandered beyond Nepal's borders, primarily as intermediaries. However, these activities have remained essentially small-scale and basically non-innovative, hardly fitting the description of the modern entrepreneur.

Before the palace evolution of 1950, large-scale entrepreneurial activity was in the trading sector and largely in the hands of foreigners, primarily the Indian Marwaris from Calcutta. As much as 90 per cent of trade was controlled by Indians. At this time, there were no taxes or other means of governmental control. This means that profits were returned to India and Indian interests continued to dominate the scene, thus failing to develop any tradition of reinvestment in Nepal or to create a reserve of capital from which resources for further investment in Nepal could be drawn.

The first opportunity for industrial entrepreneurship was provided in 1936 with the enactment of the Nepal Companies Act, which established the framework for the incorporation of public joint stock companies. Almost immediately a joint stock company was formed by the Chamaria group of the Marwaris of Calcutta for the development of the Biratnagar Jute Mills. Under the Companies Act, industries were exempt from export, income, or other taxes. Abnormal wartime shortages, which increased demand, in addition to the favourable government concessions, ensured the financial success of the mills, and most of the profits on the investment were returned to India.

The extent to which the development of entrepreneurial talent and activity has occurred among the Nepalese is not known. Even now, it appears that a significant proportion of business firms, especially in the tarai, are financed and managed by Indians or by agencies based in India. It is logical to assume, therefore, that there is a considerable drain on resources back into India, but most importantly, that a portion of the entrepreneurial function is still carried on by outsiders.

The development of local entrepreneurial talent and initiative has been slow for a number of reasons. Ethnic or traditional reluctance to engage in risk ventures has limited the flow of possible investment resources or has failed to overcome traditional values placed on land as the investment of choice. Much of the potential capital controlled by the Rana family was deliberately invested in India as a hedge against the day when political circumstances would threaten their economic security.

The lack of readily available credit facilities has made it imperative that a potential entrepreneur have access to other resources. Few non-Rana Nepalese had external contacts before the Revolution, and those who do so today are still relatively few. The lack of adequate governmental supervision of existing firms, particularly public limited companies, has in the past resulted in the temptation to take unguarded risks. This has frequently resulted in failure, thus creating the general impression that entering into such ventures carries grave and unwarranted hazards. The very paucity of entrepreneurial talent, the reluctance to enter into any venture without a prior demonstration of success (regardless of its soundness), seems to characterize the economic history of Nepal.

The time when entrepreneurial activity in Nepal becomes self generating is yet to come. Here, as in other sectors, the dependence on Indian talent has bridged the difficult transitional period, but

unless more Nepalese are willing to take the risks involved in entrepreneurial activity, Nepal's ability to become entrepreneurially self-
sufficient will be limited.

Recent industrial policy

Nepal completed a major review of its industrial policy during 1986–
1987. The new policy simplifies registration procedures, emphasizes
domestic resource-based industries, and extends incentives to export-
oriented industries. The government is particularly keen on promoting foreign collaboration and has launched a major privatization
initiative. The private purchase of the shares of public enterprises
selected for investment has been very limited and the privatization
initiative of the government appears to have stalled. This is partly
due to the fact that despite substantial increments in capital, profit-
ability levels within public manufacturing enterprises have remained
low.

Foreign investments in Nepalese manufacturing concerns are very
limited. In 1986–1987 there was a significant expansion of Chinese
participation. A rubber tire project worth $11.4 million was estab-
lished with Chinese financing. Substantial Chinese financial and technical assistance paved the way for the opening of Nepal's largest
paper mill – the Brikuti Mill – which provides 15 per cent of the
domestic demand for paper. China also provided financing for the
extension of the publicly-owned Himal Cement plant in 1986–1987. It
is hoped that the liberal, private-sector oriented industrial policy
statement in the Eighth Plan, 1992–1997 will increase the inflow of
direct investments from India and other countries.

Cottage industry and handicrafts

Nepal has a proud tradition of handicraft skills. Artisans of artistic
and decorative goods such as statues, bells, and other temple adorn-
ments maintained such a high degree of skill and aesthetic value that
such items were traded far beyond the borders of the country. These
activities were essentially highly skilled crafts, practised at the local
level with little attention to the institutionalization of the process.
Production in the far-flung mountain villages, which had to provide
their own necessities, involved traditional technology.

The isolation and stagnation of ideas, coupled with the tendency of
the inhabitants living close to the Indian border to depend on the

Indian market for goods, stifled technological advances which might have occurred through the normal process of diffusion. The seeds for the ultimate demise of a strong Nepalese textile industry were sown in the nineteenth century with the decline of Newari skills. The Anglo-Nepali trade treaty of 1923, which provided for a policy of free trade, dealt a severe blow to the craft and cottage industries.

The attempt to return hand-made goods to a position of respectability began before the Revolution. In the early phases of post-Revolution development planning, handicrafts were promoted. One of the earliest development projects was the establishment of a training centre for handicrafts in Kathmandu, with aid from the Ford Foundation (Acharya, 1984). However, the early emphasis on crafts per se was later shifted to the basic manual skills, which in some cases did not prove to be useful or realistic considering the limitations of employment opportunities. The impact of training in the cottage crafts has thus been minimal.

Cottage industries account for a significant proportion of the national income. These have recently been defined as manufacturing establishments with a fixed investment not exceeding Rs 500,000, and an annual turnover not exceeding Rs 2 million; in the case of units relying on imported raw material, the turnover ceiling is set at Rs 1 million. Cottage industries are mainly involved in food processing; cereal and oil milling and ghee (clarified butter)-making are major activities. Cottage industry production for the market consists mainly of textiles (cotton fabrics, floor coverings) and bamboo products. There is a trend towards cereal and oil milling by special mechanized units. Nepal's traditional cottage industries employ an estimated one million workers.

Ownership in cottage industries is virtually always private in the form of either a private firm, or a private limited or partnership company. In the first nine months of 1990–1991, 1,112 cottage and small industries were registered with the Department of Cottage Industry, with a total investment of Rs 122.62 million. Of these, 964 were private firms, 43 were private limited companies, and 132 were partnership firms (Central Bureau of Statistics, 1992). These figures do not cover certain specified categories which need not be registered by the owners.

Among the main categories of cottage and small-scale industries registered with the Department were polyester hosiery, woollen yarn, metallic utensils, food processing, cotton textiles, electrical appliances, stationeries, paints, bricks, tiles, stone and concrete, wax can-

Newar youth weaving in a house, Kathmandu Valley (courtesy M. Tamura)

dles, and synthetic footwear units. Among these units nylon and poly-ester hosiery, carpet-making, and units that produced basic-needs type commodities were most prominent. Among the cottage indus-trial units, hand-knitted woollen carpets and handicrafts were until recently the two leading items which contributed heavily to export earnings.

The development of cottage and small industries is essential in creating employment opportunities. A vigorous attempt to develop and expand cottage and village industries by utilizing traditional skills

Textile mill in Hetauda industrial estate (courtesy K. Inoue)

and local resources could create more employment opportunities. Export-oriented industries, such as woollen products and metal curios, could earn a significant amount of foreign exchange and also provide widespread employment opportunities. The low capital requirement is an attractive feature of cottage industries, which makes it important in any strategy for the alleviation of poverty in Nepal.

In addition, with a per capita cultivated land of only about 0.2 hectares, farming does not provide full employment to the entire rural labour force. Cottage industries and other nonfarm activities can play a very important role in augmenting the income from farming for the marginal and landless farmers. The rural poor are expected to benefit a great deal from the expansion of cottage industries (International Labour Office, 1986).

9

Transport, trade, and communication patterns

Land transportation in Nepal is handicapped by the hilly and mountainous terrain. In looking at the existing transport facilities the most significant fact that emerges is that there are few other independent nations in the world with a density of 2.68 km of road per 100 sq. km of land. Nepal has 18.50 million people and a road network of 7,330 km, of which only 2,958 km are paved (Ministry of Works and Transport, 1992). The meagre road transport facilities are supplemented by a few kilometres of railroads and by air transport (fig. 29).

Role of trails and porters

The low density of motorable roads in relation to the surface area or population has now begun to change. Historically, all transport has been by porters, pack animals, and bullock carts. The porters are generally subsistence farmers – men and women mired in mostly rural poverty. With underemployment endemic, the peasants have few means of earning cash other than by bearing loaded wickerwork baskets up and down mountain trails: oil and salt for the village merchant, pipes and tin roofing for development projects, firewood for hill markets, fodder for cattle, provisions for trekking parties, and mountaineering gear for expeditions. Farmers from isolated parts of the country also make annual treks down to the nearest roadhead to buy a year's supply of salt, calico, and cooking oil.

A porter carries baskets that weigh 85 kg or more (Rimal, 1988: 12). The basket is balanced on the back, and people of the Middle Mountains use a strap across the forehead to take most of the weight.

228

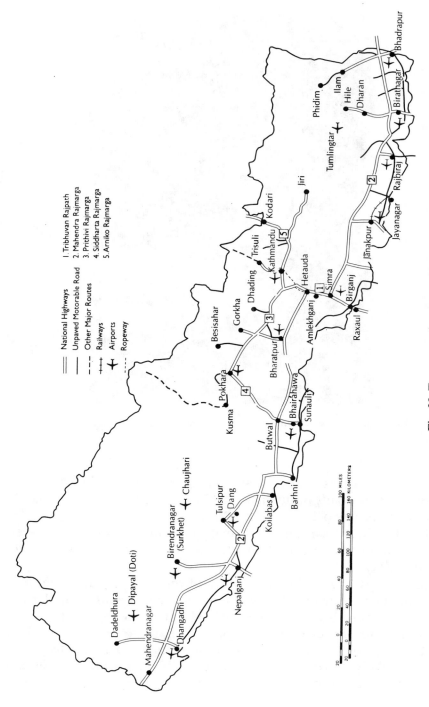

Fig. 29 **Transportation network**

National Highways
Unpaved Motorable Road
Other Major Routes
Railways
Airports
Ropeway

1. Tribhuvan Rajpath
2. Mahendra Rajmarga
3. Prithivi Rajmarga
4. Siddharta Rajmarga
5. Arniko Rajmarga

229

Porters from the Middle Mountain area carrying loads in the tarai (courtesy M. Tamura)

The Tibetans use shoulder-straps on their baskets, while the tarai people balance loads on their heads. The Newars of the Kathmandu Valley balance two baskets on a thick bamboo shoulder-pole. Increasingly, Sherpa sardars (trek managers) and porters can be seen carrying frame backpacks bought from or left behind by foreign trekkers or climbers.

The narrow mountain trails are interrupted by short breathers, when the porter slips a thick wooden cane, called a *taken*, under the basket and leans back to make a tripod out of the legs and cane. If the trail passes through a prosperous region, there will be a *chautara* – with a rock platform to place the basket on, a *pipal* tree that whispers in the slightest breeze to provide shade, and a diverted stream nearby for a quick drink. But the rest stop cannot last too long; it is time for the porter to heave the load and push off for the high pass.

The International Labour Organization in 1967 recommended 55 kg as the limit for loads being "manually transported" by an adult male. But there are wide variations that allow men to carry loads ranging from 56 kg in Mexico to 80 kg in China and 90 kg in Bangladesh and Pakistan. Dock-workers in India have a limit of 100 kg. But unlike the dock-worker, who leaves loads intermittently, a Nepali porter labours for hours at a time for days on end.

It costs the local merchants in central Nepal Rs 80 per day per porter to carry an 85-kg load of provisions. At the tourists' staging point of Pokhara, trekking agencies might pay as little as Rs 60 daily, while individual tourists pay anywhere from Rs 80 to 100. In the Arun Valley of east Nepal, the average is Rs 50 a day. During the off season, the prices are lower all over the country.

Some mountain trails are very crowded; the traffic moving on them is impressive. For example, on the trails along the Kali Gandaki, an average of more than 1,000 porters pass per day. The trails in the northern part of Nepal are still major modes of local transportation since this part of the country is not yet linked with the modern highways. Major interregional trails run east to west with the Kathmandu Valley as the focal point of these routes.

Traditionally, the network of trails was very dense in the eastern and central parts of the country, and the density was lowest in western Nepal. Until the 1950s the density of the trail network was related to population density, with the densely populated regions having the larger number of trails. These trails are supported by suspension bridges. In 1979 there were 83 suspension bridges; since then the number of suspension bridges has increased.

The importance of the trails has declined for the movement of goods and the population between the tarai and the lower Middle Mountains, where roads have replaced the traditional trails. But the trails are still an important mode of transportation between the Middle Mountains and the Great Himalaya. At the local level in the mountains, the trails play an important role in transportation.

Nepal's development efforts during the last 40 years have focused on the building of highways to link population centres. The transport of bulk goods is much easier on the roads, and the national economy has benefited immensely from road construction. For the microeconomy of the mountain villages, however, the highways have been at best a mixed blessing. Very often, income that was spread rather

Canoes crossing the Rapti River (courtesy Z. Tamura)

widely among mountain porters – all of them poor – is now shared with the urban businessmen, who run the buses, trucks, and jeeps.

Motorable roads

Nepal did not start building motorable roads outside the Kathmandu Valley until 1953–1955. The first roads were built in the tarai and inside the Kathmandu Valley. With the help of the Indian Army, the 192-km Tribhuvan Rajpath from Bhainse to Kathmandu was opened in 1956. Two other roads were built during this period: one by the British Army from Biratnagar to Dharan, and the other by US AID in the Rapti Valley from Hetauda to Narayanghat.

Among other roads that were built was the 114-km Arniko Rajmarga (constructed by China), which connected Kathmandu with Kodari on the Chinese border. The 180-km Siddhartha Rajmarga (built by India) connected the Pokhara Valley with Sunauli on the Indian border. The 200-km Prithivi Rajmarga (built by China) links Kathmandu with Pokhara. Mahendra Rajmarga, the 1,050-km east-west highway (built with assistance from UK, Russia, and India) runs mostly along the tarai and the Siwalik Range.

These main arterial roads, traversing the country from north to south and from east to west, centred on Kathmandu to connect India and China, and the roads connecting the regional headquarters to the capital form the backbone of the highway network in Nepal. The construction of these highways has barely reduced the friction of distance for the country as a whole (Stoddard, 1976: 1–9).

Feeder roads connect district headquarters to the main highways and play an important role in regional development. Out of 75 district centres, at present only 51 connect with the main highways. District roads connect one or more villages to the nearest market and provide access to the main distributor roads (Rajmarga, or feeder roads) in the network. They carry little through traffic. Nearly 35 per cent of the population of Nepal, living mostly in the mountains, has no direct vehicular access to the road network.

With the assistance of donor agencies, who provide periodic maintenance and rehabilitation, the reconstruction of the road network is being carried out, but adequate resources are not available for routine maintenance, the stabilization of slip areas, embankment repairs, and the river-training works. On an average, the Rajmargas (national highways) are closed to traffic during each monsoon for periods ranging from one to four days. Large sections of the network have a high risk of premature failure due to a combination of adverse climatic and geological conditions. While the construction of new roads has received considerable support from bilateral and multilateral donor agencies, the basic maintenance (routine and periodic repairs) has been neglected. Road maintenance, particularly emergency maintenance, is a relatively high-cost operation. Increased donor support for maintenance of the network is needed.

There is a dearth of reliable traffic data on the road network, but field observations indicate that the most heavily used arterial route – the Kathmandu-Naubise section of the Tribhuvan Rajpath – has an average daily traffic flow of nearly 1,600 vehicles approaching Kathmandu. Key links in the network, such as the Narayanghat-Mugling Road and the Arniko Rajmarga, have estimated annual average daily traffic flow levels of 900 and 350 respectively. These are low levels of traffic for the main arterial links in a national network.

The prediction of traffic growth rates, and hence the future use of the network, is also difficult in the absence of reliable data. However, given the low level of economic activity in the country, it is unlikely to change substantially in the near future. As large sections of the network are relatively underused, it will be difficult to justify economically the high levels of road maintenance cost. A reallocation of funds from new construction to maintenance is clearly indicated, but with nearly 35 per cent of the population having no direct vehicular access to the network, a decision to halt new construction further would be politically unacceptable.

Adequate maintenance of Nepal's road network is not entirely dependent on increased funding. The provision of additional funds must be accompanied by a major increase in the absorptive capacity of the government, which involves improvement in the institutional structure, in maintenance strategy, and in management and operations.

It is also important to note that roads of themselves do not produce development. Roads may be one of several factors needed for the development process, but the potential for economic improvement must already exist in the region, as the studies of the impact of the Tribhuvan Highway (Shrestha, 1980) and Siddharta Highway (Schroeder and Sisler, 1970) illustrate. If this is not the case, then the road may have the reverse effect of providing a ready means for people to leave the area. Furthermore, when the potential for growth exists, the greatest stimulus to development occurs with the provision of a basic means of vehicular access.

Railways

There are two railways in Nepal, all narrow-gauge (2'6") lines. The first railway line was constructed in 1927 from Raxaul in India to Birganj and Amlekhganj, which covers a distance of 47 km. The other line runs from Jayanagar in India to Janakpur, a distance of 29 km. The Amlekhganj to Raxaul railway has been closed to passenger traffic for the last few years but operates to carry cargo only from Raxaul to Birganj.

India is both a major source of traffic moving into Nepal and a principal market for exports. Within India, the railways are now the principal transport media, and indications are that they will remain so for many years. For this reason, the Indian Railways, and connections to them, are of importance to Nepal. It is significant that the most traffic across the Nepal-India border is close to the principal Indian railheads.

Between 1927 and 1957 the Raxaul-Birganj-Amlekhganj railway

Customs office on the Nepal-India border in Biratnagar (courtesy K. Inoue)

was part of the principal avenue of commerce between India and the Kathmandu Valley and the adjoining areas in Nepal. During this period it was a profitable undertaking, even though the track and equipment were never properly maintained and expenses were high. Following the opening of the Tribhuvan Rajpath into Kathmandu in 1956 and the paving of the road from Birganj to Amlekhganj in 1962, rail traffic and revenues fell sharply.

At Raxaul all traffic must be transshipped to and from the metre-gauge Indian Railways. Again, at Birganj, all cars are unloaded for inspection by Nepal customs, then reloaded. Goods destined for Kathmandu and the interior of Nepal must be transshipped again at Amlekhganj to trucks for further movement. Through handling or freight billing is not offered. Each shipper must make arrangements for local labour, for loading and unloading, for transshipment, and with all connecting carriers. At each handling point, some part of the shipment "disappears," and some is damaged or spoiled. The movement is slow, and long delays are common.

With the opening of the Tribhuvan Highway to Kathmandu, through truck movements became possible on a single-freight billing document, without the two intermediate handlings and with smaller in-transit losses. The savings and advantages were immediately obvious to all shippers. As a result, the Raxaul-Birganj-Amlekhganj railway has drifted into increasing disuse and disrepair.

The Jayanagar-Janakpur railway was built in the 1930s to move timber from the tarai region north of Janakpur to the Indian Railway at Jayanagar. When all of the timber in the area had been cut, the line was given to the government for continued operation. Its principal sources of traffic and revenue are the religious pilgrimages from India to the Hindu shrine at Janakpur. Freight has not been a dominant factor in this railway's operation since its discontinuance as a lumbering line. Although the line has never been well maintained, it has not fallen into complete disrepair as has the Raxaul-Amlekhganj railway. The line has been extended north of Janakpur to Bijalpur.

All freight must be transshipped to and from the metre-gauge Indian Railways at Jayanagar. Nepal customs inspection is at the far end of the line in Janakpur. Almost all traffic is destined for Janakpur and has to be off-loaded there, so this customs inspection has posed no additional problems or expense.

Railways have remained very much underdeveloped in Nepal. However, there is a possibility of converting the existing railway line from Janakpur to Jayanagar to broad gauge, and of linking it with Muzzafarpur, a major railway junction in Bihar, India. There is also the possibility of developing a railway network in the tarai. Large volumes of traffic cross the border from the Indian railheads at Raxaul, Jogbani, and the Nepalganj Road to Birganj, Biratnagar, and Nepalganj respectively. An agreement with Indian Railways to provide train operations on the three cross-border terminals would reduce the cost, time, pilferage, and damage involved in moving freight across the border at these points. The construction of new rail-truck-customs terminals at Birganj, Biratnagar, and Nepalganj would facilitate the movement of goods.

Ropeway

A ropeway, using cables to transport freight, was built in 1927 from Bhimpedi, at the end of a narrow road leading from the railhead at Amlekhganj, over the mountains and into Kathmandu. For nearly 37 years it was the only means of transporting freight into or out of the Kathmandu Valley other than by porter.

In 1960 a plan was developed for replacing the old and worn-out ropeway with a new line. It was originally planned to have the new

Ropeway from Kathmandu to Hetauda, 1968 (courtesy US AID)

ropeway extend from Amlekhganj into Kathmandu. This was later reduced in scope because of higher-than-planned costs and a lack of foreign aid funds. The line was constructed only from Kathmandu to Hetauda. The new line, which was constructed by the Riblet Tramway Company of Spokane, Washington, for US AID, was opened in April 1964, and the old line was removed. During the first few months following its opening, the operations of the new ropeway were erratic for three principal reasons: (1) derailments due to some elements of faulty design in the system; (2) power failure due to weaknesses in the basic supporting electrical power system; and (3) the lack of competent management and direction. Since November 1964, most of the mechanical problems have been solved, and the 42-km line has been operating well for the last 30 years. Its total capacity, based on 200 eight-hour working days per year, is 40,000 tons. Between 1985 and 1989 the ropeway carried approximately 12,000 tons of freight per year.

The Tribhuvan Rajpath has carried substantially more freight than has moved over the ropeway. Freight charges on the ropeway, when added to the trucking charges from Raxaul to Hetauda and delivery charges in Kathmandu, are not very different from the through rate offered by competing trucks. Ropeway management faces difficult problems in seeking and retaining traffic. A common problem is the government's practice of commandeering all ropeway capacity for days at a time, necessitating long delays in shipments destined to private industries. As a result, the ropeway has lost some of its customers, and other private shippers avoid it.

The ropeway between Hetauda and Kathmandu is a vital transport link between the tarai and the populous Kathmandu Valley. Because of the limited capacity and high cost of transport on the Tribhuvan Rajpath, it is important for Nepal to keep the ropeway in good mechanical condition and operate it efficiently. The ability to realize the maximum economic benefit from the ropeway depends heavily upon the competence of the management. The ropeway is operated as a state undertaking by the Transport Corporation of Nepal.

Air transport

Air transport plays a significant role in the development of land-locked Nepal as a supplement to surface transport. As a means of linkage between various areas, it greatly contributes to national integration, especially where surface transport is constrained by the mountainous terrain. Nepal has 42 operating airfields. Most of them are short STOL fields in the mountains, which can be used only by small planes. In the 1990s only three of the mountain airports – Kathmandu, Gurkha, and Pokhara – received regular services. In terms of traffic handled, the most important commercial airports are Kathmandu, Bhairawa, Pokhara, and Biratnagar.

Air transport in Nepal began in 1950 with the construction of an airport in Kathmandu by the Indian Aid Mission and the inauguration of services between Kathmandu and Patna. Between 1953 and 1958, Indian Airlines provided local services within Nepal, in addition to international services to and from India. In July 1958 Royal Nepal Airlines was established for the operation of domestic and international services. In 1963 the Royal Nepal Airline Corporation was formally organized as a government corporation. Tribhuvan International Airport (formerly Gaucher Field) at Kathmandu is the main gateway to Nepal. In recent years its terminal complex, tower, and runways have been considerably improved. The Royal Nepal

238

Airline carried nearly 608,000 passengers and 7,260 tons of cargo in 1990.

Although Nepal's terrain favours air transportation over other modes of transport, it also provides some major problems and obstacles. The high mountains and deep valleys present problems in air navigation, airport construction, and access to and from the airport. The four-month monsoon season from early June until early October presents some problems. In the tarai the monsoon clouds have an upper limit of 3,100 m and are usually 300 m above ground, thus allowing enough room for planes to operate either above or below the cloud base. Over the Middle Himalaya the monsoon clouds gain altitude as they move north, with their upper limit reaching about 4,575 m. The higher mountains generally remain free of clouds, though the deep river valleys, such as the Kali Gandaki and the Marsyandi, have clouds on their mountain flanks but otherwise are generally free of low-lying clouds. There have been some major air crashes during the monsoon season, which involved planes approaching the Tribhuvan International Airport.

Modern aviation makes exacting demands on aircraft maintenance, the management of airports, and the coordination of all civil aviation activities. The present civil aviation organization is not adequate to meet the growing needs of aviation in Nepal. With the growth of the National Highway system, the place of air transportation in Nepal's economy lies in the rapid movement of people and goods over longer distances. Air transport can continue to facilitate internal economic development, earn foreign exchange, and provide rapid and convenient links with neighbouring countries.

In order to reach these goals, the government should provide the capital needed for the operation and expansion of the Royal Nepal Airline, and the airline should be free from day-to-day government intervention. Equally important is the development of a domestic aviation infrastructure to feed the Tribhuvan International Airport. In addition, the more effective utilization of the existing air cargo capacity and of the associated infrastructure is impeded by the excessively slow and cumbersome customs and administrative procedures, the inadequate cargo facilities, and the generally poor or non-existent surface distribution systems for getting air freight to and from the airports.

Whereas Nepal – as a landlocked country – is at a definite disadvantage in surface transport, in trade affected by air transport it starts on an equal footing. It follows then, that Nepal should pay

239

special attention to the development of economic activities, producing goods especially suited for export by air. Traditionally, such air freight has consisted primarily of either perishable goods (such as fruits, vegetables, and flowers) and high value goods (such as precious metals and stones, leathers, carpets, and the like). The air freighting of such commodities can be made the basis for developing new or growing production and markets.

In some special instances, air freight may also be usable for less valuable commodities such as manufactured textiles and shoes, especially where charter services are available. In Nepal there are additional opportunities for benefiting significantly from international tourism. The ability to derive such benefits depends to a great extent on the provision of an adequate infrastructure and on coordination with other modes of transport.

Direction of trade and location of markets

Data on both the volume and pattern of trade in Nepal is far from satisfactory. However, some broad trends can be identified. The main flow of trade is in a north-south direction along traditional trade routes, which follow topographical conditions. The main commodities entering the trade are agricultural products – including those processed in varying degrees – and imported manufactured goods, salt, and kerosene. The traditional method of transport is by porters and pack animals in the mountains and by bullock carts in the tarai. Modern transport takes over at the railheads on the Indian border or along the main highways in Nepal.

From the forests in the tarai, the foothills, and in the Siwalik Range, forest products are exported to India. Rice, mustard, jute and jute products, small quantities of pulses, sugarcane, and tobacco are exported from the tarai to India. Because of the lack of milling facilities in the tarai, some quantities of paddy and mustard merely move across the border for processing and are reimported into Nepal. Ghee, potatoes, oranges, herbs, hides, and skin are some of the main products which move from the mountains to India. Kathmandu is an important consumer centre for cheese, woollen products, and sheep or goats coming from the mountains.

Internal trade has been greatly hampered by the geography of the country. Surplus food produced in the tarai is often transported to India rather than to the food deficit area of the Kathmandu Valley because of the difficulty of the lateral travel routes. The Kathmandu

Valley in turn imports food from India to meet the deficit. Thus, it is not unusual for Nepal to be exporting a surplus from the tarai while the Valley suffers from a food shortage.

In recent years food shortages in the Middle Mountains have resulted in greater government intervention in the movement and marketing of food grains. For supplying Kathmandu, the government has been purchasing rice from both the eastern and western tarai. This rice is shipped through India by rail and brought into Kathmandu by road. There are smaller movements of food grains within the Middle Himalayan area from the surplus to deficit areas, which are mainly carried by porters.

Little accurate information is available on market places. For agricultural products, Baitadi, Bandipur, Hetauda, Chisapani, and Sanichara appear to be of special importance. Pokhara is important for supplying imported consumer goods to the surrounding districts up to the far north. Other market centres are Butwal, Narayan Ghat and Dharan, each of which has a large hinterland. They serve as important collection points for agricultural products and are also essential for supplying the local region with imported consumer goods.

Along the Indian border in the plain there are many important market centres, which are in most cases close to an Indian railway head. Some of these centres are not only important for the collection and export of surplus products from the tarai, but also for products brought down from the Great and Middle Himalayan regions. Mahendranagar, Dhangarhi, Rajapur, Nepalganj, Koilabas, Krishnanagar, Bhairawa, Birganj, Janakpur, Rajbiraj, Hanumannagar, Biratnagar, and Bhadrapur are among the larger centres.

Organized markets for various products are still not well developed, and adequate credit and storage facilities for producers are still lacking. Some products, such as sugarcane, are either delivered by the growers to Indian mill collection points or directly to the sugar mills in Nepal. Middlemen of various kinds and numbers also play a predominant role in the trade chain of agricultural products. Traders provide cultivators with needed credit and frequently with consumer goods. This dependence of the cultivators on the merchants results in lower prices for the producer and higher profits for the middlemen. The widespread lack of market information, coupled with an absence of grading and standardization procedures, benefits the traders and hurts the producer.

The present pattern of internal trade is expected to continue and perhaps become more pronounced in the future. Products entering into trade will continue to be highly diversified and will not be confined to a small number of products outstandingly important in terms of volume. The main areas of agricultural development will continue to be in the tarai. Manufacturing activity will grow slowly and be confined primarily around Biratnagar, the Birganj-Hetauda corridor, and the Kathmandu Valley. The movement of petroleum products is from India into Kathmandu, along the Rajpath.

A new area of economic activity may emerge around the Gandak Project, if it is implemented, with Bhairawa growing in importance. One of the few developments that could alter the structure of the economy would be the Karnali Project for harnessing the hydropower potential of the Karnali. The expansion of electric power must accompany the construction of transmission lines across the country. The potential for selling excess energy to India exists, but the project would require considerable capital. It is not expected that developments in either the Gandak or Karnali projects will affect the trade and economic patterns during the next five-to-ten-year period.

Foreign trade and transit routes

Despite attempts to diversify foreign trade since the 1960s, India remains the single most important trade partner of Nepal in the 1990s. In 1988 India received 38 per cent of Nepal's exports, and supplied 36 per cent of its imports. Nepalese imports from India are mainly textiles, manufactured consumer goods, and kerosene and petrol, which are distributed to the main market centres and from there throughout the country. It is generally recognized that there is a considerable volume (estimated to be between 20 and 50 per cent) of exports and imports from India that are not recorded. This arises from the difficulty of establishing comprehensive customs control along the entire border, which is crossed by numerous tracks and paths.

The scale of trade with China is small. The Arniko Rajmarga (Kathmandu-Kodari road), which opened in May 1967 to the border of Tibet, did not yield any commercial or trade benefits for Nepal. It is not a viable alternate transit route. Small quantities of food grains and dairy products are transported from the mountains into Tibet. Some food grains also move from the eastern tarai through the mountains into Tibet. Sheep and goats are also brought in from Tibet. It would appear that the sparsely settled, arid, and mountainous areas of Tibet and the surrounding areas of south-west China will not contribute much to an export market for future Nepalese products.

The potential for developing exports for Indian markets is much greater than for any markets in the north. Nepal's large foreign trade with India already indicates its propensity towards this trading partner. Many of Nepal's current exports are agriculture and light industry from the tarai, so topographic barriers to movement are minimal. Furthermore, this is the same region that possesses the greatest promise for increased production. The prospects for specialized production from the mountainous areas are less discernible, but some have speculated that horticulture could command a large market in northern India.

Nepal's foreign trade with countries other than India involves the transit of goods to and from foreign countries through Indian territory because of the country's landlocked situation. The ways in which this situation may affect economic development have been considered (East, 1960: 1–22; Hilling, 1972: 257–264; Dale, 1968: 485–505; Glassner, 1970; Szentes, 1973: 273), but others have argued that underdevelopment is determined "less by geography than by history" (Konate, 1973: 48–49).

Under the 1950 Treaty of Trade and Commerce between India and Nepal, India provides transit facilities to Nepal and freedom from customs duties for goods in transit. A warehouse has been made available in the port of Calcutta, where all goods in transit may be stored. In 1978 separate treaties for trade and transit were negotiated between Nepal and India. Upon expiration of the 1978 treaties on trade and transit rights, Nepal and India could not agree to a new treaty (Baraith, 1989). In March 1989, upon the expiration of the 1978 treaties on trade and transit, all but two border entry points were closed.

The economic consequences of the 1989 trade and transit impasse with India was serious for Nepal. Nepal's exports to India were subjected to high tariffs, and imports from India also carried increased costs. Shortages of Indian imports such as fuel, salt, cooking oil, food, and other essential commodities soon occurred. The tourist industry was adversely affected. There were also ecological consequences since people cut trees to meet the fuel requirements in lieu of kerosene, which came from India.

With the success of the Movement for the Restoration of Democracy in 1990, economic relations with India improved. In June 1990

India announced the restoration of the status quo ante and the reopening of all border points, pending the finalization of a comprehensive arrangement covering all aspects of bilateral relations. A protocol to the 1991 Treaty of Transit lists 15 routes (fig. 30) through which all traffic in transit must pass; another Treaty of Trade, 1991, lists 21 agreed-upon routes for mutual trade along the India-Nepal border (fig. 31).

Although India in various treaties has agreed to transit rights, Nepal feels the pressure derived from its landlocked position. When the costs of transit across India are added, the financial inaccessibility of Nepal resembles its isolation of the previous century. The cost distance between Nepal and the Bay of Bengal is, indeed, much greater than is apparent from the physical distance. As one example, the cost of transporting petroleum products from Calcutta to Nepal is three times what it would cost from the Persian Gulf to Calcutta (Pant, 1976).

Nepal's exports are primarily from the agricultural base, which means that bulky items are unable to compete on the world market after incurring high overland freight costs. Even for jute, rice, hides, wheat, and other agricultural products originating in the tarai, maintaining competitive prices is difficult because of the overland hauling and for those products destined for a country other than India, through transit territory. Likewise, any products imported, whether as inputs for specialized production or in lieu of local self-sufficiency, are purchased dearly after line-haul, transshipment, and transit costs are added. Even the development of labour-intensive, low-weight exports for foreign markets seems doomed by competition from other more accessible developing countries, including India (B. P. Shrestha, 1981).

As noted earlier, the potential for developing exports for Indian markets is much greater than markets in any other country. Further, as India continues to industrialize, the demand for electrical energy will expand; thus the harnessing of Nepal's hydroelectric potential is another likely export to India. And yet another potential source of foreign earnings that depends greatly on India is the expansion of tourism. Not only does Nepal earn directly from the increasing number of Indian travellers, but the volume of tourist traffic from other countries into Nepal is closely associated with the numbers who tour India each season.

Under the circumstances, Nepal, host to SAARC nations, may wish to explore a bold vision of a common South Asia Free Trade Area, and begin with a free trade agreement with India. The com-

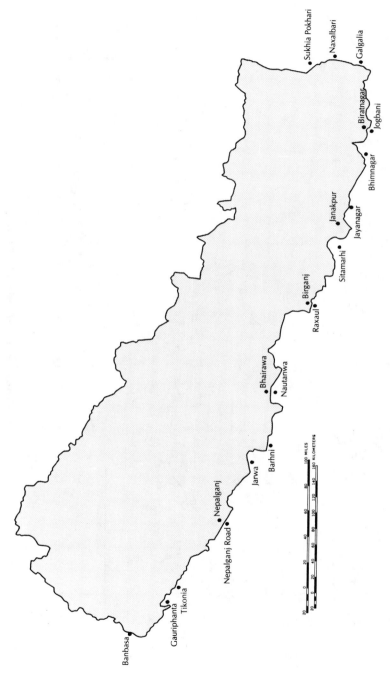

Fig. 30 **Routes for transit, 1991 treaty**

245

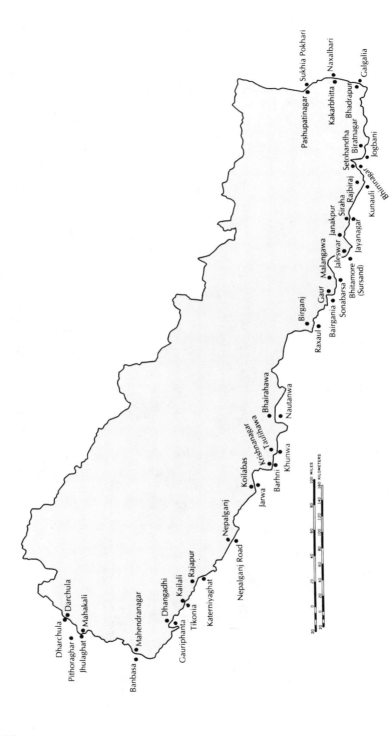

Fig. 31 **Routes for mutual trade, 1991 treaty**

246

pletion of a duty-free common market, similar to the NAFTA regime in North America, would simplify the practicalities of trade and transit between India and Nepal. Companies and investors would be able to make their long-term plans on the secure expectation that the continued integration of the closely entwined Indian and Nepalese economies would henceforth be guaranteed by treaty. Free trade would help the Nepalese economy grow, since all goods and investments would be free to travel across the border: with more and better jobs available in Nepal, there would be less incentive for the Nepalese to seek employment in India and in other countries.

Some firms will migrate to Nepal, other may move to India; it is expected that both countries will eventually benefit from the free trade arrangement. Nepal's political concerns about the Indian domination, of the disadvantages of structuring economy on the common market, and of the uncertainty surrounding the impact of the free trade agreement, are relevant. Nevertheless, Nepal's geographic problems – being small and landlocked – are geographic constants, which compound the other barriers to economic development faced by most developing nations and which leave few alternatives for the country.

Transport strategy for landlocked Nepal

Although the consequences of the landlocked situation are difficult to quantify, it is generally recognized that Nepal's lack of territorial access to the sea, compounded by its remoteness and isolation from world markets, appear to be important factors in its relative poverty. The reduction of the high transport costs facing Nepal not only requires action within Nepal but also depends heavily on improvements in the transport policy and in the facilities of neighbouring India.

A key element in a transport strategy for Nepal is, therefore, the harmonization of the planning of the transport sector with that of its transit neighbour India, within a climate of friendly relations. The transport strategy would need to be elaborated on in harmony with the overall economic development strategy, both from the viewpoint of Nepal and from that of the larger region of northern India and Bangladesh.

Nepal's need to establish and develop physical links to the sea and to world markets must be placed within the context of problems relating to the more efficient use of the existing capacity and problems of creating alternative routes through transit territory. The best basis for the development of a more effective transport strategy is a friendly relationship with the transit countries and the strengthening of the political will to cooperate.

Certain measures in the area of transit and frontier procedures could bring about considerable savings. Though Nepal has given high priority to the improvement of external trade routes, there is also the need to stress the importance of balanced growth in the internal transport network (such as feeder roads) and the external transport links. In this context, some of Nepal's problems can be viewed as part of the broader problem of the economic development of continental interiors. The development of economic cooperation in other areas can facilitate cooperation in the transport field. The benefits of such cooperation can exceed the costs for both landlocked and transit countries.

The pricing of transport services and the use of basic transport facilities (including transport infrastructure) is a major function of the national economic and social policy. Pricing has a widespread effect on the use of resources, the location of economic activity, and the distribution of real income. Landlocked Nepal has no control over transport prices and costs in the Indian transit territory. Similarly, India lacks control over prices and costs in Nepal to which it supplies transport services, and whose demand for transport services forms an additional claim on actual and future transport facilities. A bilateral agreement over pricing can serve as a partial substitute for the organizational integration of transport systems.

Communication pattern

A knowledge of the pattern and intensity of communication and information flow in Nepal is essential for the understanding of the development and integrative processes at work in the country. A close network of communication and information flow between various parts of a country creates the bonds of awareness and interdependence that promote integration of people and places within a nation. The development of communications makes a major contribution to effective territorial integration essential to sustain economic growth and the general welfare of the people. The degree to which territories are connected with each other through communication and information flow provides the integrative glue for a nation to survive and grow as a cohesive organized state. Traditional theories of

Crossing a river in the Middle Mountain area (courtesy M. Tamura)

economic and social development have emphasized the significant role of communication and information networks in accelerating self-sustained growth.

Mass communication systems have been employed to promote rural development, advance literacy, better agriculture, improved health and sanitation and accelerate adoption of family planning practices. In recent years telecommunication networks have grown to expand the interpersonal long-distance communication. Microwave signals or messages bounced off from satellites carry news, dispatches, pictures, and entertainment programmes.

Postal communications

Although the development of postal facilities has been accorded a significant place in Nepal's development plans, large areas of the country are not covered by postal services. The goal of establishing a minimum of one post office within each Village Development Com-

Buses, hand-carts, and a rickshaw, Kathmandu

mittee remains elusive. Existing mail services between principal towns remain slow due to shortage of personnel, mail vans, and poor transport network. A private postal service company (Everest Postal Care) operating in the Kathmandu Valley has relieved the pressure on government postal services. Strengthening of the postal services is a major challenge for the government, particularly in the western part of the country where large areas are not covered by postal communication.

Telecommunications

The first telephones were installed in Kathmandu at the Rana palaces in 1913. In 1914 a long-distance telephone line was installed between Kathmandu and Raxaul. Twenty-five years later in 1936 a telephone line was established between Kathmandu and Dhankuta. Wireless telephone services were set up in 1949 at Nepalganj, Bhairawa, Ilam, Dhankuta, and Biratnagar. Services were extended to Doti, Dang, Jumla, Dailekh, Salyan, Okhaldhunga, and Rajbiraj in 1951, and to Jaleshwor, Ramechap, Bandipur, Tehrathum, Taplejung, Dandeldhura, Baitadi, Baglung, Palpa, and Dhangadhi a little later. In 1950 Kathmandu was linked with Palpa by long-distance telephone.

However, at the end of the Rana rule, Nepal had few telephone services and most areas of the country were not connected by telephone with the capital city.

After the collapse of the Rana autocracy the first local telephone service became available to the public in 1955 and was expanded in 1961. In 1959 a Department of Telecommunication was established and in 1975 the Nepal Telecommunication Corporation (NTC) was formed. As of 1993 there were 47 telephone exchanges in operation serving 55 of the 75 districts in the country. There are four telephones per thousand head of population. NTC provides local and long distance public telephone services in these 55 districts. It also provides international telecommunication services through circuits operating on satellite and microwave systems. In 1992, the international outgoing telephone traffic grew by 15 per cent over the previous year. The bulk of international calls was made to India, indicating close economic and social links between Nepal and India. Nepal is now on the internet, the information superhighway.

Telex and telegraph

Telex is used mostly for transmission of texts. The telex service provided by the NTC is fully automatic. Telex services are available from Kathmandu, Birganj, Biratnagar, Pokhara Janakpur, Bhairawa, Butwal, Bharatpur, and Nepalganj. Nepal has direct telex links with seven countries and the service is available to almost all parts of the world. A domestic telegraph service is the basic means of communication in remote areas of Nepal and it plays an important role in the day-to-day administrative work of the government. Out of 75 districts only 19 district headquarters have high-frequency wireless communications. In the remaining districts telegrams are transmitted over voice circuits and telegraph circuits. An international telegraph service is available to all parts of the world through satellite and microwave telegraph circuits. Nepal has direct telegraph circuits with India and Japan.

Programme transmission

NTC provides both radio and television programme transmission services. Radio Nepal's studio is linked with NTC's circuits and Nepal Television's studio is linked with the Sagarmatha Satellite Earth Station by a microwave system.

Radio

Radio broadcasting remains the cheapest and most efficient means of mass communication in Nepal. In a mountainous country, where many of the remote villages have no access to motorable roads nor to any other communication and entertainment facilities, radio broadcasts have proved to be effective in disseminating information, educating people and entertaining the general masses.

Radio Nepal began broadcasting in 1951 after the political system changed from the Rana rule to the multi-party system. Radio broadcasts can be heard in every part of the country using medium and short waves. Broadcasting has contributed greatly to the consolidation of the nation. Nepal broadcasts news in Nepali, Hindi, and English. A second station from Radio Nepal, which uses languages such as Newari, Bhojpuri, Maithili, and Hindi, started broadcasting in 1993 to promote ethnic languages. Since 1994 Nepal Radio local stations provide programmes in eight ethnic languages.

Until 1983, Radio Nepal had to depend heavily on short-wave broadcasting to serve the whole country. Due to the unreliable characteristics of short-wave reception, it was necessary to develop nation-wide medium-wave services, which are free from fading and noise and provide reliable signals throughout the year. In the years 1980–1982, Radio Nepal started establishing medium-wave transmission. Since the establishment of these medium-wave stations, clear radio signals now reach over 90 per cent of the total population. During the daytime, short-wave signals are the only ones available for some areas not covered by medium-wave signals.

Currently, Radio Nepal broadcasts various programmes on health, education, culture, afforestation, and environment. Attempts have been made to orient the radio to meet the socio-economic needs of the scattered population living in rural communities.

Television

The influence of television has been rapid and strong in Nepal. Nepal Television Corporation (NTV) began its operation in 1985 with support from France. In addition to NTV, it is possible to receive Star TV programmes. Signals from Indian TV reach even the remote regions in the Himalaya. The influence of this transborder telecast has prompted the government to develop a mass media policy. NTV has a news exchange agreement with the CNN network of the United

States and WTN of London. A daily world news-wire service is also provided by AFP news agency of France and the national news agency RSS. About 30 per cent of NTV's broadcasting time is covered by news and related programmes.

NTV has been working towards the expansion of its service area. In the beginning, it covered only about 30 square miles. After the installation of a transmitter at Phulchoki Hill, the telecasts began to cover the entire Kathmandu Valley including some areas in the tarai in 1988. The Biratnagar transmission centre was established in 1988, and Hetauda sub-centre and the Pokhara transmission centre were established soon after. With these four centres, NTV programmes now reach over 25 per cent of the total urban population of Nepal. Biratnagar and Pokhara centres were linked with Kathmandu through microwave in 1990 and 1992 respectively. The Japan International Cooperation Agency (JICA) prepared a development plan for television network in Nepal in 1988. It suggested a four-phase development plan to be completed by 1995. During the Eighth Five-Year Plan (1992–1997) the network is to expand to cover nearly 75 per cent of the urban population. To achieve this objective, NTV will broadcast through satellite link from one transmission station and 19 transmission sub-centres to be constructed across Nepal.

In Nepal the use of video became popular even before television broadcasting started. Films came from India, the United States, and Hong Kong. Video rental shops appeared in large numbers. Since the coming of television, large parabola antennas can be seen on many roofs and more than 10 wires are often installed from each antenna for the reception of Star TV. In areas closer to the Indian border, people can receive images from India longer and more clearly than from NTV. Even in the northern areas of Nepal where NTV telecasts do not reach, people can receive world news through satellite signals.

Press

The circulation of newspapers and magazines in Nepal has increased since the decline of the Panchayat regime despite the fact that almost 70 per cent of people are illiterate. There are different degrees of circulation according to geographical areas, which attest to the existence of local diversities in political activity and inclination. No newspaper or magazine has a large circulation but various political groups with diverse principles comprise regular readers of specific papers. The constitution of 1990 clearly upholds the freedom of pub-

Parabola antennas on top of roofs in Kathmandu

lication and speech for the first time. Accordingly, publishing activity has become more widespread in major cities. The trend towards the use and revival of ethnic languages and literature has grown vigorous as well. Although the press can play an important role, in Nepal it has a more limited role than that of radio because of the low literacy rate, diversity of languages, and the small number of written languages.

Nearly two-thirds of the newspapers published in Nepal are concentrated in the Kathmandu Valley and major urban centres of the tarai. The circulation pattern is restricted due to the difficulty of transportation. A similar pattern is also true for other printed materials such as magazines and books. One major exception is textbooks written in Nepali, which have been widely distributed since the 1970s. Nepali textbooks have contributed greatly to the penetration of Nepali language as well as the value system and ideology of the government throughout the country.

Among newspapers and magazines, there are "public sector" newspapers such as *Gorkhapatra* and *Rising Nepal*, which have been and still are government papers strongly reflecting the views of the government. The need for a free and impartial press has been strongly felt since 1990. The Press and Publications Act of 1991 prohibits speeches and the publication of articles that could threaten public order and national security, promote antagonism among different religions or castes, or violate public morals. It also prevents publication of articles that may be disrespectful of the monarchy. The Act also requires journalists to be licensed. Supplementary legislation passed in 1992 established education and experience requirements for various jobs in journalism. Despite these restrictions, newspapers and magazines vigorously criticize government policies.

10

The development of tourism

Nepal's struggling economy began its quest for growth in earnest after 1950, when the country emerged from decades of isolation under the autocratic rule of the Rana family. This effort coincided with the lifting of many of the restrictions imposed on foreigners entering Nepal. In the decades that followed, the levels of growth registered in Nepal's economy proved discouraging, while the number of visitors to the country continually increased. The initial prescriptions for economic success, which relied on measures to enhance agricultural productivity and to expand overall the country's export base, proved ineffective. The actual foreign earnings generated by natural resources leaving the country – minerals, timber, agricultural products, and hydroelectric power – clearly have not met early expectations, but those earnings derived from tourists entering the country have surpassed initial projections. The high rate of tourism growth meant a 10-fold increase in its contribution to Nepal's foreign exchange receipts from the mid-1970s to the early 1990s; tourism now contributes almost one-fifth of the country's gross foreign exchange earnings.

Nepal's tourism policy predicts nearly 1 million visitors by the year 2000, despite the lack of a national tourism plan that would clearly identify how such unrealistic growth could be achieved or managed. This fact does not deter tourism's proponents in Nepal, who argue that the prevailing economic conditions dictate the need for a rapid expansion in the tourism sector. Others are properly concerned that without sufficient management and a realistic threshold placed on the number of visitors to the country, the environmental, social, and

256

equity problems associated with tourism will significantly increase and will diminish overall the developmental potential of tourism in Nepal. Clearly, the need exists for a careful analysis of tourism's potential economic benefits to the country and its possible adverse impact on local society and the natural environment. These concerns include the issue of how tourism's costs and benefits will be distributed in the country, geographically and across societal divisions.

Tourism in Nepal follows the designs of global tourism, which in addition to the conventional forms of mass or resort tourism, predict new initiatives for travel to distant places in the world. Variously called adventure tourism, alternative tourism, ethnic tourism, and most commonly, ecotourism, it remains unclear whether these forms actually represent new types of tourism or simply provide exotic new thematic and geographic destinations for tourists. Nonetheless, Nepal's tourism industry has embarked on ambitious programmes to develop ecotourism in the country. Its proponents argue that ecotourism contributes to more sustainable development in Nepal because it reconciles the pressures for economic growth with those for environmental preservation in the management of natural areas as income-generating tourist places.

Having adopted the ecotourism model in its programmes for mountain trekking, jungle wildlife viewing, and village culture study, Nepal has tried to fit it into the country's unique physical and cultural geography. Such tourism extends the touristic system in Nepal beyond the scenic and cultural resources of the Kathmandu Valley to the country's most remote frontier regions. The development prospects that such activity brings to Nepal's rural areas include the following:
1. increased linkages between the developing tourism areas located in the frontier regions and the national infrastructure, facilitated by new gateway towns and expanding roadways and communication lines;
2. expanded national and local investments in such tourism activities as tour bookings, guides and portering, lodging, and crafts;
3. heightened awareness of carrying capacity issues, the environmental impacts of tourism, and the prospective role of tourism for village conservation and for national parklands development;
4. new cultural and economic attitudes among the rural people as they increase their contact with the tourists and with tourism entrepreneurs.

In this chapter, the development of tourism in Nepal since 1950 will be reviewed and the relationship between the development of tourism and growth and change in the country will be examined. The geographic study of tourism in Nepal predicts that its role in the development of the countryside extends well beyond the economic appraisals, by considering how this activity may impact environmental conditions, culture change, and regional integration processes. An important fact in the rural transformation of Nepal is that its most distant territories, through various political, economic and social means, become more closely linked with the national space-economy. In this process, places may lose much of their autonomy as they gain modernity. The evaluation of natural and cultural resources shifts further toward the demands of the commercial economy and of national policy, inciting the potential conflicts between local traditions and national development that now unsettle many villages. Set against such changes, tourism stands as one of the most important actual and potential forces to affect life in contemporary Nepal.

Historical overview

Throughout much of its history, Nepal remained largely isolated from the rest of the world and only a few foreigners were allowed into the country. Exceptions were made for the Hindu pilgrims from India and the Buddhist pilgrims from China who have journeyed since ancient times through the country, en route to such holy places as Lumbini in the lowland tarai, Pashupatinath in the Kathmandu Valley, and Gosaikund and Muktinath in the northern mountains. Those travels, deeply rooted in complex spiritual practices, involved large-scale religious peragrinations. A network of pilgrimage routes developed that connected Nepal's sacred places to countless others scattered across the wide South Asia landscape (Bhardwaj, 1973). Historically, those journeys required the services of travel specialists, as they still do today. According to the 1908 Bengal District Gazeteer:

Most of the pilgrims ... form part of an organized tour and nothing has stimulated pilgrimage so much as the organized system of pilgrim guides. The Pandas and Pariharis of the temple have divided among themselves the whole of India, each having an allotted circle, in which they claim to possess a monopoly of pilgrims. Two or three months before the beginning of the principal festivals ... they engage agents, mostly Brahmins and sometime barbers and Gauras, and depute them to different parts of India in order to recruit pilgrims. (cited in Gurung, 1984:123–124)

In Nepal, the term *tirtha* connotes traditional pilgrimages to holy sites. To consider such pilgrims historically as tourists in Nepal helps to explain why Indian visitors have long dominated tourist arrivals in the country. As Indian pilgrim-tourists travel to the sacred Hindu sites and attend the numerous religious festivals (including Maha Shivaratri, when tens of thousands of Shiva devotees from India visit the Pashupatinath Temple in the Kathmandu Valley), they make up almost one-third of the visitors to Nepal. However, according to recent tourist statistics, more than 75 per cent of the contemporary Indian visitors list "pleasure" as the primary purpose of their visit. This reveals that modern Indian tourists now combine sacred journeys with such secular activities as sightseeing, shopping, and casino gambling.

Aside from the ancient pilgrimages of the devotees, Nepal accommodated few foreign travellers before 1949. A British representative of the East India Company was appointed to Kathmandu in 1817; thereafter, during the reign of the Rana prime ministers (1846–1951), only a few British colonialists, selected other European royalty, and occasional scientific expeditions were allowed to enter the country. Only 153 Europeans visited Nepal between 1881 and 1925. Its closed borders, mountainous terrain, and infrequent contact with the west achieved for Nepal its reputation as a forbidden land shrouded in mystery – the very qualities that became so important for the modern growth of tourism in the country.

With the return of Nepal's monarchy following the overthrow of the Rana regime in 1950–1951 and the revolutionary changes in the government that ensued, the country expanded its diplomatic ties with the rest of the world and opened its borders to foreign officials, businessmen, and tourists. Western mountaineers first came to Nepal to climb in the Himalaya in 1949, but it was not until 1955, one year after the Kathmandu airport opened, that Thomas Cook offered the first organized tour of Nepal for western visitors. In 1960 over 4,000 tourists entered the country to explore its ancient towns, temple architecture, and mountain scenery. During that time travel beyond the Kathmandu Valley was impeded by the rugged terrain and lack of motorable roads; only 125 miles of paved roadway existed in the entire country up to 1965, most of it located in the lowland tarai. The country had not yet established its comprehensive system of short take-off and landing (STOL) airstrips that now conveniently link even the most remote district centres with regional and national centres. Consequently, few visitors outside the government-sanctioned mountaineering expeditions ventured into Nepal's remote mountain regions.

It was not until 1966 that eight visitors arrived in Nepal to engage specifically in Nepal's first organized mountain trek. They were among over 12,500 visitors to the country that year, most of whom had come for general pleasure or for official business. Ten years later, in 1976, 100,000 tourists visited Nepal, over 10 per cent of whom came to trek in the mountains. Tourist statistics show steady high-growth rates midway through the 1970s, a levelling-off period during the early 1980s when the number of annual visitors reached 150,000, and then a second period of rapid growth during the late 1980s and early 1990s when the number of annual visitors exceeded 250,000. By the 1990s, Nepal's international tourism base was quite broad, dominated by Indian visitors but also including a significant number of tourists from the United States (19 per cent), Great Britain (7.5 per cent), and Germany (7.5 per cent). Other western European countries, Japan, and Australia made up the remaining tourists. By 1990 tourist spending contributed US $63.5 million to Nepal's foreign earnings, a 40 per cent increase on the mid-1980s.

The growth in tourism indicated by these figures during the past three decades has not met with an equally strong commitment by the Nepalese government to tourism management policy. The country has yet to implement tourism plans developed over 25 years ago, particularly those recommendations to improve the country's tourism infrastructure and to diffuse the government's tourism investment beyond its present concentration in Kathmandu.

The lack of any clear strategy by the government for achieving and managing the proposed scale of tourism in the country has meant that the industry itself determines the tourism capacity of the country, primarily by the number of services it provides. Clearly, this invites the prospect of overexpansion and uncontrolled growth. For example, the hotel capacity in Nepal – a common indicator of tourist services expansion – showed only 88 beds in 1959, increased to 350 in 1965, and to 1,500 in 1970. By 1980, the hotel capacity exceeded 5,000; by the early 1990s it surpassed 8,000 – almost 80 per cent of which remains concentrated in Kathmandu. The hotel capacity now exceeds the demand during many months of the year, with an annual occupancy rate of less than 50 per cent, and some planners argue that Kathmandu is already overbuilt. Similar growth has occurred in travel and trekking agencies – an increase from nine agents in 1970 to over 150 by the early 1990s. While the historical development of tourism in Nepal shows it to be an expanding industry, with a clear potential for contributing to national economic growth, it does not predict the rate of future expansion nor does it show the prospective impact that tourism will have on the Nepalese culture and the natural environment; only now are these becoming apparent.

Touristic resources

Nepal's primary attraction is its unique geographic situation. It straddles not only the Himalaya – the highest mountain range in the world – but also the great cultural traditions of India to the south and of Tibet to the north, thus providing tourists with unsurpassed opportunities for natural and cultural aesthetics. The tourist landscapes in Nepal range from wildlife parklands located among the forested plains of the subtropical tarai, to the 6,000 m trekking peaks nestled amid the icy summits of the Great Himalaya. The intervening distances contain numerous middle-elevation trekking regions, religious and historical sites, and the important tourist centres of Kathmandu and Pokhara, where cultural traditions flourish and where hotels and restaurants compete for the tourists. Gambling casinos are a growing tourist attraction in Kathmandu.

Casino Nepal, the subcontinent's first gambling hall, opened several years ago. In June 1993 Kathmandu's second Casino Anna opened its doors. Like many things in the kingdom, the gambling business is not without its share of ironies. Not the least of these is that bets, sometimes huge, are made in one of the world's poorest countries. Another is that aside from the croupiers, pit bosses, and other hangers-on, no Nepalese are allowed to set foot in a casino, let alone gamble.

Casino Nepal, along with its new cross-town rival Casino Anna, takes bets from American, Japanese, and European tourists, not to mention the Indians. Nearly 80 to 85 per cent of the gamblers are Indian tourists. For wealthy Indian tourists, the casinos serve a function other than simply entertainment. Though casino officials deny it, the gambling halls are said to enable Indians to launder "black money."

The privately-owned Casino Nepal, open round the clock, is a small, split-level gambling hall. Three rooms branch out from the foyer: the main gaming room, a slot machine area, and a room upstairs for games unique to the region. The main gaming room, tiny by Las Vegas standards, nevertheless packs in the vast majority of the Casino's 550 to 600 tourist gamblers each night. Within the room's wood-panelled walls are roulette, blackjack, baccarat, and pontoon tables. The crowd itself is the best show in Kathmandu. Turbaned Sikh businessmen lean past bemused German tourists to place their bets, while bow-tied dealers offer words of praise to the high rollers. Even an occasional trekker straggles in, his tie-dyed T-shirt wrinkled from a lengthy trek. All bets are made in either US dollars or Indian rupees and winnings may be taken out of the country. The minimum bet for most games, such as blackjack, is Rs 50. Every tourist who arrives in Nepal by plane is entitled to Rs 200 worth of free-play coupons, renewable after three days.

It may seem unusual for tourists to spend time in a casino when they could be viewing the majestic Himalaya, visiting ancient temples, or strolling about Kathmandu. But casino gambling is a growing source of income from tourists.

Natural and scenic landscapes

The fact that Nepal's territory encompasses much of the Himalaya predicts the extraordinary diversity found among its natural landscapes. With Mt. Everest, the world's highest mountain at 8,848 m, Nepal contains eight of the world's 14 8,000 m peaks, including Kanchenjunga (8,585 m), Lhotse (8,501 m), Makalu (8,470 m), Dhaulagiri (8,172 m), Cho Oyu (8,153 m), Manaslu (8,125 m), and Annapurna (8,091 m). The relief range from the high to the low spots in Nepal Himalaya is unsurpassed in other world mountain systems. For example, the summits of Dhaulagiri and Annapurna are 35 km apart, but they are separated by the Kali Gandaki River, which flows at 1,200 m above sea level. The extreme differences in elevation produce a magnificent and varied alpine terrain.

While few tourists may reach the actual summits of the high mountains, each year tens of thousands of them walk along the mountains' flanks. By crossing relatively short distances, tourists can move in Nepal through a vast range of environments – the lowland tarai, the densely-populated intermediate slopes of the Mahabharat Lekh of the Middle Mountains, the temperate evergreen forests of the transitional elevations, the snow and ice of the high passes and mountain summits, and the arid trans-Himalayan valleys north of the main Himalaya crest. The tourism industry offers such landscapes in its myriad mountain trekking programmes. The trekking programme contributes significantly to Nepal's economy. It has registered some of the highest growth rates in the tourism industry – from 27,500 trekkers in 1980 to over 70,000 in the early 1990s. During the past two decades, as the popular mountain trekking regions have become overcrowded, the new national parks have established regulations that restrict tourist movement in the mountain regions.

To the south of the Himalaya are the outer-Himalaya foothills known as the Churia and Siwalik ranges, as well as the plains and river valleys that extend the Indo-Gangetic plain and that compose Nepal's tarai region. Five national wildlife reserves and national parks are located here. The tall grasses and mixed semi-deciduous forests of the parks harbour refuge populations of such rare animals as the spotted deer, the Indian rhinoceros, sambar, Gharial crocodile and Bengal tiger, while the rivers and mud flats support numerous species of fish and migratory birds. Many of the reserves, especially the Royal Chitwan National Park, also provide visitor services for viewing the wildlife. In addition to maintaining such places as animal preserves, Nepal is deeply interested in developing the ecotourism component of the parklands, and, according to recent tourist statistics, which show, for example, that the number of visitors to Chitwan increased from 2,206 in 1975 to 34,000 in 1988, foreign tourists in Nepal are equally interested in visiting the parks.

Cultural resources

Nepal's people are a diverse group and attract as many visitors as the places they inhabit. Among the country's many ethnic groups are the Tharu, who live in the lowland tarai; the traditional Newar residents of the Kathmandu Valley; the Gurungs, Magars, Tamangs, Rais, and Limbus residing in villages at the intermediate mountain elevations, and the Tibetan groups or bhotiya, including the famous Sherpas of Khumbu, who inhabit the high elevations and trans-Himalaya valleys. Those cultures, in addition to the dominant Brahmin-Chetri communities, contribute significantly to Nepal's heritage. The Buddhist and Hindu-inspired traditions and arts, the numerous religious festivals, the *thangka* paintings, woodcarving and pottery, the music, the ethnic costumes, and the temple architecture combine to create one of the world's most compelling cultural landscapes. As extensions of Nepalese life, such features are part of the ancient and vernacular traditions of the country. They also are subject now to new economic appraisals as tourist attractions.

In some instances, cultural resources are formally identified for touristic purposes. For example, crafts and artwork such as paintings, jewellery, carpets, and woodwork, are produced exclusively for the tourist market and are sold in the numerous shops and galleries in Kathmandu and Pokhara. The entire architectural centre of Bhaktapur, a small town in the Kathmandu valley, has been designated by UNESCO as a world cultural heritage site. Exhibitions of Nepalese music, dance, and drama are frequently scheduled exclusively for tourist viewing. In other cases, however, tourist interests in Nepal's cultures are not so formalized: temple visits to observe religious rites; staying in villages to watch patterns of farming, herding, and trading; and other personal interactions with villagers and townsmen account for the many ways in which tourists enjoy the country's cultural resources. Interaction with tourists also constitutes one of the most significant means of acculturation in Nepal, leading not only to new economic opportunities for the Nepalese, but to entirely different goals, values, and lifestyles. The forms of culture change that may occur, as well as the environmental impacts, rest partially on the types of tourism at work. Thus, in considering the role of tourism in the economic and social development of Nepal, it is important to consider the various forms of tourism found there.

The old palace and temple complex of Kathmandu

Types of tourism

Recent reports by the World Tourism Organization indicate that global tourism is the world's second largest economic activity, and that it is likely to reach the number one position by the end of the next decade. The prospects that it brings to development in countries such as Nepal cannot be understated. Approximately 500 million international tourist arrivals are reported annually worldwide, with an increasing proportion of them in the third world where few alternatives for economic growth may exist. Nepal's current interest in tourism reflects these significant facts and the economic promise that tourism holds for national development.

The overall expansion of tourism into the third world – the "pleasure periphery" (Turner and Ash, 1975) – is driven by the lure of tropical environments, the availability of interesting sightseeing, and the liberal investment incentives and cheap costs that apply to tourism in those countries. Many such places develop as resort enclaves and promote the types of mass tourism that require enormous investments in destination hotels, services, and other infrastructure. The critics decry mass tourism for its adverse cultural effects and for the inequities that may derive from the economic "leakages" and capital transfers that describe the finances of international tourism. None the less, conventional tourism remains the single most important type of tourism worldwide.

Nepal is ill equipped to provide the kind of amenities that mass tourists expect, nor does it offer the kinds of "sun and surf" diversions that enclave resorts provide for tourists elsewhere in the tropical world. Recognizing its limitations for conventional mass tourism, the country's tourism industry seeks to attract other types of tourist. Pleasure-seeking visitors to Nepal still dominate the tourist arrivals, but each year more tourists come to Nepal to participate in more daring forms of tourism. Mountain trekking is the most important of these activities, followed by wildlife viewing in the tarai animal parks and whitewater rafting on Nepal's rivers. So-called adventure travel has come to dominate tourism in Nepal's rural areas and to define entirely new socio-economic agendas for the country (Zurick, 1992). In promoting such forms of tourism, Nepal follows the global tourism trends set in the 1980s and 1990s that identify alternative types of tourism, which presumably limit the negative effects of economic activity on local environments and cultures. The alternative models view tourism as a means of promoting environmental protection and meaningful cultural interaction while still achieving significant economic growth. Such models assume different names, but are called ethnic tourism when the focus is on cultural observation and nature tourism when it is on the natural environment (Whelan, 1991). In Nepal, these two primary agendas are often combined and are referred to collectively as adventure travel or ecotourism. Hector Ceballos coined the term ecotourism as:

... that segment of tourism that involves traveling to relatively undisturbed or uncontaminated natural areas with the specific object of admiring, studying, and enjoying the scenery and its wild plants and animals, as well as any existing cultural features. (Ceballos, quoted in Lindberg, 1991: 3)

Such definitions of ecotourism indicate its focus on the "pristine" world but prescribe no clear strategies for managing such tourism. Clearly, its economic benefits are what promote and sustain ecotourism in Nepal, and it should properly be considered a specialized form of tourism rather than as an alternative to it. According to a recent World Wildlife Fund report on ecotourism:

The growing demand for tourism to protected areas, combined with the need to sustain the supply of protected areas through economic activities, provides a significant opportunity to link the two trends in a beneficial way. (Boo, 1990: 1)

In Nepal, where opportunities for visiting unique natural and cultural settings abound and where the need to preserve such places is urgent, ecotourism is now an explicit development priority. The national parklands and conservation areas in the country regulate, with mixed success, tourism activities according to explicit ecotourism goals. For example, since 1986 the Annapurna Conservation Area Project (ACAP), under the auspices of the King Mahendra Trust for Nature Conservation, has implemented ecotourism programmes geared to minimize the impact of about 40,000 trekkers who annually visit the mountains and the villages situated north of Pokhara. The ACAP strategy combines environmental protection with community development and tourism management within a project area that covers 7,000 sq. km. According to ACAP guidelines, the income from tourism is used for local environmental education programmes, forest conservation, tourist awareness programmes, and alternative energy projects (Thapa, 1992).

A primary contribution of ACAP to tourism issues in Nepal is the emphasis it places on involving local people in the design and man-

266

agement of tourism goals. It appears that such participation constitutes a significant departure from conventional tourism management. If ecotourism actually represents a new alternative for more sustainable tourism in Nepal rather than simply a new marketing niche (Wight, 1993), it will be because of this element and not the promotions of the tourism industry. The pressure on Nepal to expand its tourism base predicts the opening of new touristic places. ACAP recently extended its area coverage to include the formerly closed Mustang border region. The Ministry of Tourism, through ACAP, is developing the Mustang area as a model ecotourism area. This strategy reflects Nepal's regional development plans, which make the remote border regions more accessible to tourists, and thus expands the spatial, if not structural, basis for tourism in the country.

Tourism frontiers

The Kathmandu and Pokhara valleys continue to attract the majority of tourists in Nepal, who visit such places to view the cultural traditions and ceremonies, visit the cultural sites, and shop in the markets and handicraft bazaars located there. For such tourists, the Great Himalaya provides a striking backdrop for their sightseeing excursions. The concentration of hotels, restaurants, and other tourist services in those locations reinforces the urban dominance of the touristic system. Some attempts have been made to diffuse tourism away from its concentration in Kathmandu. Affluent tourists especially are sought for the newly developed resorts in the Chitwan wildlife park, in Pokhara, and at a few other destinations such as the Dhulikhel Mountain Resort, located in the hills surrounding the Kathmandu Valley where mountain viewing is ideal.

To safeguard the touristic potential of cultural sites located in the tourist centres, the government of Nepal has sought the assistance of numerous outside agencies. The Nepali-German Bhaktapur project, begun in 1974, has played a key role in the historical preservation of Bhaktapur's temple centre, resulting in its status as a UNESCO World Cultural Heritage Site. During the 1980s the Pacific Area Travel Association supported numerous additional historical preservation projects to counter the threats of neglect, air pollution, theft, and new construction. Much of the contemporary tourism thinking in Nepal, though, is directed toward the new forms of adventure travel in the country's remote rural places. It is there that the tourism industry sees its greatest potential for growth.

The fact that tourism in Nepal is driven largely by the adventure travel industry, which seeks out "pristine" locales, means that pressure exists to continually open up new territories for tourism. In recent years, the formerly restricted areas of Dolpo, Humla, Mustang, and Makalu now welcome organized trekking. Those places are located in the remote interior mountains along the country's northern border with Tibet. The trans-Himalaya valleys situated there are isolated by high mountain passes and populated by people of Tibetan ancestry. The appeal of such places for tourists is their geographic remoteness and relatively intact cultures. Other ecotourism destinations are planned in the lowland tarai plain, where wildlife reserves are developed to accommodate more tourists. Overall, the primary frontiers into which tourism is currently expanding include the mountain regions where mountaineering and trekking are already popular, the new mountain destinations not yet developed for trekking, the tarai animal parks, and the whitewater rivers for rafting expeditions (fig. 32).

Mountain trekking regions

The most important regions for mountain tourism in Nepal are Annapurna in the west-central region (primarily the Annapurna Conservation Area), Khumbu in the vicinity of Sagarmatha (Mt. Everest), and Langtang-Helambu, situated north of Kathmandu. The government of Nepal requires that all western tourists obtain permits to enter those areas. The three regions combined accounted for over 95 per cent of all mountain trekking permits issued in the early 1990s. The remaining 5 per cent of trekkers visited Rara Lake National Park in far-western Nepal and the newly opened regions in Dolpo, Humla, Makalu, and Kanchenjunga. Relatively few tourists actually climb the mountains in those regions, although the Nepal Mountaineering Association issues permits to foreign trekkers for 18 different peaks located throughout the country. Mountaineering, meanwhile, continues to be an important tourism-related activity in select areas that contain popular climbing peaks, and it often contributes to early tourism development throughout the mountains. The well-established mountain trekking regions are now fully incorporated into Nepal's fledgling national park system. The most important of these – Khumbu, Langtang-Helambu, and Annapurna – constitute significant new policy arenas as well as recreation areas, precisely because they demonstrate the difficulties encountered when converging the inter-

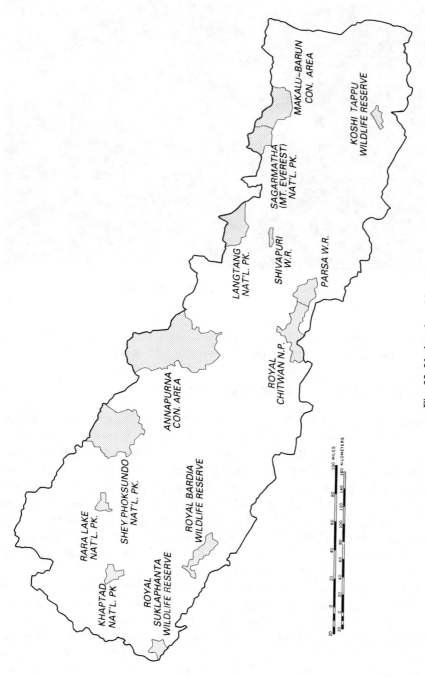

Fig. 32 **National parklands**

Trekking permit checkpoint, Dhunche

ests of tourists, national development, environmental conservation, and the needs of the native people who reside in the parklands.

Sagarmatha National Park, Khumbu

Sagarmatha National Park, established in 1976 to safeguard the unique natural and cultural heritages of the Mt. Everest region, contains 1,243 sq. km in the Khumbu area of north-east Nepal. In addition to the famous Himalayan peaks, Khumbu is home to about 3,000 Sherpas, who have become famous during the past several decades as mountaineers and trekking guides. The Sherpa economy, traditionally based on transhumance and trading, now includes tourism as one of its mainstays. Each year about 8,000 tourists reach Sagarmatha from Kathmandu via flights to Lukla, a two-day walk away, or by hiking for a week from the roadhead at Jiri.

In the park area, tourists visit the Mt. Everest Base Camp, the adjoining ridge lines that offer superior views of the Everest massif, the Sherpa villages, and some of the larger monasteries, such as Tengboche. Tourism has had a mixed impact on the Khumbu Sherpa. Lifestyles and status have changed as a result of the new economic opportunities and greater exposure to western culture, but the

Sherpas have managed to keep intact such fundamental aspects of their culture as the language, religious practices, community relations, and self-identity (Stevens, 1991; Fisher, 1990). The environmental disruptions linked to tourism in Khumbu, while not yet fully understood, are considerable (Karan and Mather, 1985). The Sagarmatha National Park, in alliance with the local people, has instituted for both the Sherpas and tourists numerous regulations on forest use, rubbish disposal, sanitation procedures, and other environmental activities. As the first national park in Nepal to gain worldwide attention, the problems and successes encountered in the management of Sagarmatha National Park help to guide the development of mountain parklands elsewhere in Nepal.

Langtang National Park

Situated in the central Himalaya 32 km north of Kathmandu, Langtang-Helambu is the most accessible mountain park in Nepal. None the less, it receives less than 15 per cent of all trekkers in the country. Langtang was designated as the first Himalaya National Park in 1971, but was not gazetted until 1976. The complex topography of the region, numerous lakes, and its diverse ethnic base of primarily Tibetan origin are Langtang-Helambu's chief attractions for tourists. Its relatively low popularity among western tourists can be attributed partly to its lack of tourist amenities, the relatively small size of its territory, and the limited coverage it receives in the tourism advertisements.

Annapurna Conservation Area

Over 38,000 tourists flock to the Annapurna mountain region each year, making it Nepal's most popular mountain tourism region. That number almost equals the 40,000 inhabitants of the region. Building on the experiences of Sagarmatha and Langtang, where many local residents have suffered from inappropriate park policies, the government of Nepal, through the King Mahendra Trust for Nature Conservation, manages the region as the integrated Annapurna Conservation Area Project (ACAP) rather than as a national park. The primary reason is to elicit the fuller participation of the local people in resource conservation and ecotourism.

The Annapurna tourist region is a vast area, encompassing several districts, numerous watersheds, and the Annapurna massif, in its

Mt. Machapuchare in the Annapurna Range

7,000 sq. km. Major trekking routes encircle the area, following the Marsyandi and Kali Gandaki river valleys. Information centres have been established for tourists in Pokhara, Siklis, and at the regional headquarters in Ghandruk to provide visitors with the cultural and natural histories of the region and to educate them about ways to minimize their local impact. The primary goal of ACAP is to blend tourism with traditional subsistence activities rather than to replace them. Given the large numbers of tourists who visit Annapurna each year, ACAP considers such an approach essential in order to upgrade the local living standards and to enable the sustainable development of the Annapurna region.

Other mountain tourism regions

Several other less travelled regions contribute to Nepal's mountain touristic system. The hills around the Kathmandu Valley are popular day-hike regions. A two-week trekking route through the Middle Mountains connects the Kathmandu and Pokhara Valleys, bypassing numerous mountain villages. Rara Lake National Park, located 30 km north of Jumla in far-western Nepal, was established in 1976 on 106 sq. km that includes the 3,000 m high Rara Lake. Khaptad National Park in western Nepal occupies a middle-elevation grassland plateau of considerable cultural as well as natural historical importance. Such places are well off Nepal's beaten trekker paths.

Nepal tourism, through numerous international adventure travel agencies as well as the Nepalese tourism industry, promotes the perceptions of isolation, pristine natural conditions, and intact cultures that attract visitors to the mountain regions. In their quests for "authenticity," such tourists are propelled into the most remote regions of Nepal and thus contribute to the geographic expansion of tourism into the peripheral locations. The government of Nepal responds to this compelling quest by frequently opening formerly closed border regions to tourists. During the late 1980s and early 1990s, several new tourism regions were made available for organized tours. The newly opened tourism regions include the following: the Shey-Phoksundo National Park, which covers the areas of Dolpo and Mugu districts in the trans-Himalayan zone; the Humla region along Nepal's northwest border with Tibet; the Makalu-Barun Conservation Area in eastern Nepal; Mustang district in the Annapurna Conservation Area, and the Kanchenjunga region along the Sikkim border to the east. The new areas restrict tourists to organized tours, require them to pay high entry fees, and schedule tourist activities according to the new ecotourism criteria. The current numbers of tourists visiting the new trekking territories are small, but the trends noted elsewhere in Nepal predict gains in popularity for all of them.

Tarai wildlife parks

Five important wildlife reserves have been established in the forests of Nepal's lowland tarai. Some originated as Royal Hunting Reserves – as far back as 1846 in the case of Chitwan. They became established sanctuaries in the mid-1970s, and soon thereafter several developed as tourist destinations.

Royal Chitwan National Park

Located about 90 km south-west of Kathmandu in the inner tarai, Chitwan was gazetted in 1973 and extended in 1977 to its present size of 932 sq. km. The park contains portions of the Churia Hills, and the valleys of the Rapti, Narayani, and Reu rivers. Along with advancements in game management, Chitwan's popularity as a tourist destination increased significantly during the 1980s, reflected in the numbers of tourists visiting the park: from less than 5,000 in 1980 to about 40,000 in 1990. A few concessionaires operate tourist lodges within the Park boundaries. The largest and most luxuriant of them is the Tiger Tops Jungle Lodge and Tented Camps, which, in addition to the regular lodge amenities, provides opportunities for wildlife viewing on elephant back, land-rover drives, boat trips, and jungle treks. Around the perimeter of the park, numerous small-scale tourist operations are established, notably in the agricultural village of Saurha, which is now almost completely devoted to wildlife tourism.

Other tarai parks

The other wildlife parks in the tarai are less developed for tourism than Chitwan, although the current interest in attracting tourists to them reveals the likelihood of future tourism expansion. In the western tarai lies the Royal Suklaphanta Wildlife Reserve, one of Nepal's least accessible nature parks with little current tourism investment. The Royal Bardia Wildlife Reserve and the smaller Parsa Wildlife Reserve are both situated in the central tarai and share many ecosystem characteristics with Chitwan. To the east is the Koshi Tappu Reserve, gazetted in 1976 to cover about 100 sq. km along the Sapta-Koshi River. It contains such large mammals as wild boar, spotted deer, and hog deer, the last surviving population of wild buffalo, and Nepal's sole elephant-breeding facility. Apart from a small lodge maintained at the reserve for tourist use, there is little in the way of tourism services yet at Koshi Tappu Reserve or among the other less-known tarai parks. With the increasing popularity of Chitwan, however, the tourism industry envisions further expansion of the alternative wildlife reserves in the tarai in order to diffuse tourism pressures on Chitwan.

River rafting

Some of the main rivers that drain the Himalaya watersheds provide whitewater rafting experiences for an increasing number of adventure tourists. Between the mid-1980s and the early 1990s, the number of rafters increased almost twofold. Over 5,000 tourists now annually raft on Nepal's rivers, including the two most popular rafting rivers – the Trishuli River, located near the Kathmandu Valley, and the Sun

Kosi River, located in the eastern part of the country. The rafting expeditions are often combined with other tourism activities and are offered as packages by over 20 rafting agencies in Kathmandu. The contribution of the rafting tours to the local economies is quite minor since little or no money is spent en route, but for the travel agencies in Kathmandu, they constitute a new arena of tourism involvement.

Economic development potential of tourism

While tourism now contributes a significant share of Nepal's total foreign earnings, in 1965 it accounted for less than US$400,000 of the total revenue in convertible currencies. By 1975, tourism earnings had surpassed US$15 million, and in the late 1980s they reached US$65 million. Tourist expenditures are about evenly distributed in lodging (27 per cent), handicrafts and other purchases (25 per cent), food (26 per cent), and miscellaneous sightseeing (22 per cent). These numbers are offset, though, by the import investments required of the tourism sector and the operating expenses of tourism agencies. The fact that many of these expenditures involve foreign purchases reveals a net contribution to Nepal's economy that is considerably less than was hoped for.

The dependency of Nepal's tourism industry on foreign imports is a common feature of third world tourism (Britton, 1982). This is especially true for Nepal because its tourist sector is heavily dependent on foreign-made goods. Moreover, the industry relies heavily on bookings made by foreign agencies, where payments are made overseas. According to an economic evaluation of tourism by the Nepal Rastra Bank, about half of the tourists visiting Nepal are catered for by non-Nepalese agencies (Nepal Rastra Bank, 1989). The report recommends that Nepalese travel agencies be encouraged to link more directly with foreign agencies. This is difficult for Nepal for two primary reasons. One reason is that Indians continue to dominate visitor arrivals, catered for almost exclusively by Indian agents. This is unlikely to change in the near future. The second reason is that westerner arrivals in Nepal are dominated by adventure tourists, who either visit the country as a stopover on a longer Asian journey or come as participants in the many adventure travel itineraries developed by agencies based in western countries. In the latter case, the foreign agencies may have local representatives who handle the logistics of the tour, but the bulk of payments are made in the originating countries.

Nepal's trekking industry is a good case in point. There are approximately 90 trekking agencies in Nepal registered by the Trekking Agents Association of Nepal and another 20 or so non-registered agencies. Together, they handle over 20,000 trekkers annually, or one-third of the total number of trekkers in Nepal each year. The remainder come in pre-packaged tours without local representation or as individual trekkers who do not employ the services of any trekking agency.

The total investment in trekking agencies increased sharply during the past decade, from Rs 7 million in 1983 to almost Rs 30 million by the early 1990s. This increase reflects the continued interest in mountain trekking among the country's tourism sector. The trekking earnings have increased proportionally, totalling approximately US$10 million by 1990. These are derived primarily from direct services provided (80 per cent) and from equipment hiring (19 per cent). Despite these gains, the potential earnings of Nepal's trekking agencies are hindered by the fact that a strong adventure travel industry exists in the generating countries where most of the finances for Western trekkers are arranged. Without adequate representatives in Nepal, the flow of earnings will be diminished by the overseas operations. Since trekkers spend the longest time in Nepal, averaging 26 nights, and constitute a high proportion of total visitor arrivals (23 per cent), the trekking industry is widely recognized to be critical for the development of tourism in the country. Moreover, because trekking contributes to the most widespread dispersion of tourists into Nepal's rural areas, it may constitute a key factor in the diffusion of tourism earnings to the remote areas of the country.

The aggregate national statistics on tourism described above fail to assess its local economic impact. Mountain tourism, wildlife ecotourism, and the other forms of adventure travel in Nepal may provide alternative opportunities for rural people to find employment as guides, porters, and small-scale entrepreneurs. The infrastructural improvements necessary for tourism – bridges, roads, pathways, and lodges – may provide additional employment. However, tourism provides mainly seasonal work for most of those employed in it. For example, about 70 per cent of trekking permits are issued for the periods October to December and March to April; this dependency on tourism employment reveals underemployment for much of the year. To offset this phenomenon, some tourism planners in Nepal advocate a more diversified tourism base to attract tourists during the off-season.

In addition to seasonality problems, the flow of tourism earnings through the regional and local economic systems tends to favour those wealthy individuals who already have the investment capital and political influence to build new lodges and to equip the tourists with guides and to contract the portering services. By exacerbating disparities in the local economy and by promoting a greater dependency on economic externalities, tourism may in fact erode the sustainability of the village agrarian economies. Finally, it appears that Nepal is moving toward more resort developments. These are highly expensive endeavours, which Nepal can little afford to manage. In the end, a continued reliance on the touristic assets Nepal already has – the mountains and the wildlife – may prove to be the most sustainable features of tourism growth in the country.

Social impacts of tourism

In addition to its economic potential, Nepal's tourism system introduces to the remote regions new interactions between local people and foreigners. It fosters acculturation, the diffusion of ideas, innovations, and new technologies that could prompt new lifestyles and aspirations. Consequently, the potential for social impacts is great. Critics of tourism argue that the consequences for the local people may be negative when tourism views local traditions mainly as colourful assets to be exploited by the tourism industry. According to anthropologist Greenwood (1989: 179):

Treating culture as a natural resource or a commodity over which tourists have rights is not simply perverse, it is a violation of the peoples' cultural rights ... the commoditization of culture in effect robs people of the very meanings by which they organize their lives.

Such a view predicts a gradual erosion of cultural identity, world views, social interactions, and self-determinism among those traditional populations adversely affected by tourism. Tourism proponents, however, argue that traditional communities are exposed to all kinds of outside forces and that tourism at least represents one activity by which the local people can benefit. For example, the Nepalese geographer Gurung believes that the country's primary problem is poverty and that a dynamic tourism industry should be vigorously pursued without sentimentality over its potential cultural impacts (Gurung, 1984). The catalogue of potential social impacts of tourism, both negative and positive, is quite large and varies considerably from one locale to another. None the less, several broad themes show the nature of the tourism impact on Nepalese society.

Cultural identity

Many of the individual changes brought by tourism are superficial: the adoption of new clothing styles, food preparation, handicraft designs, cassette players, and others. Such material changes can be expected with or without tourism when seen as part of the broader historical assimilation of Himalayan cultures by lowlanders (Allan, 1988). Of greater concern are the fundamental shifts in identity that may occur precisely because of the secular interests of tourism. For example, early reports on the impact of tourism on Sherpa society indicated that the maintenance of religious practices, traditional cultural knowledge, and ethics have been eroded with the advance of tourism in Khumbu (Coppock, 1978; Fürer-Haimendorf, 1975). More recent accounts based on longer-term observation emphasize, however, the maintenance of such traits among the Sherpas. Some reports indicate that religious observation has actually increased among the Sherpas with the growth of tourism (Stevens, 1991), and that the total identity of the Sherpa culture has intensified (Fisher, 1990). Cultural identity changes associated with tourism throughout Nepal Himalaya are difficult to assess due to the lack of detailed information. However, local circumstances do show the tenacity of the mountain cultures in the face of the rather wide-spreading modernity that accompanies the tourists.

Lifestyle changes

The most dramatic change that tourism has introduced to Nepal's local economies is the additional employment it provides. The new careers and seasonal work opportunities of tourism predict changes in the patterns of living among traditional people. The severity of such changes, however, can be debated. Adams (1992) argues that tourism has not dramatically altered the traditional patterns of labour among the Sherpas, while both Stevens (1991) and Fisher (1990) show that concepts of time, mobility, work status, and levels of disposable income have upset to some degree the traditional production and trade arrangements found in Khumbu. Brower (1991: 80) noted:

Tourism has brought extraordinary opportunity to the Sherpa people. The rise in tourist visits coincided with a radical restructuring of a traditional

278

cornerstone of the Khumbu economy, trans-Himalayan trade.... The growth of a new trekking industry has provided yet more jobs for Sherpas, and the diversification of trekking styles has only expanded the money-making opportunities for Sherpa entrepreneurs.

While the Sherpas provide perhaps the best example of the role of the tourism economy, the changes in lifestyle associated with tourism can be seen throughout Nepal at places visited by large numbers of tourists. In the Annapurna region, the numbers of new lodges, the electrification of villages, the seasonal demands for porters, the hiring of ponies for tour groups, and the new practices of horticulture and growing food for tourists all point to dramatic shifts in the way the mountain people conduct their lives. Such changes are not restricted to the mountain regions either. In the tarai, for example, the demand for nature guides at the wildlife parks and the growth of tourist services point to new opportunities for young people. In the urban centres of Kathmandu and Pokhara, where much of the tourism is centred, the number of persons employed by travel agencies, airlines, hotels, restaurants, cargo agencies, and handicraft shops has grown dramatically over the past three decades.

Undoubtedly, the changes in lifestyle that occur in Nepal as a result of tourism are geographically widespread but their precise nature remains localized. Consequently, to consider lifestyle changes as social impacts requires that they be assessed in the context of the individual village societies as well as from the perspective of national economic development. Most reports from rural places indicate that the lifestyle changes associated with tourism do not necessarily reflect the abandonment of traditional cultural values. Young people often bridge their cultures by maintaining local traditions and adopting Western ways. This is less clear in those places, especially the towns, where both the economic and social life are shaped almost exclusively by the commerce of tourism.

Material culture

The impact of tourism on culture will depend upon how the tourists "channel" cultural norms into consumptive norms. As shown above, it is not certain whether tourism changes fundamental cultural views as it modifies material life. Some forms of culture, such as handicrafts and ceremonies, may even benefit from tourism if they are favourably received by tourists. For example, in Nepal the religious ceremonies, temple architecture, and philosophies of Buddhism and Hinduism are

279

Buddhist Samyak festival in Patan

of great interest to many tourists. The value and esteem of these religions may be bolstered by tourism. However, it is also possible that tourism may safeguard the artifacts of religious life – temples and icons – but erode the spirit that initially created them. In effect, the meaning of religious articles shifts to material interests. In extreme cases, the theft of religious sculptures is prompted by tourist sales. In less severe instances, religious icons are made exclusively to be sold to tourists in the handicraft shops in Kathmandu and Pokhara.

Various aspects of Nepalese material culture may benefit from tourism. For example, traditional textiles and weaving, woodcarving, pottery, and other handicrafts and artwork are supported by tourist sales. Cultural performances that traditionally related to indigenous audiences now command the attention of international tourists. These new touristic evaluations of culture are important issues in the growth and management of tourism in Nepal. They constitute the surfaces of culture that reflect tourist interests. Consequently, they are the aspects of social change that are most readily identified with tourism.

Environmental impacts of tourism

Extensive literature exists on the environmental costs of tourism, much of which focuses on the ecological consequences of tourist numbers exceeding the carrying capacity of recreational areas (Farrell and Runyan, 1991). Our knowledge of the impact of tourism in Nepal is derived mainly from the effect of mountain tourism on the natural environment. Forest destruction, through increased fuelwood-cutting, pollution created by trash and waste dumping, sanitation problems, vandalism, stone-quarrying and other resource depletions, trail-side erosion, and poaching, has been attributed in part to the increased numbers of trekkers in the mountain areas. The most widespread reports of these problems are from the Khumbu area where tourism has a fairly long history (Coppock, 1978; Richter, 1989). More recent detailed studies show the complexity of tourism's environmental consequences in Khumbu, especially as they relate to the regulatory demands of Sagarmatha National Park (Brower, 1991; Bjonness, 1980; Pawson et al., 1984; Stevens, 1993). The environmental impacts of tourism are less well known in other parts of Nepal, although new insights have been gained by the Annapurna Conservation Area Project.

In addition to the specific localized impacts it may have on the environment, tourism growth contributes to new indirect costs. It promotes lodge construction in such tourism centres as Nauje (Namche Bazaar) in the Khumbu region, Dhunche and Kyanjin in the Langtang-Helambu area, and at Ghandruk, Ghorapani, Siklis, and other centres in the Annapurna region. The new buildings require significant amounts of timber and stone, often portered from distant sources. Hydropower developments in Khumbu and Annapurna have now brought electricity to many villages and tourist lodges along the popular trekking routes. Since these projects require diversions in stream-flow, pipelines, and possibly overhead transmission lines, without careful construction management their environmental impact may be significant. For example, the ACAP Ghandruk Electrification Project launched in 1990 is reported to have caused water shortages at Chane village and disrupted the watermills located there. The increased wealth that derives from tourism has allowed some villagers to increase the size of their livestock herds. This is true especially among the Sherpa yak herders in Khumbu. The increased herd size may have an adverse impact on the environment due to overgrazing in the pastures and fodder-cutting in the forests. The employment opportunities of tourism may also cause conflicts with traditional resource management, especially during the busy tourism season when field preparation, trail maintenance, and other resource activities suffer from the lack of available workers.

Such potential conflicts between tourism, traditional resource management, and environmental quality are the primary motivations behind the establishment of Nepal's system of national parklands. These institutions seek to resolve the often contradictory aims of economic development, environmental conservation, and cultural adaptation. The trade-offs between the economic and ecological benefits of tourism are not yet clear, although proponents of eco-tourism argue that it provides an important economic rationale for conservation development (Lindberg, 1991).

The national parks in Nepal will require proper management in order to meet their environmental goals. For example, the restrictions on wood fires in Khumbu introduced by the Sagarmatha National Park guidelines are not effectively enforced for various cultural and touristic reasons. In central Nepal, the ACAP guidelines cover such a large region that it is difficult to monitor them outside of a few central villages. ACAP distributes an informational pamphlet to the trekkers that explains the kinds of tourist activities leading to environmental problems. ACAP also supports an important environmental education programme in the region's primary and secondary schools to increase the levels of conservation awareness among the villagers. ACAP regulations on fuelwood-cutting incorporate the development of 10 project-owned village nurseries, the technical support provided to other private nurseries, and the establishment of plantation forests on about 70,000 hectares of land. These diverse activities link the development of tourism with the broader environmental needs of the people who live in the ACAP region.

The environmental impacts of tourist activities in the parts of Nepal that lie outside the major mountain parklands are less known. The other mountain areas frequented by tourists lack studies to show their environmental impact, although presumably such places will share the same characteristics as the Khumbu and Annapurna regions. Whitewater rafting on Nepal's rivers is likely to have a minimal impact on the environmental impact. In the tarai, visitors to the wildlife parks employ the services of guides who restrict their tours to well-established trails, thus minimizing the impact of tourists over the larger region. Apart from those tourists who stay at the resort lodges in the tarai parks, visitors spend their nights outside the park, usually in nearby towns and villages, where their environmental impact remains unknown. While some writers argue that tourism is inevitably destructive of the environment (Cohen, 1978), it is important also to understand that both the negative and positive impacts of tourism are locally determined and may vary considerably between host places and cultures.

Tourism prospects

With a per capita income of US$150, Nepal is one of the world's poorest countries. Its development prospects are constrained by high population densities, limited natural resources, and low industrial output. Against these rather bleak conditions, tourism is being promoted as a primary development asset for the country. Since its first Five-Year Plan (1956–1960), the Government of Nepal has sought to increase the foreign exchange earnings from tourism. Despite geopolitical crises, inflation, and natural hazards, the continued growth in tourism indicates that it can, indeed, play an important role in the economic development of the country. Some experts argue that such growth is necessary and overshadows any negative effects that tourism may have on the country's natural and cultural systems. The development of the tourism sector will require a costly investment in such tourist services as lodges and guides, improvements in the road and communications infrastructure, and employment training. A comprehensive plan is necessary to address these concerns.

The sustainable development of tourism in Nepal requires a balanced approach that blends the interests of the national economy with the local economies and environmental protection. The flow of tourism earnings through Nepal's touristic system tends to favour urban places and contributes to further economic inequality in rural areas because not everyone has access to the benefits of tourism. The tourism model most widespread in the country is ecotourism. Because it occurs notably in the country's most remote regions and includes not only nature tourism but also village stays, ecotourism brings to the issue of tourism growth the key factors of environmental and cultural sustainability. Such examples as the Annapurna Conservation Area Project and Sagarmatha National Park show how these interests can be combined into regional development plans. The eventual success of such tourism-related projects depends on how well their management resolves the often contradictory aims of the local populations, environmental preservation, national economic development, and the tourists themselves.

11

Development challenges

In the preceding chapters we have analysed Nepal's growth and change during the last four decades in resource development, land use, deforestation, agriculture, population, cultural patterns, urbanization, industrial growth, transport systems, tourism, and associated environmental management issues, which have characterized the patterns of development.

Politically, the past four decades have marked the end of a journey in which Nepal emerged from being a secluded fief into a modern political state. The process of change began in 1950 when a palace revolution (Leuchtag, 1958) overthrew a century-old government of hereditary rulers, which had usurped power from the Shah royal family. The present King Birendra's grandfather, King Tribhuvan, was restored to the throne with Indian assistance. Tribhuvan shepherded the country through a decade of experimental democracy. King Birendra's father, King Mahendra, however, dissolved an elected Parliament in December 1960 and instituted the partyless panchayat system of tiered villages, districts, and national councils. The system succeeded in establishing stability and attracting a large amount of foreign development aid to Nepal, but it also centralized power in the palace. Between 1978 and 1990 Nepal was buffeted by recurring bouts of protests from the educated and frustrated urban youth, who found ultimate inspiration in the sweeping changes for democracy in Eastern Europe. Widespread pro-democracy forces toppled Nepal's absolute monarchy and King Birendra put his seal on a new constitution that enshrines multiparty democracy and human rights as hallmarks of the political system. Nepal had indeed reached an important historical benchmark.

Economically, despite seven five-year development plans between 1956 and 1990, Nepal remained one of the poorest countries of the world. It was ranked 152 among 173 nations in the 1993 UN Human Development Report, which computes a nation's economic health in a new way, using a number of social and economic variables instead of the traditional figures on per capita income, GDP, and trade balance. Gender and urban-rural disparities remained significant in regard to access to social services such as health, education, and economic employment opportunities. Population density per unit of agricultural land increased by about two-and-a-half times over the last two generations. The availability of agricultural land declined from 0.6 hectares per person in 1950 to 0.24 hectares in 1990. About 40 to 50 per cent of the population, an estimated 8 million out of a population of 18.49 million, live in absolute poverty (World Bank, 1991: 8). The rapid population growth, which has doubled since 1952 and is expected to double again in about 25 years, has led to encroachment on forests and marginal lands, congestion in urban areas, and an increasing flow of migrants – mainly to Indian cities – in search of employment opportunities.

Within the political and economic framework outlined above, Nepal must face several development challenges in the 1990s as the nation prepares to enter the twenty-first century. Three major challenges facing Nepal are the formulation and implementation of policies: (1) for sustainable development and conservation to meet the needs and improve the quality of life of its present population and future generations; (2) to integrate its poverty alleviation programme with development strategies; and (3) to integrate population issues with its development planning. National action on a fairly broad front will be required to meet these challenges. Some of the major policy areas will include the location of industries, land use policy, rural-urban interaction, community development, income growth and employment, public health, nutritional standards, housing, social services, welfare-oriented public goods, and greater provision for political participation at local, regional, and national levels.

Sustainable development and conservation

Since the 1950s the philosophy and practice of environmental management in Nepal's development planning may be described as a "frontier economics model" – a term coined by Kenneth Boulding (1966). Under this model, if local resources or absorptive capacities should exhaust, people could move on to the next untapped frontier or create a new one with a new source of energy or new technology. The model involved shifting the carrying capacities technologically. Development under the frontier economics paradigm treated the environment as an infinite supply of physical resources (water, soil, air, energy, and raw materials) to be used for the benefit of the people and as an infinite sink for the by-products of the development and consumption of these benefits in the form of various types of pollution (waste) and ecological degradation.

Large resettlement projects in the tarai involved a transformation of the environment in order to solve the increasing population problems in the Middle Mountains. In the 1950s the construction of a new road, together with the DDT-spraying programme in the malarious Rapti Valley, opened up land for the settlement of thousands of farmers from the Middle Mountains. Previously, the Valley was used mainly as a hunting preserve for the Ranas. They would move the high government officials, along with their wives and as many as 800 elephants, to the Valley for a month of hunting. Resettlement schemes were partly responsible for the loss of forest area in the tarai during the past four decades (Metz, 1991).

The opposite of the frontier economics paradigm in environmental management is the "deep ecology" philosophy, which espouses a value system based on environmental ethics (Nash, 1989) rather than the money and material orientation of economics (Devall and Sessions, 1985). The deep ecology school of thought emphasizes a different relationship between nature and human socio-economic activity, one which focuses on ethical, social, and spiritual aspects which have been largely ignored in the frontier economics view. Deep ecology has provided the conceptual basis for several successful new environmental movements in India, such as the Chipko movement in the Himalaya (Barthelemy, 1982) and the Save the Narmada movement (Estava and Prakash, 1992), and in other Asia-Pacific countries (Rush, 1991; Karan, 1994).

The application of deep ecology concepts would lead to radical changes in the traditional approach to development. The new approach tends to focus on the least human modification of the environment and strives to achieve a symbiosis with nature. At the current levels of population and rural land degradation in Nepal, the deep ecology approach to development planning appears highly impractical. It is difficult enough to stabilize the population and land degradation, let alone decrease them to achieve a symbiosis with nature.

Ecodevelopment, another paradigm of environmental management in development, attempts to integrate the social, ecological, and economic concerns in development for the future (Riddell, 1981). This approach tends to incorporate many of the social equity and cultural concerns raised in deep ecology. The basic premise of the paradigm is that solutions to environmental and economic problems must come from and fit into the local context. This fledgling ecodevelopment paradigm is still relatively obscure, but it can provide a fully integrated sustainable development model for Nepal. By addressing the problems of depleting resource levels, the degradation of the environment, the destruction of life-support systems, and the aesthetic impact of development processes, the concept forces the need to ecologize the economy.

The ecodevelopment model implies that ecological calculations need to be embodied much more substantively into the economic, political, and social decision-making processes. Cooperation between the natural and social sciences are needed to develop the understanding of how social institutions are to incorporate ecological concerns. The development of sustainable practices will demand methods of ecological calculation that draw on the scientific understanding of natural processes and the social and scientific understanding of the social processes.

These methods of ecological calculation will need to be translated into policy instruments for achieving sustainable development, which in turn raises the question of what is the appropriate institutional structure. The making of development policy in Nepal is split between many agencies. The current institutional mix is not well suited to the integration of social, ecological, and economic considerations into policy making. This is a complex issue and unlikely to be resolved quickly. As a first step, however, it might be useful to undertake a series of local studies that would try to integrate ecological, economic, and social concerns. The aim should be to integrate local and general forms of knowledge in the most appropriate way in order to allow the adoption of sustainable technologies and practices. The challenge ahead is quite simply the development of detailed strategies for the application of the ecodevelopment concept across the range of the environmentally unsustainable uses of the resources and of the inequity within the society.

In addition to the ecodevelopment paradigm for environmental management in development, three strategic approaches are required to solve the priority environmental and natural resource problems in Nepal. First, basic economic and environmental policy reform is needed to reverse the current mismanagement of the environment and natural resources. Policies must be changed to reflect the real value of the natural resources and their products, including the environmental costs of production and use. Emphasis must be placed on strengthening the implementation and enforcement of environmental regulations and the development of incentives to improve the quality of the environment and the management of resources. This includes establishing incentives for the greater empowerment and participation of the local populations and increased land and resource ownership and management rights.

Secondly, the human and institutional capacity in Nepal to analyse and manage natural resources and environmental problems needs strengthening in both the public and private sectors. A better balance is required between the institutions responsible for resource use as well as those involved in protecting, rehabilitating, and planning for sustainable development. Solutions will involve better monitoring and the enforcement of regulations, the development of incentives for improved environmental stewardship in public and private institutions and communities, public participation in environmental impact assessments, improved technological capacity, and training for the private sector and government authorities.

National and international policy development for Nepal is severely hampered by the lack of information on trends in the conditions of the natural resources and environmental systems and on the economic and social costs of depletion and degradation.

Thirdly, improved public access to information on development plans and decisions are essential to ensure government accountability and open decision-making. Responsible public policies on the environment and natural resource use can be enhanced by an informed public and a political system open to the concerns and participation of those affected by the development programmes, which will require increased attention to the environmental education of all levels of society in Nepal.

Integration of poverty alleviation programmes with development strategies

There is significant potential for integrating the poverty alleviation programmes with development activities in the rural areas. The potential for this integration is high, both in the selection of activities and in their effective implementation. The implementation would be far more important than the selection of activities. Devising appropriate institutional mechanisms for planning activities under the poverty alleviation programmes within the framework of area development planning, and more particularly, for their effective implementation, constitutes a major development challenge for Nepal.

The integration of poverty alleviation programmes such as food, fertilizer, and credit subsidies, the indirect subsidies of irrigation operations, integrated rural development projects, employment creation projects, and small income generating projects with development will ensure that the programmes as they operate will result in a sustained increase in GDP through the increased productivity of resources, the conservation of the environment, and in human development. Inadequate integration with the goals of development has led to the inefficient use of resources allocated to the poverty alleviation programmes due to weak linkages with growth, a low potential for the sustained employment generation, an insufficient impact on social development, and the protection of the environment. Existing subsidies have not provided substantial benefits to the poor in Nepal (World Bank, 1991: 96). This trend, if unchecked, can undermine the objectives of economic growth as well as the alleviation of poverty.

The link between agricultural development and the alleviation of poverty is clearly visible in Nepal. Land reform, irrigation development, the increasing yield per hectare of cropped areas, and increasing cropping intensity should contribute to higher incomes and the absorption of labour. Redistribution or welfare measures have limited scope for reducing poverty in Nepal. A development strategy for growth, within which specific poverty alleviation policies and programmes can be framed, is essential.

Agricultural growth programmes such as the Pocket and Block production programmes of the Ministry of Agriculture and the Lumle and Pakhribas Agricultural Centres are located in relatively more accessible developed regions, which are better endowed in terms of agroeconomic characteristics. These programmes are not directed to help the poor specifically. The Lumle and Pakhribas Centres have developed methods to integrate research and extension services to provide the local farmer with the most effective technologies available. The Centres are not really concerned with small farmers or with extending technologies and practices that increase employment in areas where poverty is widespread.

One does not find an adequate concern in Nepal for undertaking activities, such as soil conservation including afforestation, water harvesting, and the drainage and construction of field channels to raise agricultural productivity, which improve the land resource base and the ecosystem in rural areas. These are best undertaken in the framework of watershed development in which mini or micro watersheds can serve as regional units for development, using technologies that are area specific, cost effective, ecologically sound, and locally acceptable. This kind of approach will ensure sustainable production and restoration of the ecological balance through employment-oriented production systems such as multiple cropping, agroforestry, and horticulture. In the field one often finds that each department views the other as a rival, competing for staff and other resources. This approach is detrimental to the raising of agricultural productivity as well as to the alleviation of rural poverty on a sustained basis.

The poverty alleviation programmes in Nepal are essentially top-down ventures, heavily dependent on government bureaucracy. As a consequence, the perceived needs of the people do not get sufficient attention. The activities chosen are often ill suited to the local resource endowments, which results in large leakages and inefficiencies in the implementation of programmes. The employment creation projects are weakly integrated, with area development showing a lack of flexibility both in selecting activities to suit the local resource endowments and in devising methods for their implementation. The Special Public Works Program, sponsored by the ILO, has provided work for 10–20,000 rural poor persons in construction jobs on irrigation projects. The assets created do not have the potential for sustained increased employment over a period of time. Further, the upper-income households with larger landholdings in the rural areas seem to have been the major beneficiaries from the assets created, whereas the assets created exclusively for the benefit of the poor, such as housing and programmes to help the marginal and poor farmers, are relatively rare.

The integration of poverty alleviation programmes with agricultural development can be made effective by strengthening the land base for the poor, particularly the women, through the effective implementation of the existing legislation on land reform. Since there is an active land market in the countryside where farmers who have access to resources are able to augment their landholdings, it would be desirable to advance long-term loans on liberal terms to the landless poor for the purchase of land.

In integrating the poverty alleviation programmes with development, the biggest challenge for Nepal lies in an appropriate institutional mechanism for policy and programme implementation. Nepal's civil service faces a number of problems that will affect all development-related activities and their implementation. These problems include inadequate renumeration and operating funds, patronage in promotion and posting practices, excessive centralization, and attitudinal and communication problems that prevent effective contact between public servants and poor, illiterate farmers. Considering past experience, improvement in this area is bound to be slow. However, the implementation or delivery of socio-economic programmes designed to bring about structural changes in rural society, improvement in literacy and awareness levels of the poor, and progress towards group endeavours on the part of the poor themselves will determine the degree of success in the implementation of the poverty alleviation programmes.

The dilemma facing Nepal is clear and unmistakable: the development of integrated poverty alleviation programmes is needed most under conditions of widespread poverty, the prevalence of unorganized activities, illiteracy, and ignorance. It is precisely these conditions which render the integration of the poverty alleviation programmes with development strategies, and more so, the implementation of the programmes, very difficult. Administrative decentralization can help the rural poor to the extent that resources are moved closer to the poor beneficiaries. The large number of international non-governmental organizations (NGOs) can provide programmes to help the poor. But they do not have the resources or capacity to design or implement poverty alleviation efforts that would integrate with the development goals of the country. At the present time there are large numbers of foreign NGOs operating in Nepal whose coordination with the government's general development programmes is inadequate.

Integration of population and development planning

Unrelenting population growth, widespread poverty, and tardy growth in employment continue to plague the Nepalese economy more than 40 years after the end of the Rana autocracy. Nepal's planning strategy was designed to tackle these very issues. Why did years of planning fail to lower the rate of population growth? What went wrong with the elaborate planning exercises that paid particular attention to social objectives and sectoral development?

A major factor contributing to poverty in Nepal has been the rapid increase in population, which nearly doubled in the last 20 years and will double again by 2020. No serious effort has been made in Nepal to integrate population issues with development planning. Social and human development play crucial roles in influencing fertility rates, and Nepal's planning placed little emphasis on promoting these objectives.

The process of demographic transition is a result of the interaction of a number of diverse aspects of psychological, social, economic, technological, and institutional factors. Essentially it involves the collective decision of a society to shift from a large family-size norm to a small-size norm. The earliest explanations attributed this shift to modernization, urbanization, and industrialization. A recent view stresses psychological modernity as an important factor which contributes to health and demographic transition (Mechanic, 1992).

The psychological factors relate to one's attitude towards the practice of family limitation, the number of children one wishes to have, the attitude towards health care, and the ability to handle children's illnesses. These psychological factors may be closely related to the historical and expected probabilities of child survival in a given society. If parents are convinced that survival probabilities are high then they may decide to have fewer children. Therefore, the preconditions for a falling birthrate are: (1) access to the means of reducing infant and child mortality, and (2) measures leading to changes in the psychological and social attitudes regarding health care and family size.

Reductions in infant and child mortality depend upon the availability and quality of maternal and child health care, the extent and quality of medical attention during childbirth, and the immunization of children for infections and other childhood diseases. Basically, it is the access to health care and the attitudes towards childhood illnesses and child care that might finally help bring down the infant mortality rate.

Access to health care involves three components: (1) locational access, (2) economic access, and (3) social access. Locational access is particularly important for low income groups in Nepal since it can increase their opportunity cost of treatment. For instance, if an agricultural labourer must seek medical assistance from afar, he might be required to forgo a day's earnings, which might be his only source of income. In such a situation, he might either hesitate or not even seek medical assistance for himself or his family unless in an emergency. Nepal has paid scant attention to this question in its development planning. It is hardly necessary to point out the arguments in favour of economic access. The provision of free or subsidized health care on the basis of income is an accepted principle in most societies. In Nepal social access assumes great significance because of the country's past history of the denial of such services to certain castes and social groups.

Attitudinal changes concerning health and family size seem to be determined by the level of education and the spread of literacy, especially among women. Studies from different countries show that the number of children born to a woman declines as her educational level rises. So does the infant mortality rate. Thus access to health care and female education appear to be the most critical factors in the decline of the birth rate. Female education not only initiates changes in one's attitude toward family size and children's health, but also enables women to improve their status within the family and in society. Demographic transitions are preceded by health and educational transitions.

The importance of the woman's status for the reduction of fertility and the alleviation of poverty needs to be explicitly recognized in Nepal's development programmes. Women constitute not only about half the population of the country, but they also bear the brunt of poverty. Women's status and level of education in society and in the family are vital for the success of the policy of reducing the population growth.

Nepal's official policy has so far treated population growth essentially as exogenous to the developmental process. However, the experience of other countries has shown that the decline in fertility levels and the success of population policies are influenced by the levels of social and human development. Therefore it is essential to integrate the population policy within the development strategy. Accordingly, it will be necessary to integrate policies to reduce the growth of population in the rural areas with social development, employment programmes such as those concerning small-scale rural industries, and capital construction in agriculture and for ecodevelopment. All of these factors will ultimately make a favourable impact on the acceptance and practice of family planning and in reducing population growth. An increase in female employment and income would raise the food and nutritional intake and would reduce malnutrition and the incidence of sickness arising from it. Thus women's employment can be a potent weapon for breaking the linkages between population growth and poverty in Nepal.

The real shortcomings of Nepal's planning lie in its general neglect of social sector planning and thus its failure to integrate population issues with development programmes and policies. The failure to reduce illiteracy, to improve the status of women in society, and to ensure access to health care have also accounted for its failure to reduce the rate of population growth.

References

Acharya, P. K. 1920. *Encyclopedia of Hindu Architecture*. Leiden: E. J. Brill.

Acharya, R. 1984. *Cottage Industry in Nepal*. Kathmandu: Centre for Economic Development and Administration.

Adams, V. 1992. "Tourism and Sherpas, Nepal: Reconstruction of Reciprocity." *Annals of Tourism Research* 19: 534–554.

Agrawal, G. R. and A. K. L. Das. 1986. *Transport Linkages in Nepal: Prospects for Regional Cooperation*. Kathmandu: Centre for Economic Development and Administration, Tribhuvan University.

Aitchison, C. U. 1929. *A Collection of Treaties, Engagements and Sanads Relating to India and Neighboring Countries*, XIV. Calcutta.

Allan, N. J. R. 1988. "Highways to the Sky: the Impact of Tourism on South Asian Mountain Culture." *Tourism Recreation Research* 13(1): 11–16.

Asian Development Bank. 1982. *Nepal: Agriculture Sector Strategy Study*. Manila.

Bajracharya, M. K. 1986. *Forestry in Nepal: an Introduction*. Kathmandu.

Banister, J., and S. Thapa. 1981. *The Population Dynamics of Nepal*. Honolulu, Hawaii: East-West Center.

Baraith, R. S. 1989. *Transit Politics in South Asia: a Case Study of Nepal*. Jaipur: Aalekh.

Barthelemy, G. 1982. *Chipko: sauver les forêts de l'Himalaya*. Paris: Editions L'Harmattan.

Bhandari, B. 1992. "Mortality in Nepal: Patterns, Trends and Differentials." In K. C. Bal Kumar, ed. *Population and Development in Nepal*. Kathmandu: Central Department of Population Studies, Tribhuvan University, pp. 37–50.

Bhardwaj, S. M. 1973. *Hindu Places of Pilgrimage in India: a Study in Cultural Geography*. Berkeley, CA: University of California Press.

Bhattarai, S. 1988. *Development and Environment: an Identification of Acute Problem Areas in Nepal*. Bulletin No. 9. Nepal National Committee for Man and the Biosphere, Kathmandu, pp. 21–26.

Bista, D. B. 1972. *People of Nepal*. Kathmandu: Ratna Pustak Bhandar.

——— 1991. *Fatalism and Development: Nepal's Struggle for Modernization*. Calcutta: Orient Longmans.

Bjonness, I. M. 1980. "Ecological Conflicts and Economic Dependency on Trekking in Sagarmatha (Mount Everest) National Park, Nepal." *Norsk Geografisk Tiddscrift* 34: 119–138.

Blaikie, P. 1976. *The Effects of Roads in West Central Nepal.* Norwich: Overseas Development Administration.

—— 1980. *Nepal in Crisis.* New Delhi: Oxford.

—— 1981. "The Crisis of Regional Planning in a Double-Dependent Periphery." In: *Development from Above or Below.* New York: John Wiley, pp. 231–258.

Boo, E. 1990. *Ecotourism: the Potential and Pitfalls*, vols. 1 and 2. Washington, D. C.: World Wildlife Fund.

Boulding, K. 1966. "The Economics of the Coming Spaceship Earth." In: H. E. Jarrett, ed. *Environmental Quality in a Growing Economy.* Baltimore: John Hopkins University Press.

Britton, S. G. 1982. "The Political Economy of Tourism in the Third World." *Annals of Tourism Research* 9(3): 331–358.

Brower, B. 1991. *Sherpa of Khumbu: People, Livestock and Landscape.* Delhi: Oxford University Press.

Buchanan, F. 1819. *An Account of the Kingdom of Nepal and of the Territories Annexed to this Dominion by the House of Gorkha.* Edinburgh: Archibald Constable and Co.

Campbell, J. G., R. J. Shrestha, and F. Euphrat. 1987. "Socio-Economic Factors in Traditional Forest Use and Management: Preliminary Results From a Study of Community Forest Management in Nepal." *Banko Janakari* 1(4). Kathmandu: Forestry Research and Information Centre, Forest Survey and Research Office.

Caplan, L. 1970. *Land and Social Change in East Nepal: A Study of Hindu-Tribal Relations.* Berkeley and Los Angeles, CA: University of California Press.

—— 1975. *Administration and Politics in a Nepalese Town: The Study of a District Capital and its Environs.* London: Oxford University Press.

Carter, J. 1987. *Organizations Concerned with Forestry in Nepal.* Kathmandu: Forestry Research and Information Centre, Occasional Paper No. 2/87.

Central Bureau of Statistics. 1957. *Population Census of Nepal.* Kathmandu. (In Nepali.)

—— 1967. *Results of the 1961 National Census of Population.* Kathmandu. (In Nepali.)

—— 1975. *Population Census – 1971: Social Characteristics Tables*, part II. Kathmandu.

—— 1977. *The Analysis of the Population Statistics of Nepal.* Kathmandu.

—— 1984. *Population Census – 1981: Social Characteristics Tables*, vol. I, part III. Kathmandu.

—— 1985a. Intercensal Changes of Some Key Census Variables, Nepal 1952/54–81, vols. I and II. Kathmandu.

—— 1985b. *National Sample Survey of Agriculture 1981/82.* Kathmandu: National Planning Commission.

—— 1987. *Population Monograph of Nepal.* Kathmandu.

—— 1988. *Migration Statistics from Demographic Sample Survey, 1986–87.* Kathmandu.

—— 1989. *Statistical Year Book of Nepal.* Kathmandu.

—— 1992a. *Population Census – 1991*, vol. I. Kathmandu.

—— 1992b. *Annual Census of Manufacturing, 1990–91.* Kathmandu.

—— 1992c. *Nepal Statistical Yearbook*. Kathmandu.

—— 1992d. *Statistical Pocket Book, Nepal*. Kathmandu.

—— 1993a. *The Analysis of the 1991 Population Census (Based on Advance Tables)*. Kathmandu.

—— 1993b. *Statistical Year Book of Nepal*. Kathmandu.

Centre for Economic Development and Administration. 1977. *Migration in Nepal: A Study of Far Western Development Region*. Kathmandu: Tribhuvan University.

Clark, R. D. 1983. "Urban Primacy and Socio-Economic Development in India: a Case for Reexamination." *Demography India* 11(1): 1–15.

Coburn, B. 1982. *Nepali Aama*. California: Ross-Erikson.

Cohen, E. 1978. "Impact of Tourism on the Physical Environment." *Annals of Tourism Research* 5(2): 215–237.

Conway, D., and N. Shrestha. 1980. "Urban Growth and Urbanization in Least Developed Countries: the Experience of Nepal." *Asian Profile* 8(5): 477–494.

Cooke, M. T. 1985. "Social Change and Status Emulation among the Nisyangte of Manang." *Contributions to Nepalese Studies* 13(1): 45–56. Kathmandu: Research Centre for Nepal and Asian Studies, Tribhuvan University.

Coppock, R. 1978. "The Influence of Himalayan Tourism on Sherpa Culture and Habitat." *Zeitschrift für Kulturaustausch* 3: 61–8.

Dahal, D. R. 1985. "Population Growth, Land Pressure and Development of Cash Crops in a Nepali Village." *Contributions to Nepalese Studies* 13(1): 1–10. Kathmandu: Research Centre for Nepal and Asian Studies, Tribhuvan University.

Dale, E. H. 1968. "Some Geographical Aspects of African Land-locked States." *Annals, Association of American Geographers* 58(3): 485–505.

Dangol, B. D. S. 1992. "Is the 1991 Population Census in Nepal Really Under-enumerated? A Critical Review." *Tathyanka Gatividhi* (Statistical Bulletin published by Central Bureau of Statistics, Nepal) 43(2): 1–5.

Davis, S. H. 1993. *Indigenous Views of Land and the Environment*. World Bank Discussion Papers 188. Washington, D.C.: The World Bank, pp. 1–9.

Deo, R. N. 1993. "Improving Access of the Poor to Groundwater in Nepal: Socio-political and Managerial Issues." In: F. Kahnert and G. Levine, eds. *Groundwater Irrigation and the Rural Poor: Options for Development in the Gangetic Basin*, Washington, D.C.: The World Bank, pp. 101–110.

Department of Food and Agricultural Marketing Services. 1983. *Agricultural Statistics of Nepal*. Kathmandu.

Department of Statistics. 1957. *Census of Population 1952/54*. Kathmandu. (In Nepali.)

Devall, B., and G. Sessions. 1985. *Deep Ecology: Living as if Nature Mattered*. Salt Lake City, UT: Peregrine Smith Books.

Dixit, A. 1992. "Little Water, Dirty Water." *Himal* 5(1): 8–10.

Dutt, B. B. 1977. *Town Planning in Ancient India*. New Delhi: New Asian Publishers.

East, W. G. 1960. "The Geography of Land-locked States." *Transactions and Papers, The Institute of British Geographers* 28: 1–22.

Economic and Social Commission for Asia and the Pacific. 1980. *Population of Nepal*. ESCAP Country Monograph Series, No. 6. Bangkok.

Economic Survey (1992). 1992. Kathmandu: Ministry of Finance.

El-Shakhs, S. 1972. "Development, Primacy and System of Cities." *Journal of Developing Areas* 7:11–36.

297

Estava, G., and M. Prakash. 1992. "Grassroots Resistance to Sustainable Development, Lesson from the Banks of Narmada." *Ecologist* 22(2): 45–47.

Farrel, B. H., and Runyan, D. 1991. "Ecology and Tourism." *Annals of Tourism Research* 18(1): 26–40.

Fisher, J. F. 1986a. "Tourists and Sherpas." *Contributions to Nepalese Studies* 14(1): 37–62. Kathmandu: Research Centre for Nepal and Asian Studies, Tribhuvan University.

―――― 1986b. *Trans-Himalayan Traders: Economy, Society and Culture in Northwest Nepal*. Berkeley, CA: University of California Press.

―――― 1990. *The Sherpas: Reflections on Change in Himalayan Nepal*. Berkeley, CA: University of California Press.

Fisher, R. J. 1989. *Indigenous Systems of Common Property Management in Nepal*. Honolulu: East West Center, Environment and Policy Institute Working Paper No. 18.

Fletcher, L. B., and D. F. Sahn 1984. *An Assessment of Food Aid as a Development Resource in Nepal*. Ann Arbor: Community Systems Foundation.

Fürer-Haimendorf, C. von. 1956a. "Ethnographic Notes on the Tamangs of Nepal." *Eastern Anthropologist* 9: 166–177.

―――― 1956b. "The Inter-relations of Castes and Ethnic Groups in Nepal." In: *Man and Nature: Selected Papers of the 5th International Congress of Anthropological and Ethnological Sciences*. Philadelphia, PA: University of Pennsylvania Press, pp. 526–532.

―――― 1960. "Caste in the Multi-Ethnic Society of Nepal." *Contributions to Indian Sociology* 4: 12–32.

―――― 1964 (1979). "The Sherpas of Nepal." Berkeley, CA: University of California Press, 2nd edn. New Delhi: Sterling.

―――― ed. 1974. *Contribution to the Anthropology of Nepal*. Warminster: Aris and Phillips.

―――― 1975. *Himalayan Traders: Life in Highland Nepal*. London: John Murray.

Gautam, K. H., and N. H. Roche. 1987. "The Community Forestry Experience in Dolakha District." *Banko Janakari* 1(4). Kathmandu: Forestry Research and Information Centre, Forest Survey and Research Office.

Ghimire, K. 1992. *Forest or Farm?: The Politics of Poverty and Land Hunger in Nepal*. Delhi: Oxford University Press.

Gilmour, D. A. 1987. *Not Seeing the Trees for the Forest: A Reappraisal of the Deforestation Crisis in Two Hill Districts of Nepal*. Nepal-Australia Forestry Project Discussion Paper.

―――― 1989. *Forest Resources and Indigenous Management in Nepal*, Working Paper No. 17. Honolulu: East West Center, Environment and Policy Institute.

Gilmour, D. A., and R. J. Fisher. 1991 (1992). *Villagers, Forests and Foresters: The Philosophy, Process and Practice of Community Forestry in Nepal*. Kathmandu: Sahayogi Press.

Glassner, M. I. 1970. *Access to the Sea for Developing Land-locked States*. The Hague: Martin Nijhoff.

Goldman, N., A. J. Coale, and M. Weinstein. 1979. *The Quality of Data in the Nepal Fertility Survey*, Scientific Reports No.6. London: International Statistical Institute/World Fertility Survey.

Government of Nepal. 1957. (2014). *Nepalko Janaganana* (Population Census of Nepal). Kathmandu: Samkhya Vibhag. (In Nepali.)

—— 1972a. *Agricultural Statistics of Nepal, 1972.* Kathmandu: Economic Analysis and Planning Division.

—— 1972b. *Agricultural Statistics.* Kathmandu: Department of Agricultural Statistics.

—— 1977. *Agricultural Statistics of Nepal, 1977.* Kathmandu: Economic Analysis and Planning Division.

Greenwood, D. J. 1989. "Culture by the Pound: an Anthropological Perspective on Tourism as Culture Commoditization." In: V. L. Smith, ed. *Hosts and Guests: the Anthropology of Tourism.* Philadelphia, PA: University of Pennsylvania Press, pp. 171–186.

Gubhaju, B. B. 1975. "Fertility and Mortality in Nepal." *Journal of Nepal Medical Association* 13: 115–128.

Gurung, H. 1968. "Geographical Foundations of Nepal." *The Himalayan Review* 1(1): 1–9.

—— 1984. *Nepal: Dimensions of Development.* Kathmandu: Sahayogi Press.

Gutschow, N., and B. Kölver. 1975. *Ordered Space: Concepts and Functions in a Town of Nepal.* Wiesbaden: Kommissionsverlag Franz Steiner Gmbh.

Hagen, T. 1961. *Nepal, the Kingdom in the Himalayas.* Berne: Kummerly and Frey.

Hilling, D. 1972. "Routes to the Sea for Landlocked States." *Geographical Magazine* 44: 257–264.

Höfer, A. 1979. *The Caste Hierarchy and the State in Nepal: A Study of the Muluki Ain of 1854.* Innsbruck: Universitätsverlag Wagner.

Holmberg, D. H. 1989. *Order in Paradox: Myth, Ritual and Exchange among Nepal's Tamang.* Ithaca and London: Cornell University Press.

Iijima, S. 1963. "Hinduization of a Himalayan Tribe in Nepal." *Kroeber Anthropological Papers* 29: 43–52.

—— 1977. "Ecology, Economy and Culture Change among the Thakalis in the Himalayas of Central Nepal." *Changing Aspects of Modern Nepal,* Monumenta Serindica No. 1. Tokyo: Institute for the Study of Languages and Cultures of Asia and Africa, Tokyo University of Foreign Studies.

—— 1982. "The Thakalis: Traditional and Modern." *Anthropological and Linguistic Studies of the Gandaki Area in Nepal,* Monumenta Serindica No. 10: 21–39. Tokyo: Institute for the Study of Languages and Cultures of Asia and Africa, Tokyo University of Foreign Studies.

Industrial Promotion and Productivity Centre. 1961. *Industrial Enterprises Act, 1961.* Kathmandu.

Inoue, K. 1983. "Nepal's Development Plans: Hardships for the Growth." *Asian Trends* 24: 98–119. (In Japanese.)

International Cooperation Administration. 1958. *Nepal Corporation and Company Act with Industrial Development Corporation Act Bye-Laws and Operational Procedure.* Washington, D.C.

International Labour Office. 1986. *Employment Expansion through Cottage Industries in Nepal.* Geneva.

Ishii, H. 1980. "Recent Economic Changes in a Newar Village." *Contributions to Nepalese Studies* 8(1): 157–179. Kathmandu: Research Centre for Nepal and Asian Studies, Tribhuvan University.

—— 1982. "Agricultural Labour Recruitment in a Parbate Village in Nepal." *Anthropological and Linguistic Studies of the Gandaki Area in Nepal*, Monumenta Serindica No. 10: 40–80. Tokyo: Institute for the Study of Languages and Cultures of Asia and Africa, Tokyo University of Foreign Studies.

Jefferson, M. 1939. "The Law of the Primate City." *Geographical Review* 29: 226–232.

Joshi, A. R., and S. L. Shrestha. 1988. *Environmental Impact of Development: Nepal's Lessons from Experience*. Bulletin No. 9. Nepal National Committee for Man and Biosphere, Kathmandu, pp. 7–20.

Joshi, B. L., and L. E. Rose. 1966. *Democratic Innovations in Nepal: A Case Study of Political Acculturation*. Berkeley, CA: University of California Press.

Joshi, T. R. 1973. "Kathmandu, Nepal: A Socioeconomic Ecology of the Modernizing Pre-industrial City." *Proceedings of the Association of American Geographers* 5: 126–130.

K. C., Bal Kumar, 1992. "Migration and Urbanization in Nepal." *Population and Development in Nepal*. Kathmandu: Central Department of Population Studies, Tribhuvan University, pp. 130–158.

Kanesalingam, V. 1991. *Privatisation, Trends and Experiences in South Asia*. Delhi: Macmillan.

Kano, K. 1979. *Rolwaling Sherpa no Keizai to Shakai* (Economy and Society of the Rolwaling Sherpas), Little World Series No. 3. Nagoya: Little World. (In Japanese.)

Kansakar, V. V. S. 1973–1974. "History of Population Migration in Nepal." *The Himalayan Review* 6: 58–68.

—— 1979. *Effectiveness of Planned Resettlement Program in Nepal*. Kathmandu: Centre for Economic Development and Administration.

—— 1989. "Population of Nepal." In: K. P. Malla, ed. *Nepal: Perspectives on Continuity and Change*. Kirtipur: Research Centre for Nepal and Asian Studies, pp. 28–50.

Karan, P. P. 1960a. *Nepal: a Physical and Cultural Geography*. Lexington, KY: University of Kentucky Press.

—— 1960b. "Land Use Reconnaissance in Nepal with Aero-Field Techniques and Photography." *Proceedings of the American Philosophical Society* 104(2): 172–187.

—— 1961. "Population, Land Utilization and Possible Expansion of Cultivated Area in Nepal." *Pacific Viewpoint* 2: 41–58.

—— 1973. "Kathmandu-Patan: The Twin Cities Urban System." Map Supplement. *Himalayan Review* 6.

—— 1994. "Environmental Movements in India." *Geographical Review* 84: 32–41.

Karan, P. P., and W. A. Bladen. 1982. "Perception of the Urban Environment in a Third World Country." *Geographical Review* 72: 229–232.

Karan, P. P., and S. Iijima. 1983. *Map – Kingdom of Nepal*, Monumenta Serindica. No. 11. Tokyo: Institute for the Study of Languages and Cultures of Asia and Africa, Tokyo University of Foreign Studies.

—— 1984. "A New Map of Nepal." *Explorers Journal* 62: 82–85.

Karan, P. P., and C. Mather. 1985. "Tourism and Environment in Mount Everest Region." *Geographical Review* 75: 93–95.

Katwal, B. B. 1986. *Landlessness in Rural Nepal*. Dhaka: Centre on Integrated Rural Development for Asia and the Pacific.

Kawakita, J. 1955. "Crop Zone." In: *Land and Crops of Nepal Himalaya*. Kyoto: Kyoto University, Fauna and Flora Research Society.

—— 1974. *Hill Magars and their Neighbours*. Tokyo: Tokai University Press.

—— 1984. *A Proposal for the Revitalization of Rural Areas Based on Ecology and Participation through the Experiences of ATCHA in the Nepalese Hill Area*. Tokyo: Association for Technical Cooperation to the Himalayan Areas, Research Report No. R-84-2.

Kenting Earth Sciences Ltd. 1986. *Land Resource Mapping Project*. Government of Nepal and Canadian International Development Agency.

Kernan, H., W. L. Bender, and B. R. Bhatt. 1986. *Report of the Forestry Private Sector Study*. Kathmandu: U.S. Agency for International Development Mission to Nepal.

Khan, A. R., and E. Lee. 1983. *Poverty in Rural Asia*. Bangkok: International Labor Organization.

Khanal P., and A. Chitrakar. 1987. "The Valley Chokes: Pollution in Kathmandu." *Himal*, May, pp. 3–8.

Kobayashi, M. 1991. "Recent Changes of Economic Activities in Hill Villages of Nepal." *Regional Views* 4: 87–106. (In Japanese.)

—— 1992. "Patterns of Migration and Employment under Development in Nepal." *Proceedings of the Department of Humanities, College of Arts and Sciences, University of Tokyo* 95: 55–83. (In Japanese.)

Konate, Y. 1973. "Are Landlocked Countries Condemned?" *Ceres* 6(5): 48–49.

Krotki, K. J., and Thakur, H. N. 1971. "Estimates of Population Size and Growth from the 1952–54 and 1961 Censuses of the Kingdom of Nepal." *Population Studies* 25(1): 89–103.

Kumar, S. K., and D. Hotchkiss. 1988. *Consequences of Deforestation for Women's Time Allocation, Agricultural Production, and Nutrition in Hill Areas of Nepal*, Research Report 69. Washington, D.C.: International Food Policy Research Institute.

Leuchtag, E. 1958. *Erika and the King*. New York: Coward McCann. See also, *With a King in the Clouds*. London: Hutchinson.

Levy, R. I. 1990. *Mesocosm: Hinduism and the Organization of a Traditional Newar City in Nepal*. Berkeley, CA: University of California Press.

Lindberg, K. 1991. "Policies for Maximizing Nature Tourism's Ecological and Economic Benefits." Washington, D.C.: World Resources Institute Working Paper.

McDougal, C. 1969. *Village and Household Economy in Far Western Nepal*. Kirtipur: Tribhuvan University.

Macfarlane, A. 1976. *Resources and Population: a Study of the Gurungs of Nepal*. Cambridge: Cambridge University Press.

McGee, T. G. 1971. *The Urbanization Process in the Third World*. London: Bell.

Mahat, T. B. S. 1985. Human Impact on Forests in the Middle Hills of Nepal. Ph.D. Dissertation, Australian National University.

Malla, U. M. 1978. "Settlement Geography of Kathmandu Valley from 600 B.C. to 1000 A.D." *Geographical Journal of Nepal* 1(1): 28–36.

—— 1987. *Natural Resources of Nepal*, MAB Bulletin No. 8. Nepal National Committee for Man and the Biosphere, Kathmandu.

—— 1988. *Environmental Planning and Management with Special Reference to Sus-*

tainable Development, Bulletin No. 9. Nepal National Committee for Man and Biosphere, Kathmandu, pp. 27–37.

Mechanic, D. 1992. "Research Possibilities on Facilitating the Health Care Transition." In: L. C. Chen et al., eds. *The Role of Social Research*. Westport, CT: Auburn House Publishing Company.

Messerschmidt, D. 1980. "Gateway-Hinter Relations in Changing Nepal." *Contributions to Nepalese Studies* 8(1): 21–39.

Metz, J. J. 1991. "A Reassessment of the Causes and Severity of Nepal's Environmental Crisis." *World Development* 19(7): 805–820.

Minami, M. 1990. "Productive Cooperation and Subsistence Activities among the Magar in Western Nepal." *Journal of Asian and African Studies* 39: 29–68. (In Japanese.)

Ministry of Economic Planning. 1967. *Mobility of Agricultural Labour in Nepal*. Kathmandu.

Ministry of Health. 1987. *Fertility and Family Planning Survey Report, 1986*. Kathmandu.

Ministry of Works and Transport. 1992. *The Future of the Nepalese Road Network*. Kathmandu: Department of Roads, Maintenance and Rehabilitation Coordination Unit.

Nash, R. F. 1989. *The Rights of Nature: A History of Environmental Ethics*. Madison, WI: University of Wisconsin Press.

National Commission on Population. 1983. *Internal and International Migration in Nepal: Summary and Recommendations*, Report of the Task Force on Internal and International Migration in Nepal. Kathmandu: National Planning Commission.

National Planning Commission. 1991. *Approach to the Eighth Plan, 1992–97*. Kathmandu: His Majesty's Government.

—— 1992. *Highlights of the Eighth Plan (1992–97)*. Kathmandu.

Nelson, D. et al. 1980. *A Reconnaissance Inventory of the Major Ecological Land Units and Their Watershed Condition in Nepal*. Kathmandu: Integrated Watershed Management Project, Department of Soil and Water Conservation.

Nepal Rastra Bank. 1989. *Income and Employment Generation from Tourism in Nepal*. Kathmandu: Nepal Rastra Bank.

Nepal Trading Corporation. 1959. *Nepal: Trade Directory, 1950*. New Delhi.

Nield, R. S. 1985. *Working Paper for the Water and Energy Commission Secretariat (WECS)*. Kathmandu: Water and Energy Commission, Seminar on Fuelwood and Fodder – Problems and Policy.

Numata, M. 1987. "Present Status of Environmental Conservation in Nepal and Future Trends." *Population, Development and Environment in Nepal*. Tokyo: The Asian Population and Development Association, pp. 35–40.

Ojha, D. P. 1982. Planned and Spontaneous Land Settlement in Nepal: A Study of Two Tarai Settlements in the Kanchanpur District. Unpublished Ph.D. dissertation, Cornell University.

Okada, F. E. 1957. "Ritual Brotherhood: A Cohesive Factor in Nepalese Society." *Southwestern Journal of Anthropology* 13: 212–222.

PADCO. 1986. *Kathmandu Valley Urban Land Policy Study*. Prepared for the Government of Nepal and US AID. Washington, D.C.: PADCO.

Pant, Y. P. 1962. *Planning for Prosperity*. Kathmandu: Navayuga Sahitya Mandir.

—— 1976. "Energy Crisis in a Water-Rich Country." *The Rising Nepal*, 5 May.

Pawson, I. G., D. D. Stanford, and V. A. Adams. 1984. "Growth of Tourism in Nepal's Everest Region: Impact on the Physical Environment and Structure of Human Settlements." *Mountain Research and Development* 4(3): 237–246.

Pieper, J. 1975. "Three Cities of Nepal." In: P. Oliver, ed. *Shelter, Sign and Symbol.* London: Barrie and Jenkins, pp. 52–69.

Pradhan, B. B. 1982. *Problems and Prospects of Public Enterprises in Nepal.* Kathmandu: Centre for Economic Development and Administration.

Rai, N. K. 1985. *People of the Stones: The Chepangs of Central Nepal.* Kathmandu: Research Centre for Nepal and Asian Studies, Tribhuvan University.

Rajbhandary, H. B., and S. C. Shah. 1981. "Trends and Projections of Livestock Production in the Hills." In: *Nepal's Experience in Hill Agricultural Development.* Kathmandu: Ministry of Food and Agriculture.

Rauch, E. 1954. *Report to the Government of Nepal on Farm Enterprises.* Rome: Food and Agriculture Organization.

Reed, H. B., and M. J. Reed. 1968. *Nepal in Transition.* Pittsburgh, PA: University of Pittsburgh Press.

Regmi, D. R. 1950, 1958. *A Century of Family Autocracy in Nepal.* Banaras. Also published in 1958 in Kathmandu by the Nepali National Congress.

Regmi, M. C. 1963. *Land Tenure and Taxation in Nepal,* vol. 1. Berkeley, CA: University of California Press.

—— 1971. *A Study of Nepalese Economic History, 1776–1846.* New Delhi: Munjushri Publishing House.

—— 1976. *Landownership in Nepal.* Berkeley, CA: University of California Press.

Richter, L. K. 1989. *The Politics of Tourism in Asia.* Honolulu, HI: University of Hawaii Press.

Riddell, R. 1981. *Ecodevelopment: Economics, Ecology, and Development: an Alternative to Growth Imperative Models.* London: Gower.

Rimal, M. 1988. "Burdens of the Poor." *UN Development Forum,* July-August 1988: 12.

Robbe, E. 1954. *Report to the Government of Nepal on Forestry,* United Nations Food and Agricultural Organization Report No. 209. Rome.

Rush, J. 1991. *The Last Tree: Reclaiming the Environment in Tropical Asia.* New York: Asia Society.

Savada, A. M., ed. 1993. *Nepal and Bhutan: Country Studies,* Area Handbook Series. Washington, D.C.: U.S. Government Printing Office.

Scharff, M. R., and F. S. Leerberger. 1962. *Report on Power Development Project: Nepal.* New York: Scharff and Leerberger.

Schroeder, M. C., and D. G. Sisler. 1970. *The Impact of the Sonauli-Pokhara Highway on the Regional Income and Agricultural Production of Pokhara Valley, Nepal,* Occasional Paper No. 32. Department of Agricultural Economics, Cornell University.

Schumpeter, J. 1961. *The Theory of Economic Development.* New York: Oxford University Press.

Sharma, C. K. 1989. "Nepal's Hydro Schemes: Progress and Plans." *Water Resources Journal,* September, pp. 83–84. ESCAP, United Nations.

Sharma, P. 1989. *Urbanization in Nepal.* Papers of the East-West Population Institute, No. 110. Honolulu, HI: East-West Center.

Sharma, P. R. 1978. "Nepal: Hindu-Tribal Interface." *Contributions to Nepalese*

References

Studies 6(1): 1–14. Kathmandu: Research Centre for Nepal and Asian Studies, Tribhuvan University.

Shrestha, A., J. Stoeckel, and J. M. Tuladhar. 1991. "The KAP-Gap in Nepal: Reasons for Non-use of Contraception among Couples with an Unmet Need for Family Planning." *Asia-Pacific Population Journal* 6: 25–38.

Shrestha, B. P. 1967. *The Economy of Nepal*. Bombay: Vora and Company, p. 16.

—— 1981. *An Introduction to Nepalese Economy*. Kathmandu: Ratna Pustak Bhandar.

Shrestha, C. B. 1973–1974. "The System of Central Places in Arniko Rajmarga Area." *The Himalayan Review* 5(6): 19–39.

—— 1975. "Urbanization Trends and Emerging Patterns in Nepal." *The Himalayan Review* 7(7): 1–13.

—— 1990. "Ridge-to-Valley Migration in Nepal: A Case Study of the Chack Khola Valley Area." In: Aijazuddin Ahmad et al., eds. *Mountain Population Pressure*. Delhi: Vikas Publishing House, pp. 146–165.

Shrestha, K. P. 1992. "Critical Review on 1991 Population Census of Nepal." *Tathyanka Gatividhi* (Statistical Bulletin published by Central Bureau of Statistics) 43(2): 10–13.

Shrestha, M. N. 1981. "Nepal's Traditional Settlement: Pattern and Architecture." *Journal of Cultural Geography* 1(2): 26–43.

—— 1982. "Rural Migration in Nepal." *The East Lakes Geographer* 17: 25–31.

—— 1984. Urbanization in the Kathmandu Valley: A Historical Perspective. Paper presented at the 13th Annual Conference on South Asia. Madison, Wisconsin.

—— 1985. Patterns of Urban Growth in Nepal. Paper Presented at the International Conference on Asian Urbanization. University of Akron, Ohio.

Shrestha, N. R. 1985. "The Political Economy of Economic Underdevelopment and External Migration in Nepal." *Political Geography Quarterly* 4(4): 289–306.

—— 1990. *Landlessness and Migration in Nepal*. Boulder, CO: Westview.

Shrestha, R. L. 1980. *Impact of Kathmandu Raxaul Highway (Tribhuvan Rajmarg) on Nepalese Economy (1956–1975)*. Kathmandu: G. S. Agrawal.

—— 1986. *Socioeconomic Factors Leading to Deforestation in Nepal*. Research and Planning Series No. 2. HMG-USAID-GTZ-IDRC-Winrock Project.

Shrestha, R. L. J. 1982. The Relationship between the Forest and the Farming System in Chautara, Nepal, with Special Reference to Livestock Production. Unpublished thesis, Australian National University.

Shumshere, P., and M. Mohsin. 1967. *A Study Report on the Pattern of Emerging Leadership in Panchayats*. Kathmandu: Home Panchayat Ministry.

Stevens, S. 1991. "Sherpas, Tourism and Cultural Change in Nepal's Mount Everest Region." *Journal of Cultural Geography* 12(1): 39–58.

—— 1993. *Claiming the High Ground: Sherpas, Subsistence, and Environmental Change in the Highest Himalaya*. Berkeley, CA: University of California Press.

Stoddard, R. H. 1976. "A Measure of Highway Expansion in Nepal." *The Himalayan Review* 8(8): 1–9.

Svejnar, J., and E. Thorbecke. 1986. *Economic Policies and Agricultural Performance: the Case of Nepal, 1960–1982*. Paris: Development Centre of the Organization for Economic Cooperation and Development.

Szentes, T. 1973. "The Economic Problems of Land-locked Countries." In: Z. Cervenka, ed. *Land-locked Countries of Africa*. Uppsala: The Scandinavian Institute of African Studies.

Takayama, R. 1960. "Economy of the Agro-Pastoral Tibetans in the Torbo Region, N.W. Nepal." Torbo Ethnography No.2. *Minzokugaku-Kenkyu* (The Japanese Journal of Ethnology) 24(3). Tokyo: The Japanese Society of Ethnology. (In Japanese.)

Tamura, M. 1986. "Tibeto-Burman Ethnic Groups." *Motto Shiritai Nepal* 109–136. (In Japanese.)

Thapa, G. B., and K. Weber. 1986. *Land Settlement in Nepal.* Bangkok: Asian Institute of Technology.

Thapa, G. J., ed. 1992. *Two Year Progress Report, January 1990-December 1991. Annapurna Conservation Area Project.* Kathmandu: The King Mahendra Trust for Nature Conservation.

Thapa, S., and R. Retherford. 1982. "Infant Mortality Estimates Based on the 1976 Nepal Fertility Survey." *Population Studies* 36(1): 61–80.

Thapa, S., and A. O. Tsui. 1990. "Family Planning Needs and Costs: Nepal, 1985–2000." *Asia-Pacific Journal* 5(2): 17–30.

Tuladhar, J. M. 1989. "The Onset of Fertility Decline in Nepal?" *Asia-Pacific Population Journal* 4: 15–30.

Turner, L., and J. Ash. 1975. *The Golden Hordes: International Tourism and the Pleasure Periphery.* London: Constable.

United Nations. 1985. *The Least Developed Countries.* New York.

——— 1987. *The Law of the Sea. Rights of Access of Land-locked States to and from the Sea and Freedom of Transit.* New York.

——— 1989. *Development and Conservation of Ground-Water Resources and Water-Related Natural Disasters and Their Mitigation in Selected Least Developed Countries in the ESCAP Region,* Water Resources Series No. 66. New York.

UN-ESCAP. 1985. *Role of Participatory Organizations in Agrarian Reform.* Bangkok.

UNICEF. 1987. *Children and Women of Nepal: A Situational Analysis.* Kathmandu.

——— 1989. *The State of the World's Children.* Oxford: Oxford University Press.

United States Bureau of the Census. 1979. Country Demographic Profile. *Nepal.*

Upadhyay, S. K. 1993. "Use of Groundwater Resources to Alleviate Poverty in Nepal: Policy Issues." In: F. Kahnert and G. Levine, eds. *Groundwater Irrigation and the Rural Poor: Options for Development in the Gangetic Basin.* Washington, D.C.: The World Bank, pp. 91–99.

Upreti, B. C. 1993. *Politics of Himalayan River Waters.* New Delhi: Nirala Publications.

Vaidyanathan, K. E., and F. H. Gaige. 1973. "Estimates of Abridged Life Tables, Corrected Sex-age Distribution and the Birth and Death Rates for Nepal 1954." *Demography* (India) 2: 2.

Vajracarya, D. 1973 (2030). *Licchavikalka Abhilekha* (Inscriptions of the Licchavi Era). Kathmandu: Research Centre for Nepal and Asian Studies, Tribhuvan University. (In Nepali.)

Water and Energy Commission. 1986. *Land Use in Nepal: A Summary of the Land Resource Mapping Project Results (With Emphasis on Forest Land Use).* Kathmandu: Ministry of Water Resources.

——— 1987. *Fuelwood Supply in the Districts of Nepal.* Kathmandu: Ministry of Water Resources.

——— 1988. *Energy Sector Synopsis Report 1985/86.* Kathmandu: Ministry of Water Resources.

Weiner, M. 1973. "The Political Demography of Nepal." *Asian Survey* 13(6): 617–630.

Weller, G. A. 1991. "The Development of a National Hydropower Industry in Nepal." *Water Resources Journal*, March, pp. 93–96. ESCAP, United Nations.

Whelan, T. 1991. *Nature Tourism: Managing for the Environment*. Washington, D.C.: Island Press.

Wight, P. 1993. "Ecotourism: Ethic or Eco-sell?" *Journal of Travel Research* 31(3): 3–9.

World Bank. 1974. *Agricultural Sector Survey of Nepal*, Report No. 519a-NEP. Washington, D.C.

—— 1978. *Nepal Forestry Sector Review*, Report No. 1952-NEP. Washington, D.C.

—— 1989. *World Development Report, 1989*. New York: Oxford University Press.

—— 1991. *Nepal: Poverty and Incomes*. Washington, D.C.

Wyatt-Smith, J. 1982. *The Agricultural System in the Hills of Nepal: The Ratio of Agricultural to Forest Land and the Problem of Animal Fodder*, Occasional Papers No. 1. Agricultural Projects Services Centre, Kathmandu.

Yadav, R. P. 1987. *Agricultural Research in Nepal: Resource Allocation, Structure, and Incentives*. Washington, D.C.: International Food Policy Research Institute.

Yamamoto, Y. 1983. "Inter-Caste Marriages in Pokhara: Sanskritization or Urbanization?" *Journal of Asian and African Studies* 25: 1–38.

Zaman, M. A. 1973. *Evaluation of Land Reform in Nepal*. Kathmandu: Ministry of Land Reforms.

Zipf, G. K. 1941. *National Unity and Disunity*. Bloomington: Principia Press.

Zurick, D. 1992. "Adventure Travel and Sustainable Tourism in the Peripheral Economy of Nepal." *Annals of the Association of American Geographers* 82(4): 608–628.

Tables

Table 1 **Nepal, other least developed countries, developing countries, and developed market economy countries: A comparison**

	Nepal	LDCs	Developing countries	Developed countries
Population growth rate (% per year), 1970–1980	2.3	2.6	2.6	0.8
Life expectancy at birth (years), 1970	44	41	50	71
Number of radios per 1,000 persons, 1980	1.8	29	101	952
Per capita GDP (US$), 1981	157	220	970	9,681
Average rate of change in per capita GDP (% per year), 1970–1980	−0.2	0.6	3.3	2.5
Share of agriculture in GDP (%), 1981	63	47	17	4
Average rate of change in per capita agriculture production (% per year), 1970–1980	−1.4	−1.1	0	0.6

Source: United Nations (1985: 50).

Table 2 **Monthly rainfall, evapotranspiration, and water deficits in the tarai (in mm)**

Month	Rainfall	Evapotranspiration	Deficit
Jan.	17	37	20
Feb.	12	53	41
Mar.	31	175	144
April	74	182	108
May	138	197	59
June	502	194	—
July	751	201	—
Aug.	536	170	—
Sept.	472	153	—
Oct.	145	104	—
Nov.	8	76	68
Dec.	2	44	42

Source: Kenting Earth Sciences Ltd. (1986).

Table 3 **Land use pattern, 1954–1990 (in '000 ha.)**

	1954 (Robbe)	1960 (Karan)	1964 (GON)	1970 (GON)	1974 (GON)	1978–1979 (Kenting)	1990 (GON)
Forest	4,532	4,537	4,532 32.07%	4,475 31.78%	4,823 45.20%	6,295 42.69%	5,533 37.60%
Cultivated land	2,382	1,777	1,931 13.67%	1,980 14.06%	2,326 16.49%	2,968 20.00%	2,653 18.00%
Land snow	4,584	2,203	2,131 14.97%	2,112 15.00%	2,125 14.97%	—	2,246 15.30%
Barren land	—	—	—	—	2,629 18.64%	—	—
Grazing land	—	—	—	—	1,785 12.66%	1,701 11.54%	1,978 13.40%
Other lands	1,762	6,094	5,563	5,538	3,046	2,729 18.51%	2,306 15.70%
Total area	13,260	14,611	14,157	14,105	14,105	14,748	14,718

Sources: Robbe (1954); Karan (1960); Government of Nepal (1972a, 1972b, 1977); Central Bureau of Statistics (1992c); Kenting Earth Sciences Ltd. (1986).

Note: The total area may not add up because all land categories are not included in each survey.

Table 4   **Change in forest area, 1964–1965 and 1978–1979 (in '000 ha.)**

Regions	1964–1965	1979–1979	Area change	Per cent change	Annual change
Mountains	5,683.1	5,492.0	−191.1	−3.4	−0.2
High and Middle Himalaya	3,943.8	4,016.1	72.3[a]	1.8	0.1
Siwaliks	1,739.3	1,455.9	−263.4	−15.1	−1.2
Tarai	783.8	552.9	−190.9	−24.4	−2.0
Nepal	6,466.9	6,084.9	−382.0	−5.9	−0.4

Source: Water and Energy Commission (1987: 62).
a. Does not include 221.8 ha. of forest in the High Himalaya in the 1978–1979 survey.

Table 5 **Cultivated land and population, 1971 and 1991**

	Great Himalayan valleys		Middle Himalaya		Tarai		Nepal	
	1971	1991	1971	1991	1971	1991	1971	1991
Cultivated land[a] ('000 ha.)	97	130	606	756	1,293	1,440	1,996	2,326
	4.86%	5.59%	30.36%	32.52%	64.78%	61.89%	100%	100%
Population ('000)	1,139	1,444	6,071	8,411	4,346	8,606	11,556	18,462
	9.86%	7.80%	52.53%	45.60%	37.61%	46.60%	100%	100%
Households ('000)	205	276	1,091	1,567	794	1,501	2,090	3,345
Per capita cultivated land (ha.)	0.085	0.09	0.1	0.089	0.297	0.167	0.173	0.125
Per household cultivated land (ha.)	0.473	0.471	0.555	0.482	1.628	0.959	0.955	0.695

Sources: Central Bureau of Statistics (1985b, 1992c); National Planning Commission Secretariat (1974).
a. Cultivated land data are for 1971 and 1991.

Table 6   **Cultivated land and agricultural density, 1981**

District name	Cultivated land in sq. km	Cultivated land (%)	Agricultural density per sq. km
Achham	82.23	4.89	2,252
Arghakhanchi	104.56	8.76	1,504
Baglung	106.24	5.96	2,026
Baitadi	143.66	9.46	1,247
Bajhang	76.15	2.23	1,628
Bajura	36.39	1.66	2,051
Banke	434.04	18.57	473
Bara	799.08	67.15	399
Bardiya	582.14	28.75	342
Bhaktapur	93.39	78.48	1,711
Bhojpur	172.08	11.42	1,120
Chitawan	554.19	24.99	468
Dadeldhura	130.11	8.46	668
Dailekh	90.15	6.00	1,847
Dang	527.55	17.85	505
Darchula	97.71	4.21	923
Dhading	500.38	25.98	486
Dhankuta	407.23	45.70	319
Dhanusa	695.45	58.94	622
Dolakha	110.68	5.05	1,360
Dolpa	42.38	0.54	520
Doti	84.34	4.16	1,816
Gorkha	128.80	3.57	1,796
Gulmi	186.87	16.26	1,274
Humla	9.07	0.16	2,238
Ilam	599.86	35.22	297
Jajarkot	60.35	2.71	1,646
Jhapa	1,163.27	72.43	412
Jumla	51.76	2.05	1,329
Kailali	515.38	15.93	500
Kalikot	92.16	5.29	951
Kanchanpur	310.16	19.26	545
Kapilbastu	822.10	47.30	328
Kaski	388.37	19.25	570
Kathmandu	251.52	63.68	1,679
Kavrepalanchok	625.74	44.82	491
Khotang	91.13	5.73	2,333
Lalitpur	152.96	39.73	1,205
Lamjung	141.95	8.39	1,076
Makwanpur	414.92	17.10	587
Manang	18.96	0.84	370
Mohottari	697.67	69.63	518
Morang	1,076.95	58.06	496

Table 6 (*cont.*)

District name	Cultivated land in sq. km	Cultivated land (%)	Agricultural density per sq. km
Mugu	15.04	0.43	2,906
Mustang	67.59	1.89	191
Myagdi	120.52	5.25	804
Nawalparasi	479.02	22.16	645
Nuwakot	453.03	40.41	448
Okhaldhunga	104.09	9.69	1,322
Palpa	480.47	34.99	446
Panchthar	495.34	39.91	310
Parbat	79.51	16.10	1,615
Parsa	495.25	36.60	574
Pyuthan	101.35	7.74	1,556
Ramechhap	527.23	34.10	306
Rasuwa	89.93	5.82	336
Rautahat	848.20	75.33	392
Rolpa	112.07	5.96	1,501
Rukum	63.93	2.22	2,072
Rupandehi	851.16	62.59	445
Salyan	99.33	6.79	1,531
Sankhuwasabha	153.29	4.40	844
Saptari	953.82	69.98	397
Sarlahi	649.79	51.61	614
Sindhuli	152.41	6.12	1,205
Sindhupalchok	121.17	4.77	1,917
Siraha	837.95	70.53	448
Solukhumbu	148.26	4.48	595
Sunsari	721.09	57.37	478
Surkhet	300.38	12.26	553
Syangja	169.81	14.59	1,601
Tanahu	490.48	31.73	456
Taplejung	95.33	2.61	1,267
Terhathum	333.31	49.09	277
Udayapur	356.94	17.30	448
NEPAL	24,637.17	16.74	610

Source: Central Bureau of Statistics (1989).

Table 7 **Farm size and income, 1984–1985**

	Large	Medium	Small	Marginal	Non-cultivator
Tarai					
Farmsize (ha.)	>5.4	2.7–5.4	1.0–2.7	<1.0	—
Per cent of households	3	9	23	38	27
Per capita Monthly income (Nepalese Rs)	277	202	174	143	136
Middle Himalaya					
Farm size (ha.)	>1.05	0.5–1.05	0.2–0.5	<0.2	—
Per cent of households	16	24	50	11	—
Per capita Monthly income (Nepalese Rs)	162	139	128	108	150

Source: World Bank (1991: 12).

Table 8 **Land distribution by size of holding**

Holding size	Households (%)	Cultivated land (%)
Less than 1 ha.	63.1	10.6
1–5 ha.	26.5	26.9
5 or more ha.	10.4	60.5

Source: Zaman (1973: 27).

313

Table 9 **Redistribution of land under the 1964 Land Reform Programme (in ha.)**

Region	Cultivated area	Above ceiling	Appropriated or confiscated	Area distributed
Tarai				
eastern	167,247	9,153	4,676	3,380
central	364,879	6,645	943	377
western	194,717	11,651	3,124	495
far-western	133,382	25,173	23,880	18,723
inner	658,560	6,291	1,053	559
Subtotal	1,518,785	58,913	33,676	23,534
Kathmandu				
Valley	42,577	7,062	149	54
Other mountains	764,638	405	6	—
Total	2,326,000	66,380	33,831	23,588

Source: Ministry of Land Reforms.

Table 10 **Population growth, 1911–1991**

Year	Population	Exponential growth rate	Change (%)	Doubling time (yr)
1911	5,638,749			
1920	5,573,788	−0.116	−1.152	
1930	5,532,574	−0.074	−0.739	
1941	6,283,469	1.273	13.572	54.47
1954	8,361,194[a]	2.857	33.067	24.27
1961	9,471,350[b]	1.247	13.277	55.60
1971	11,555,983	1.989	22.010	34.85
1981	15,022,839	2.624	30.001	26.42
1991	18,491,097[c]	2.077	23.087	33.37
2000	22,935,078[d]	2.154	24.033	32.19

Source: Central Bureau of Statistics (1987: 7).

a. This figure was adjusted for 1954 by adding population of western Nepal (4,970,968), population of eastern Nepal projected forward for two years (3,373,493) and people recorded as absent from their homes but living in Nepal (18,733).
b. Includes persons absent from home but present in the country (58,354).
c. Central Bureau of Statistics (1993b: 5).
d. Projected with estimated TRF = 4.00 in 2000 A.D.

Table 11 **Population by region, 1971–1991**

Region	Land in		1971 Population		1981 Population		1991 Population		Annual growth rate		Population density per	
	sq. km	%	'000	%	'000	%	'000	%	1971–1987	1981–1991	sq. km 1991	Arable land/ha. 1981
Mountain	51.8	35	1,139	9.9	1,303	8.7	1,444	7.8	1.36	1.03	28	10.6
Middle Mountain	61.3	42	6,080	52.5	7,163	47.7	8,411	45.5	1.67	1.62	137	7.6
Tarai	34.1	23	4,337	37.6	6,557	43.6	8,606	46.7	4.20	2.76	252	4.7

Source: Central Bureau of Statistics (1989: tables 1.2 and 2.1; 1993a: table 1.2).

315

Table 12 **Population change by district, 1971–1991**

District name	Area in sq. km	Population 1971 area adjusted	Population 1981	Change 1971–1981	Change % 1971–1981	Population 1991	Change 1981–1991	Change (%) 1971–1981
Achham	1,680	163,597	185,212	21,615	13.21	198,188	12,976	7.01
Arghakhanchi	1,193	130,212	157,304	27,092	20.81	180,884	23,580	14.99
Baglung	1,784	179,040	215,228	36,188	20.21	232,486	17,258	8.02
Baitadi	1,519	156,654	179,136	224,482	14.35	200,716	21,580	12.05
Bajhang	3,422	108,623	124,010	15,387	14.17	139,092	15,082	12.16
Bajura	2,188	61,342	74,649	13,307	21.69	92,010	17,361	23.26
Banke	2,337	130,516	205,323	74,807	57.32	285,604	80,281	39.10
Bara	1,190	233,401	318,957	85,556	36.66	415,718	96,761	30.34
Bardiya	2,025	102,772	199,044	96,272	93.68	290,313	91,269	45.85
Bhaktapur	119	122,320	159,767	37,447	30.61	172,952	13,185	8.25
Bhojpur	1,507	177,887	192,689	14,802	8.32	198,784	6,095	3.16
Chitawan	2,218	183,644	259,571	75,927	41.34	354,488	94,917	36.57
Dadeldhura	1,538	60,535	86,853	26,318	43.48	104,647	17,794	20.49
Dailekh	1,502	149,397	166,527	17,130	11.47	187,400	20,873	12.53
Dang	2,955	186,639	266,393	79,754	42.73	354,413	88,020	33.04
Darchula	2,322	75,118	90,218	15,100	20.10	101,683	11,465	12.71
Dhading	1,926	213,121	243,401	30,280	14.21	278,068	34,667	14.24
Dhankuta	891	110,448	129,781	19,333	17.50	146,386	16,605	12.79
Dhanusa	1,180	332,610	432,569	99,959	30.05	543,672	111,103	25.68
Dolakha	2,191	134,223	150,576	16,353	12.18	173,236	22,660	15.05
Dolpa	7,889	19,110	22,043	2,933	15.35	25,013	2,970	13.47
Doti	2,025	127,499	153,135	25,636	20.11	167,168	14,033	9.16
Gorkha	3,610	188,221	231,294	43,073	22.88	252,524	21,230	9.18
Gulmi	1,149	206,051	238,113	32,062	15.56	266,331	28,218	11.85
Humla	5,655	25,757	20,303	−5,454	−21.17	34,383	14,080	69.35

316

District								
Ilam	1,703	147,367	178,356	30,989	21.03	229,214	50,858	28.51
Jajarkot	2,230	85,728	99,312	13,584	15.85	113,958	14,646	14.75
Jhapa	1,606	248,953	479,743	230,790	92.70	593,737	113,994	23.76
Jumla	2,531	61,218	68,797	7,579	12.38	75,964	7,167	10.42
Kailali	3,235	136,063	257,905	121,842	89.55	417,891	159,986	62.03
Kalikot	1,741	71,552	87,638	16,086	22.48	88,805	1,167	1.33
Kanchanpur	1,610	68,863	168,971	100,108	145.37	257,906	88,935	52.63
Kapilbastu	1,738	205,216	270,045	64,829	31.59	371,778	101,733	37.67
Kaski	2,017	164,590	221,272	56,682	34.44	292,945	71,673	32.39
Kathmandu	395	342,406	422,237	79,831	23.31	675,341	253,104	59.94
Kavrepalanchok	1,396	245,490	307,150	61,660	25.12	324,329	17,179	5.59
Khotang	1,591	200,084	212,571	12,487	6.24	215,965	3,394	1.60
Lalitpur	385	142,835	184,341	41,506	29.06	257,086	72,745	39.46
Lamjung	1,692	125,489	152,720	27,231	21.70	153,697	977	0.64
Makwanpur	2,426	169,770	243,411	73,641	43.48	314,599	71,188	29.25
Manang	2,246	7,436	7,021	−415	−5.58	5,363	−1,658	−23.61
Mohottari	1,002	285,709	361,054	75,345	26.37	440,146	79,092	21.91
Morang	1,855	292,473	534,692	242,219	82.82	647,823	140,131	26.21
Mugu	3,535	29,485	43,705	14,220	48.23	36,364	−7,341	−16.80
Mustang	3,573	10,393	12,930	2,537	24.41	14,292	1,362	10.53
Myagdi	2,297	87,120	96,904	9,784	11.23	100,552	3,648	3.76
Nawalparasi	2,162	184,021	308,828	124,807	67.82	436,217	127,389	41.25
Nuwakot	1,121	176,702	202,976	26,274	14.87	245,260	42,284	20.83
Okhaldhunga	1,074	123,925	137,640	13,715	11.07	139,457	1,817	1.32
Palpa	1,373	178,932	214,442	35,510	19.85	236,313	21,871	10.20
Panchthar	1,241	145,809	153,746	7,937	5.44	175,206	21,460	13.96
Parbat	494	114,489	128,400	13,911	12.15	143,547	15,147	11.80
Parsa	1,353	202,123	284,338	82,215	40.68	372,524	88,186	31.01
Pyuthan	1,309	136,306	157,669	21,363	15.67	175,469	17,800	11.29
Ramechhap	1,546	157,385	161,445	4,060	2.58	188,064	26,619	16.59

Table 12 (cont.)

District name	Area in sq. km.	Population 1971 area adjusted	Population 1981	Change 1971–1981	Change % 1971–1981	Population 1991	Change 1981–1991	Change (%) 1971–1981
Rasuwa	1,544	26,732	30,241	3,509	13.13	36,744	6,503	21.50
Rautahat	1,126	249,683	332,526	82,843	33.18	414,005	81,479	24.50
Rolpa	1,879	155,478	168,166	12,688	8.16	179,621	11,455	6.81
Rukum	2,877	102,666	132,432	29,766	28.99	155,554	23,122	17.46
Rupandehi	1,360	243,346	379,096	135,750	55.78	522,150	143,054	37.74
Salyan	1,462	140,944	152,063	11,119	7.89	181,785	29,722	19.55
Sankhuwasabha	3,480	118,964	129,414	10,450	8.78	141,903	12,489	9.65
Saptari	1,363	292,768	379,055	86,287	29.47	465,668	86,613	22.85
Sarlahi	1,259	285,075	398,766	113,691	39.88	492,798	94,032	23.58
Sindhuli	2,491	148,999	183,705	34,706	23.29	223,900	40,195	21.88
Sindhupalchok	2,542	205,614	232,326	26,712	12.99	261,025	28,699	12.35
Siraha	1,188	300,295	375,358	75,063	25.00	460,746	85,388	22.75
Solukhumbu	3,312	79,406	88,245	8,839	11.13	97,200	8,955	10.15
Sunsari	1,257	237,693	344,594	106,901	44.97	463,481	118,887	34.50
Surkhet	2,451	105,822	166,196	60,374	57.05	225,768	59,572	35.84
Syangja	1,164	248,692	271,824	23,132	9.30	293,526	21,702	7.98
Tanahu	1,546	167,754	223,438	55,684	33.19	268,073	44,635	19.98
Taplejung	3,646	111,360	120,780	9,420	8.46	120,053	–727	–0.60
Terhathum	679	92,662	92,454	–208	–0.22	102,870	10,416	11.27
Udayapur	2,063	115,361	159,805	44,444	38.53	221,256	61,451	38.45
NEPAL	147,181	11,555,983	15,026,801	3,470,818	30.03	18,495,079	3,468,278	23.08

Source: Central Bureau of Statistics (1989: table 1.2; 1993a: table 1.2).

Table 13a **Internal migration pattern by region, 1981**

Origin	Destination: Mountains				
	En.	Cn.	Wn.	Mid.	Far.
Mountains					
eastern	—	5,558	126	4,655	6,183
central	53	—	17	12	21
western	15	29	—	49	21
mid-western	12	8	3	—	651
far-western	6	8	2	580	—
Middle Mountains					
eastern	21,290	408	58	354	1,352
central	1,047	3,800	101	149	149
western	65	124	648	158	97
mid-western	621	34	9	859	649
far-western	17	11	4	145	1,274
Tarai					
eastern	639	213	13	142	371
central	108	174	18	138	57
western	23	39	78	34	32
mid-western	9	16	2	46	13
far-western	2	3	1	9	16
Total in-migration	23,907	10,425	1,080	7,330	10,886

Source: Central Bureau of Statistics (1984: Vol. II, table 8).

Table 13b **Internal migration pattern by region, 1981**

Origin	Destination: Middle Mountains				
	En.	Cn.	Wn.	Mid.	Far.
Mountains					
eastern	18,220	32,602	33,890	18,282	7,971
central	411	10,186	400	102	90
western	96	1,377	5,526	138	100
mid-western	37	185	508	1,153	846
far-western	33	131	61	65	1,844
Middle Mountains					
eastern	—	9,766	5,411	2,622	887
central	3,815	—	4,448	767	440
western	343	5,512	—	1,638	300
mid-western	121	607	1,537	—	910
far-western	52	330	134	2,364	—
Tarai					
eastern	7,414	4,206	2,399	2,351	349
central	713	5,123	6,884	653	195
western	99	761	1,174	253	91
mid-western	44	994	158	1,014	95
far-western	25	93	42	98	441
Total in-migration	31,423	71,873	62,572	31,500	14,559

Source: Central Bureau of Statistics (1984: Vol. II, table 8).

Table 13c **Internal migration pattern by region, 1981**

| Origin | Destination: Tarai | | | | | Total out-migration |
	En.	Cn.	Wn.	Mid.	Far.	
Mountains						
eastern	69,869	16,939	9,567	6,402	5,723	235,987
central	1,146	8,651	224	241	182	21,736
western	415	5,953	22,659	1,174	667	38,219
mid-western	96	163	133	651	1,466	5,912
far-western	248	197	52	114	9,900	13,241
Middle Mountains						
eastern	202,592	15,270	1,654	1,368	2,328	265,360
central	12,803	83,290	4,010	1,976	2,480	119,275
western	2,627	63,210	64,328	6,968	4,086	150,104
mid-western	327	709	4,549	31,110	12,486	54,528
far-western	347	264	173	971	41,285	47,371
Tarai						
eastern	—	18,140	970	672	1,076	38,955
central	9,715	—	2,651	1,889	735	29,053
western	332	843	—	613	300	4,672
mid-western	189	742	430	—	9,486	13,238
far-western	129	102	35	215	—	1,211
Total in-migration	300,835	214,473	111,435	54,364	92,200	1,038,862

Source: Central Bureau of Statistics (1984: Vol. II, table 8).

Table 14 **Regional net migration, 1981**

Geographic region	Net migration 1981
Eastern Mountain	−212,080
Central Mountain	−11,311
Western Mountain	−37,139
Mid-western Mountain	1,418
Far-western Mountain	−2,355
Eastern Middle Mountain	−233,937
Central Middle Mountain	−47,402
Western Middle Mountain	−87,532
Mid-western Middle Mountain	−23,028
Far-western Middle Mountain	−32,812
Eastern Tarai	261,880
Central Tarai	185,420
Western Tarai	106,763
Mid-western Tarai	41,126
Far-western Tarai	90,989

Source: Central Bureau of Statistics (1984: vol. II tables 7 and 8).

Note: Moved within the same geographic region: 233,426; moved to different geographic region: 1,038,862.

Table 15 **Taranagar Village, Gorkha district: Population and caste structure**

		Total	Ward								
			1	2	3	4	5	6	7	8	9
Population	1971	2,889	517	159	406	331	217	232	250	200	377
	1984	3,999	737	230	413	428	516	417	386	355	517
	1992	5,326	1,038	223	567	519	515	524	518	521	901
Households	1984	600	91	37	69	59	66	82	61	56	79
	1992	895	172	38	98	94	90	88	74	95	146
Household by caste, 1992											
Kumal		231/5[a]	61/1				5/	9/1	58/1	51/2	49/
		12/12[b]	1/1		1/1	2/2	2/2	1/1	2/2	3/3	13/13
Magar		200/82	20/10	21/	55/8	20/2	11/2	35/22	10/10	15/15	
		19/18	4/3		4/4	2/2	1/1	1/1		5/5	2/2
Bahun		106/118	30/12	9/2	12/9	14/9	46/37	4/4		15/15	30/30

323

Table 15 (*cont.*)

	Total	1	2	3	4	5	6	7	8	9
							Ward			
Chetri	12/11 72/49	4/3 20/17	 1/1	1/1 7/1	1/1 9/2	1/1 10/7	 7/3		4/4 5/5	1/1 13/13
Newar	25/25 49/44	8/8 18/18		1/1 4/1	10/10 10/10	2/2 4/2	 3/3	 1/1	2/2 2/2	1/1 7/7
Gurung	6/6 15/15	1/1 2/2	4/4		1/1 2/1	3/3 3/3	 2/2	 1/1		1/1 1/1
Sarki	52/26	6/6	2/	10/	13/7	3/3	14/6			4/4
Kami	30/20	1/1		8/5	7/1	3/3	1/			10/10
Total	85/85 895/405	21/19 172/77	38/7	7/7 98/24	21/21 94/38	10/10 90/61	5/5 88/44	2/2 74/19	14/14 95/43	5/5 146/92

Source: Based on field survey by Kobayashi.

a. The number on the left-hand side of the slash indicates the number of the total households for each category and the number on the right-hand side indicates that of the households from other villages.

b. The small numerals above those of the ordinary size indicate the numbers of store managers; those on the left of the slash indicating the total number of store managers for the category and those on the right indicating the number of store managers who came in from other villages.

Note: Main castes only are listed separately.

Table 16 **Price of farmland in Gorkha district ('000 rupees per ha.)**

Year	1978	1980	1982	1987	1990	1991
R. Village		W 68.8		W 133.6	W 196.5	
In Hill area			D 47.2		D 94.3	
D. Village	W 49.1		W 78.6		W 245.6	W 271.1
In Besi area	D 29.5		D 35.4		D 117.9	
National price index	100	124.5	157	253		

Source: Field Survey by Kobayashi, and *Statistical Yearbook of Nepal.*

W = Wet land; D = Dry land; Price index (1978) = 100; Besi: Riverside low area in the Hill region, altitude of R. Village is 980 m, D. Village is 440 m.

Table 17 **Taranagar: Type of job and destination of out-migrants**

Period of migration	1971	1972–1976	1977–1981	1982–1986	1987–1991	Total
To India	9	8	11	28	65	121
military	(2)	(2)	(3)	(3)	(4)	(14)
Other countries		1	2	3	4	10
military		(1)	(2)	(1)	(2)	(6)
Domestic	1	9	12	34	55	111
military		(1)	(6)	(8)	(3)	(18)
police		(3)	(1)	(7)	(4)	(15)
officer			(2)		(4)	(6)
others	(1)	(3)	(5)	(19)	(44)	(72)
Kathmandu		[2]	[2]	[11]	[23]	[38]
Total	10	18	25	65	124	242

Source: Based on field survey by Kobayashi.

( ): details by type of job.
[ ]: details by destination.

Table 18   **Changes of population by mother tongue, 1952/54–1991**

Mother tongue	1952/54	1961	1971	1981	1991	Percentage in 1991
Nepali	4,013,567	4,796,528	6,060,758	8,767,361	9,302,880	50.31
Maithili	1,024,780	1,130,401	1,327,242	1,668,309	2,191,900	11.85
Bhojpuri	477,281	577,357	806,480	1,142,805	1,379,717	7.46
Tamang	494,745	518,812	555,056	522,416	904,456	4.89
Abadhi	328,408	447,090	316,950	234,343	374,638	2.03
Tharu	359,594	406,907	495,881	545,685	993,388	5.37
Newari	383,184	377,727	454,979	448,746	690,007	3.73
Magar	273,780	254,675	288,383	212,681	430,264	2.33
Rai, Kirati	236,049	239,749	232,264	221,353	439,312	2.38
Gurung	162,192	157,778	171,609	174,464	227,918	1.23
Limbu	145,511	138,705	170,787	129,234	254,022	1.37
Bhote, Sherpa	70,132	84,229	79,218	73,589	121,819	0.66
Rajbansi	35,543	55,803	55,124	59,383	85,558	0.46
Satar	16,751	18,840	20,660	22,403	25,302	0.14
Danuwar	9,138	11,624	9,959	13,522	23,721	0.13
Sunwar	17,299	13,362	20,380	10,650	—	—
Chepang	14,261	9,247	—	—	25,097	0.14
Thami	10,240	9,046	—	—	14,400	0.08
Thakali	3,307	4,134	—	5,289	7,113	0.04
Jirel	2,721	2,757	—	—	4,229	0.02
Lapcha	—	1,272	—	—	—	—
Others	178,142	156,953	490,253	770,606	995,356	5.38
Total	8,256,625	9,412,996	11,555,983	15,022,839	18,491,097	100.00

Source: Department of Statistics (1957) and Central Bureau of Statistics (1967, 1975, 1984 and 1993b).

Table 19 **Livestock per household in villages of different ethnic/language groups**

Ecological zone	Location	Village	Ethnic/language groups	Average livestock numbers	Year of research	Source
Great Himalaya	Dolpo	Tsarka	Tibetan	33.1	1958	Takayama (1960: 46)
Great Himalaya	Rolwaring	Beding	Sherpa	14.9	1973	Kano (1979: p. xv)
Higher Middle Mountains		Thak	Gurung	7.6	1969	Macfarlane (1976: 89)
Middle Mountains	Kathmandu Valley	Satungal	Newar	1.3	1970	Ishii (1980)
Lower Middle Mountains		Bahuntar	Parbate Hindus	8.1	1978	Ishii (1982: 45)
Tarai		Ganguli	Maithili	1.5	1989	Ishii (original)
Tarai	Kailali	(Samples)	Tharu	14.6	1967–1968	McDougal (1969: 98)

Tables

Table 20 Growth of urban population 1952/54–1991

Name	1952/54	1961	1971	1981	1991
Dhankuta				13,836	17,073
Banepa		5,688			12,537
Bhadrapur			7,499	9,761	15,210
Bhaktapur	32,320	33,877	40,112	48,472	61,405
Bharatpur				27,602	54,670
Bidur					18,694
Biratnagar	8,060	35,355	45,100	93,544	129,388
Birendra Nagar				13,859	22,973
Birganj	10,037	10,769	12,999	43,642	69,005
Butwal			12,815	22,583	44,272
Damak					41,321
Dhangadhi				27,274	44,753
Dhankuta				13,836	17,073
Dharan		13,998	20,503	42,146	66,457
Dhulikhel					9,812
Dipayal					12,360
Hetauda			16,194	34,792	53,836
Ilam			7,299	9,773	13,197
Inaruwa					18,547
Jaleswor					18,088
Janakpur	7,037	8,928	14,294	34,840	54,710
Kalaiya					18,498
Kathmandu	106,579	121,019	150,402	235,160	421,258
Kirtipur	7,038	5,764			
Lahan				13,775	19,018
Lalitpur (Patan)	42,183	47,713	59,049	79,875	115,865
Mahendra Nagar				43,834	62,050
Malangwa	5,551	6,721			14,142
Matihani		5,073			
Nepalganj	10,813	15,817	23,523	34,015	47,819
Pokhara		5,413	20,611	46,642	95,286
Rajbiraj		5,232	7,832	16,444	24,227
Siddhartha Nagar (Bhairawa)			17,272	31,119	39,473
Tansen		5,136	6,434	13,125	13,599
Taulihawa					17,126
Thimi	8,657	9,719			
Tribhuvan Nagar				20,608	29,050
NEPAL	238,275	338,183	463,909	958,702	1,697,710

Source: Department of Statistics (1957) and Central Bureau of Statistics (1967, 1975, 1984 and 1993b).

Note: In 1993 three more cities, Gaur (20,434), Byas (20,124), and Tulsipur (22,654) are added. They are not included in the discussion here.

Table 21 **Decennial changes in urban population 1952/54–1991**

Name	Change (%) 1952/54–1961	Change (%) 1961–1971	Change (%) 1971–1981	Change (%) 1981–1991
Banepa				
Bhadrapur			30.16	55.82
Bhaktapur	4.82	18.40	20.84	26.68
Bharatpur				98.07
Bidur				
Biratnagar	338.65	27.56	107.41	38.32
Birendra Nagar				65.76
Birganj	7.29	20.71	235.73	58.12
Butwal			76.22	96.04
Damak				
Dhangadhi				64.09
Dhankuta				23.40
Dharan		46.47	105.56	57.68
Dhulikhel				
Dipayal				
Hetauda			114.85	54.74
Ilam			33.90	35.04
Inaruwa				
Jaleswor				
Janakpur	27.00	60.10	143.74	57.03
Kalaiya				
Kathmandu	13.55	24.28	56.35	79.14
Kirtipur	−18.10			
Lahan				38.06
Lalitpur (Patan)	13.11	23.76	35.27	45.06
Mahendra Nagar				41.56
Malangwa	21.08			
Matihani				
Nepalganj	46.28	48.72	44.60	40.58
Pokhara		280.77	126.30	104.29
Rajbiraj		49.69	109.96	47.33
Siddhartha Nagar (Bhairawa)			80.17	26.85
Tansen		25.27	103.99	3.61
Taulihawa				
Thimi	12.27			
Tribhuvan Nagar				40.96
NEPAL	41.11	37.39	107.11	77.24

Source: Central Bureau of Statistics (1957, 1967, 1975, 1984 and 1993b).

Table 22 **Native born and foreign born migrants in urban areas, 1971 and 1981**

Name	Migrants 1971				Migration in 1981			
	Foreign born	%	Native born	%	Foreign born	%	Native born	%
Banepa								
Bhadrapur	3,032	40.43	1,069	14.26	1,491	15.28	2,544	26.06
Bhaktapur	32	0.08	1,132	2.82	6	0.01	1,610	3.32
Bharatpur					991	3.59	14,126	51.18
Bidur								
Biratnagar	14,262	31.62	7,151	15.86	9,007	9.63	14,282	15.27
Birendra Nagar					47	0.34	2,048	14.78
Birganj	2,118	16.29	2,086	16.05	2,834	6.49	5,544	12.70
Butwal	2,349	18.33	6,254	48.80	2,130	9.43	5,310	23.51
Damak								
Dhangadhi					1,473	5.40	9,130	33.48
Dhankuta					74	0.53	1,986	14.35
Dharan	2,354	11.48	6,678	32.57	3,593	8.53	16,451	39.03
Dhulikhel								
Dipayal								
Hetauda	724	4.47	5,923	36.58	576	1.66	8,753	25.16
Ilam	128	1.75	262	3.59	175	1.79	1,043	10.67
Inaruwa								
Jaleswor								
Janakpur	1,426	9.98	1,084	7.58	2,884	8.28	5,528	15.87
Kalaiya								
Kathmandu	3,750	2.49	15,751	10.47	2,862	1.22	29,127	12.39
Kirtipur								
Lahan					543	3.94	1.415	10.27
Lalitpur (Patan)	1,230	2.08	1,866	3.16	398	0.50	6,397	8.01
Mahendra Nagar					782	1.78	12,902	29.43
Malangwa								
Matihani								
Nepalganj	3,246	13.80	4,983	21.18	1,021	3.00	1,582	4.65
Pokhara	215	1.04	463	2.25	700	1.50	5,600	12.01
Rajbiraj	1,099	14.03	1,047	13.37	1,251	7.61	1,802	10.96
Siddhartha Nagar (Bhairawa)	2,817	16.31	5,482	31.74	2,908	9.34	5,874	18.88
Tansen	98	1.52	517	8.04	74	0.56	1,412	10.76
Taulihawa								
Thimi								
Tribhuvan Nagar					35	0.17	1,299	6.30
Total	38,880	8.42	61,748	13.37	35,855	3.75	155,765	16.28

Sources: Central Bureau of Statistics, 1975: vol. 5, table 40 and vol. 2, pt. 1, table 10).

Note: Data on 1981 migrants are as cited by P. Sharma (1989: table 10).

Table 23   **Area, population, and density in cities, 1991**

Name	Total area in sq. km	Built up area (%)	Population 1991	Density/sq. km (total area)
Banepa	5.3	6.6	12,537	2,365.47
Bhadrapur	11.2	27.9	15,210	1,358.04
Bhaktapur	6.9	27.7	61,405	8,899.28
Bharatpur	55.2	12.7	54,670	990.40
Bidur	34.9	8	18,694	535.64
Biratnagar	59.9	19.9	129,388	2,160.07
Birendra Nagar	36.1	8.7	22,973	636.37
Birganj	22.3	23.3	69,005	3,094.39
Butwal	38.4	11.6	44,272	1,152.92
Damak	75.1	4.5	41,321	550.21
Dhangadhi	93	4.1	44,753	481.22
Dhankuta	47.9	1.6	17,073	356.43
Dharan	12.2	56.4	66,457	5,447.30
Dhulikhel	10.9	4.2	9,812	900.18
Dipayal	34.7	4.8	12,360	356.20
Hetauda	55.5	14.6	53,836	970.02
Ilam	27.7	5.9	13,197	476.43
Inaruwa	17.5	10.8	18,547	1,059.83
Jaleswor	15.1	7.8	18,088	1,197.88
Janakpur	21.1	29.5	54,710	2,592.89
Kalaiya	11.4	16.2	18,498	1,622.63
Kathmandu	47.8	61.9	421,258	8,812.93
Lahan	18.4	6	19,018	1,033.59
Lalitpur (Patan)	16.1	52	115,865	7,196.58
Mahendra Nagar	192.6	3.6	62,050	322.17
Malangwa	7.7	10.7	14,142	1,836.62
Nepalganj	12.3	30.9	47,819	3,887.72
Pokhara	52.5	28	95,286	1,814.97
Rajbiraj	11.1	22.3	24,227	2,182.61
Siddhartha Nagar (Bhairawa)	35.7	13.4	39,473	1,105.69
Tansen	11.3	8.8	13,599	1,203.45
Taulihawa	20.6	6.6	17,126	831.36
Tribhuvan Nagar	54.4	4.1	29,050	534.01

Sources: Central Bureau of Statistics (1993b: 9).

Note: Data on total area and built up area are cited by K.C. (1992: 153).

Table 24 **Regional pattern of rural–urban population, 1991**

Regions	Population density in sq. km	Rural population	Urban population	Urban population (%)
Mountains				
eastern	34.41	359,156	0	0.00
central	75.04	471,005	0	0.00
western	3.38	19,655	0	0.00
mid-western	12.20	260,529	0	0.00
far-western	41.95	332,785	0	0.00
Total	27.85	1,443,130	0	0.00
Middle Mountains				
eastern	132.96	1,398,868	30,270	2.12
central	226.99	1,931,522	693,407	25.88
western	132.15	2,311,993	108,885	4.50
mid-western	88.95	1,196,582	22,973	1.88
far-western	99.19	658,359	12,360	1.84
Total	137.25	7,497,324	867,895	10.31
Tarai				
eastern	365.72	2,344,287	314,168	11.82
central	325.19	2,841,782	246,239	6.32
western	252.88	1,246,400	83,745	6.30
mid-western	127.15	853,461	76,869	8.26
far-western	139.48	568,994	106,803	15.80
Total	253.63	7,854,924	827,824	9.59
NEPAL	125.64	16,795,378	1,695,719	9.17

Source: Central Bureau of Statistics (1993b, table 1.2 and 1.3).

Table 25 **Rank order of urban areas, 1952/54–1991**

1952/54	1961	1971	1981	1991
Kathmandu	Kathmandu	Kathmandu	Kathmandu	Kathmandu
Lalitpur (Patan)	Lalitpur (Patan)	Lalitpur (Patan)	Biratnagar	Biratnagar
Bhaktapur	Biratnagar	Biratnagar	Lalitpur (Patan)	Lalitpur (Patan)
Nepalganj	Bhaktapur	Bhaktapur	Bhaktapur	Pokhara
Birganj	Nepalganj	Nepalganj	Pokhara	Birganj
Thimi	Dharan	Pokhara	Mahendra Nagar	Dharan
Biratnagar	Birganj	Dharan	Birganj	Mahendra Nagar
Kirtipur	Thimi	Siddhartha Nagar (Bhairawa)	Dharan	Bhaktapur
Janakpur	Janakpur	Hetauda	Janakpur	Janakpur
Malangwa	Malangwa	Janakpur	Hetauda	Bharatpur
	Kirtipur	Birganj	Nepalganj	Hetauda
	Banepa	Butwal	Siddhartha Nagar (Bhairawa)	Nepalganj
	Pokhara	Rajbiraj	Bharatpur	Dhangadhi
	Rajbiraj	Bhadrapur	Dhangadhi	Butwal
	Tansen	Ilam	Butwal	Damak
	Matihani	Tansen	Tribhuvan Nagar	Siddhartha Nagar (Bhairawa)
			Rajbiraj	Tribhuvan Nagar
			Birendra Nagar	Rajbiraj
			Dhankuta	Birendra Nagar
			Lahan	Lahan
			Tansen	Bidur
			Ilam	Inaruwa
			Bhadrapur	Kalaiya
				Jaleswar
				Taulihawa
				Dhankuta
				Bhadrapur
				Malangwa
				Tansen
				Ilam
				Banepa
				Dipayal
				Dhulikhel

Table 26 **Early industrial enterprises**

Industrial enterprises	Date incorporated	Source of capital[a]	Present status
Biratnagar jute	1936	Indian	Operating
Juddha match	1937	Indian	Operating
Sugar mill	1937		Liquidated 1944–45
Morang cotton	1942	Joint	Liquidated
Cotton mill, Birganj	1942	Indian	Liquidated 1947
Morang hydel	1942	Indian	Operating
Himalayan mining	1943	Indian	Liquidated 1951
Plywood/bobbin	1943	Indian	Liquidated 1952[b]
Miscellaneous: Ayurvedic drugs, soap, ceramics	War period	Nepalese	Liquidated

Source: Shrestha (1967:184–193).
a. Much of the Indian investment was in the Nepalese name.
b. Later rejuvenated.